Praise for *Dream to Destiny*

My pastor and dear friend Robert Morris has done it again. His writing is founded on universal and biblical truths that educate, motivate, and mobilize readers of all ages and backgrounds. God is glorified, and His plan is realized when we act upon the dreams He places in our hearts. In *Dream to Destiny*, Robert Morris shows us the way.

Samuel Rodriguez

Lead Pastor, New Season Church and President/CEO, NHCLC

Author of *Persevere with Power: What Heaven Starts, Hell Cannot Stop!*

Executive Producer, *Breakthrough* and *Flamin' Hot* Movies

So many can become lost, distracted, and even disillusioned on the journey from taking their dreams into their destiny. We all need help at times to navigate this terrain that can test our character, perseverance, and priorities. Pastor Robert not only provides a road map within these pages, but also breathes hope back into every dreamer's future. Thank you, Pastor Robert, for living out all that this message now powerfully passes along.

Charlotte Gambill

International Speaker and Author

Robert Morris is a master teacher like no other. He has the ability to present even the most difficult of topics in such a way that people leave with a clear understanding and having heard from the throne of God. His latest work, *Dream to Destiny*, is no exception. Dreams can die without a plan, and this book will have a plan for your dream that sees the vision through to your purpose and God's plan for your life.

Jentezen Franklin

Senior Pastor, Free Chapel

New York Times Bestselling Author

I am so grateful for the tremendous impact Pastor Robert Morris has made on my life and ministry. I am moved again by his reminder that God has a meaningful and powerful destiny for each of us. God never stops our growth or progress, but instead continues to shape and mold us for His glory.

Chad Veach
Lead Pastor, Zoe Church
International Speaker and Author

In *Dream to Destiny*, Pastor Robert walks you through the life of Joseph in a clear, compelling, and Christ-centered way. This book will inspire and challenge you to move from your dream to your destiny.

Dr. Derwin L. Gray
Co-founder & Lead Pastor, Transformation Church
Author of *God, Do You Hear Me? Discovering the Prayer God Always Answers*

Dream to Destiny is a book for such a time as this! From the story of the life of Joseph, Pastor Robert Morris provides biblical and practical keys for the process of seeing the dream God gave you come alive. This is a book I will put in the hands of every one of my leaders and that I would love for every believer in Christ to read!

Joakim Lundqvist
Pastor, Word of Life Church Sweden

God often uses seasons of hardship to prepare us as a people of destiny. God dreams require courage and strategy. In his newly revised and expanded book, *Dream to Destiny*, Pastor Robert Morris helps us identify ten tests each of us will face and the tools and insight necessary to navigate them correctly.

Lisa Bevere
New York Times Bestselling Author
Cofounder, Messenger International

DREAM
TO
Destiny

DREAM TO ✳ *Destiny*

✦ **A Proven Guide to** ✦
Navigating Life's Biggest Tests
✦ ✳ **and Unlocking Your**
God-Given Purpose ✳ ✦

ROBERT MORRIS

BETHANYHOUSE
a division of Baker Publishing Group
Minneapolis, Minnesota

Dream to Destiny: A Proven Guide to Navigating Life's Biggest Tests and Unlocking Your God-Given Purpose

Copyright © 2023 by Robert Morris.

New and Expanded Edition. Portions of content previously published as *From Dream to Destiny: The Ten Tests You Must Go Through to Fulfill God's Purpose for Your Life*. Copyright © 2019 by Robert Morris. Published by Gateway Press®, 500 S Nolen, Suite 300, Southlake, Texas 76092. gatewaypublishing.com. Original published by Regal Books. Copyright © 2005 by Robert Morris.

Distributed by Bethany House Publishers, Minneapolis, Minnesota. www.bethanyhouse.com. Bethany House Publishers is a division of Baker Publishing Group, Grand Rapids, Michigan.

Additional copyright information on page 303.

Library of Congress Control Number 2023023211

ISBNs: 9780764242946 (Hardcover), 9781493445455 (eBook)

Study Guide also available.
Study Guide ISBNs: 9780764242953 (Study Guide), 9781493445462 (Study Guide eBook)

We hope you hear from the Holy Spirit and receive God's richest blessings from this book by Gateway Publishing®. Our purpose is to carry out the mission and vision of Gateway Church through print and digital resources to equip leaders, disciple believers, and advance God's kingdom. For more information on other resources from Gateway Publishing, visit gatewaypublishing.com.

Gateway Publishing
500 S Nolen, Suite 300
Southlake, TX 76092
gatewaypublishing.com

Cover illustration by Joshua Noom.

Visit dreamtodestiny.com for bonus content.

Printed in the United States of America.
23 24 25 26 27—5 4 3 2 1

TABLE OF CONTENTS

Get Ready for the Journey!

I t caught me by surprise.

I was scheduled to speak to a large group of young adults at church, and I started preparing by praying for direction. I really wanted to bring these young adults a message from the heart of God Himself. Perhaps it was because I knew how many critical, life-changing decisions are made at that age. Maybe it was because at nineteen years old, I had been a foolish, self-destructive young man when the Lord finally captured me with His love and completely transformed my life. Whatever the reason, I desperately wanted to know what God desired to say to this group. That's when the surprise came.

The Holy Spirit began to flood my mind with an outline for a message about a young man in the Bible named Joseph and the journey he took on the way to fulfilling his destiny. I thought about how Joseph went through tests that measured and forged his character. The message themes came faster than I could write them down.

In that encounter with the Holy Spirit, I began to see with fresh eyes how Joseph had been destined to be an instrument of God's deliverance for humanity, yet he had to endure great testing along the way. At the young age of seventeen, Joseph received a glimpse of his destiny in a dream. Not only did he fail to understand the dream's true meaning, he also didn't know the journey had just begun.

If you're familiar with the biblical account of Joseph in Genesis, you know it wasn't until he was thirty years old that he stepped into the first phase of the extraordinary destiny God had planned for his life, and it wasn't until much later that his full destiny came to pass! But the hard lessons learned in those years of testing equipped and purified him. It was only through these tests that Joseph was found faithful to fulfill his God-given destiny.

After I preached this message to that group of young adults, I realized this message was not just for them—it was for *everyone*! Every one of us has a dream, and every one of us has a destiny. Perhaps you have some dreams that are yet to be fulfilled or a destiny you may have only caught a glimpse of so far. You may have even compared yourself with others who seem to be walking in their destinies and perhaps wondered what's hindering you from stepping into yours.

So the question is, *How do we travel from the dream to the destiny and what happens along the way?*

I believe the book you now hold in your hands will give you exciting answers to many of the questions you may have. From the life of Joseph, you will learn vital truths about the tests that wait for you on the road to your destiny—tests you must pass if you are to step into the fullness God has planned for you.

We all have dreams—dreams for our families, dreams for our finances, and dreams for our chosen vocations, but right now I want to challenge you to dream a little bigger. Allow God to stir in your heart *His* dream for you. I promise, His dream for you is better. His destiny for you is bigger.

You see, God's thoughts for you are higher than your thoughts. His plans for you are better than your plans. He has a destiny in mind for you, and it's bigger than you *can ever* imagine. You can't dream a bigger dream than God can dream!

Discovering God's Dream

God revealed His dream for my life at a very young age. When I was three years old, I came into my parents' bedroom one night and said, "Jesus visited me."

"Oh really? What did He say to you?" they asked.

"He told me He wants me to preach to the whole world."

They weren't too surprised by what I said because on the day I was born, my mom and dad dedicated me to the Lord and named me Robert after my mother's father, who was murdered when my mom was a young girl. He was a businessman and a preacher, so they named me after him and prayed I would carry on the ministry my grandfather never had the chance to finish.

Growing up, I would set up a tape recorder and record myself preaching. (My dad still has one of these tapes!) God put a dream in my heart as a very young child, but I wasn't ready to fulfill it right then. I needed to walk through these character-building tests (a few of them more than once!), and through them, God has taught me that it's not really about me preaching to people. In fact, it's not about me at all. It's about *people* coming into closer relationship with God.

I know not everyone is given a dream like this as a three-year-old! If you're not sure about God's dream for your life, the best way to find out is to get to know Him. Get to know the One who is the Creator of dreams. Spend time with Him. He will give you a dream!

> Hear now My words:
> If there is a prophet among you,
> I, the LORD, make Myself known to him in a vision;
> I speak to him in a dream.
> Not so with My servant Moses;
> He is faithful in all My house.
> I speak with him face to face,
> Even plainly, and not in dark sayings;
> And he sees the form of the LORD.
> Why then were you not afraid
> To speak against My servant Moses? (Numbers 12:6–8)

This passage states that God spoke to Moses "face to face" and "plainly" (v. 8) because Moses was "faithful in all My house" (v. 7). In other words, because Moses sought God first, God spoke to him as a friend. Moses was not seeking the dream or the destiny—he was seeking a *relationship* with God. Because of that, God said He would reveal Himself to Moses.

If you're not sure about God's dream for your life, the best way to find out is to get to know Him.

Psalm 103:7 says, "He made known His ways to Moses, His acts to the children of Israel." Notice there's a big difference between "His ways" and "His acts." The children of Israel knew *what* God did—parting the Red Sea and miracles like that—but Moses knew *why* He did it.

Moses knew God as a Person and understood there is something much more important than knowing God's dream for your life. *It's actually knowing God.* If you're not certain of what God has dreamed for your life, I encourage you to pursue the Giver of dreams. Pursue the One who will not only reveal the dream to you but will also bring it to pass. As you get to know God as a friend, He will speak to you. He will reveal His dream for you, and then He will give you the ability to carry it out.

Discerning Which Dreams Are from God

Before we go any further, I want to talk about some dreams you may be holding on to that are not from God. We all have dreams, perhaps from our childhood, that are really just personal desires or fantasies. For example, you may have played football in high school and had big dreams of becoming a famous NFL player. Well, I hate to be the one to break it to you, but if you're over thirty-five, the Dallas Cowboys are probably not going to call! As we grow in faith and maturity, we must let go of those fantasies to fully embrace the dreams God has given us.

You may wonder, *How can I know the difference between my dreams and God's dreams for me?* The best thing to do with any dream is to put it on the shelf and continue to spend time with God. He will confirm His dream for your life in time. It's not that you don't have faith for it or that you forget about the dream. You simply submit it to the Lord, trusted friends, and an authority figure in your life. You don't have to try to figure it out on your own. But you do have to remember the dream itself is not your destiny. You'll learn throughout this book that the dream is what gets you started on the character-building journey toward your destiny.

When you focus too much on the dream, you're often focusing too much on yourself. As you get to know the Lord—the Giver of the dream—and make a habit of speaking to Him heart to heart, He will reveal His deepest thoughts and confirm His dreams for you.

Everyone's Dream Is Unique

Whatever dream God has given you is incredible and special and just for *you*. Yet, each one of our dreams is supernaturally intertwined with our loving heavenly Father's ultimate dream of reconciling His lost children to Himself. God has assigned a role—a destiny—for each one of us that is essential to His plans. No two roles are exactly alike, but they are all equally important to God. There are things He has created you to do that only you can accomplish. The same is true for me.

You may not pastor a church or preach on a regular basis like I do, but that doesn't mean your assignment is any less important than mine. If your destiny is outside of the church or organized ministry (and most are), it's still a holy, God-inspired destiny.

Sadly, many people live *with* the dream instead of *in* the destiny. That's why this message about Joseph is so vital. Each of us has a part to play, and our parts will be fulfilled only to the extent that our God-given destinies are fulfilled.

As I said, this message is for all of us—for me and for you, wherever you are, whatever your age. Every one of us is on a journey toward a destiny, and every one of us is destined to do great things for God and His kingdom. Like Joseph, you are destined for great power and great influence. Like Joseph, you have to pass ten important tests to step into your destiny and help the people God has placed in front of you. Like Joseph, you will find your destiny waiting on the other side of these tests.

Are you ready to find out how? Read on.

CHAPTER ONE

The Pride Test

I t was early Sunday morning, and things were beginning to quiet down at the prayer center for James Robison's ministry. Volunteers were finishing their shifts and heading off to church, and the only two people left to answer the phones were myself and Terry Redmon—a good friend, who also happens to be James Robison's son-in-law.

An interesting series of events had led me to the prayer center that day. I was only in my twenties, but I had been involved in ministry for several years. Things happened pretty fast after I surrendered my life to Jesus Christ. I got saved at the age of nineteen, and ten months later, I started working for James Robison, an evangelist who was preaching in citywide evangelistic crusades. He asked me to start traveling with him and speaking at junior and senior high school assemblies. I had only been a Christian for a year when I began to travel and preach the gospel. Pretty heady stuff for someone so young (and even younger in the Lord!).

Though I started out speaking at public schools, it wasn't long before I was preaching at crusades. James was even gracious enough to give me a title: associate evangelist. Wow! I was only twenty years old, but because of my association with James, I was already involved in television and preaching to large crowds. And now I had a title to prove I was a bona fide evangelist!

It seemed to me that the favor of God was on everything I touched. What a destiny lay before me! What could stop me now?

In retrospect, it's clear that an enemy called pride had begun to creep into my life. Slowly, prideful thoughts began to take up residence in my mind—thoughts that could not coexist with a proper reverence for a holy God.

By the time I was twenty-five, I had become far too accustomed to hearing people tell me how gifted I was. I began to listen to their praise. Worse, I began to *expect* it! People would say to me, "You're so gifted! You can do anything!" And with all the wisdom of my twenty-five years, I began to believe them. I started thinking, *Man, I'm something. I'm really successful!*

Deep down, I knew I was prideful, but I didn't know what to do about it. The more my pride grew, the more it seemed to stand in my way. I began to pray about it, asking God for help. I said, "God, I know I have pride. I know my insecurity makes me vulnerable to it. I need to be free of this, but I don't know what to do!" 11-26-23

One day as I was praying, I asked the Lord, "What can I do about this? Is there anything I can do to deal with the pride in my life?"

His answer didn't exactly thrill me. I sensed God telling me, "Well, here's a thought. You could step out of ministry and take a regular job."

I suppose my response didn't exactly thrill Him either. I said, "Yes, that is a thought, Lord. It's a *bad* thought, but it *is* a thought."

The religious part of me couldn't imagine it would be God's will for me to leave ministry. (After all, I was being used so mightily by Him!) But try as I might, I could not get rid of that thought. It grew stronger and stronger until the Lord orchestrated the circumstances for me to step out of ministry. I finally did what the Lord suggested: I started looking for a "regular" job.

But I couldn't find one!

I quickly discovered I wasn't as valuable as I had presumed. Think about it. When all you've been is an evangelist, what do you list as your skills on a job application? Strong preaching ability? Gives excellent altar calls? Exegetes well? From a practical standpoint, I simply didn't have a lot of qualifications for a regular job.

After much searching, I finally found a position as a security guard at a Motel 6. That was the only job I could get. Now you must remember, people had told me I was so gifted that I could do *anything*. But it didn't take long for me to learn it wasn't true. I learned that without God's blessing, I can't do anything. It's only through the blessing of God that we can have true success. This is a valuable lesson I never would have learned without first stepping out of ministry.

It's only through the blessing of God that we can have true success.

After a month of working nights as a security guard at Motel 6, I felt I had made great strides toward humility, and I decided I was ready to return to ministry. I checked back with James Robison's ministry to see if they had any job openings. I was happy to discover they needed a morning supervisor at their prayer center, from 5:00 a.m. to 2:00 p.m. That sure sounded better than the graveyard shift I had been working at Motel 6, so I took the job.

Keep in mind, I had been an associate evangelist. Now I was back at the ministry but working as a prayer partner. It was clear God was continuing to do His pride-killing work in my heart.

As I said, on that particular morning Terry and I were the only ones left in the room, and I was busy on the phone, talking with a woman who had called for prayer. Before ending the call, she said to me, "You sound so familiar." I began to fill her in on exactly who I was. "Oh, you probably recognize me from one of the times I traveled and preached with James," I said. "I'm an associate evangelist here at the ministry."

The room seemed strangely quiet as I hung up the phone. Terry turned to me, and I noticed he had taken his phone off the hook.

"Can I talk to you a minute?" Terry asked.

I nodded.

"Robert," he continued gently, "I am so happy you're working here again. I realize most people would not be willing to do it, and I'm so glad to see you're allowing God to work in this area of your life. But I want to ask you something. Why did you tell that woman you're an associate evangelist? That's no longer your title, and you know that. You know what you are—you're a prayer partner."

Feeling defensive, I said, "Well, I *used* to be an associate evangelist, and I just thought it would bless her to know that." Bless *her*! My words seemed hollow and contrived, even to me.

I wasn't quite sure why I had told her that, so I asked Terry a question: "When you're on the phone with someone, don't you ever tell them that you're James Robison's son-in-law?"

"No, I don't."

"Don't you think it would bless someone who calls in to know they got to pray with James's son-in-law?" I asked.

Terry drew a deep breath. "Well," he replied, "if they are blessed by *that*, then they are being blessed for the wrong reason." I will never forget the words that followed.

"Robert, I love you, man. But you are going to have to get to the place where you have your identity in Christ and not in what you do or in who you are." *(or what u weigh...)*

The words Terry spoke to me that day pierced my heart. Yet God took those words and began to use them in my life. In fact, He continues to use them to this day.

You see, although I didn't know it at the time, I was in the very early stages of a journey toward my destiny. God had given me a glimpse of how He wanted to use me and the destiny He had in mind for me. But I was in the middle of an important test, and I would have to pass it before I could move into the next phase along the path to my destiny.

At that point I had yet to learn that a great destiny carries with it great responsibilities—responsibilities that require strong character. It's easy to get excited about God's plans without having any idea about the strengths we will need to fulfill them. But God knows. He knows everything about us. He knows the dreams He has for us and what it will take to get the job done, and He wants to fully equip us.

Seasons of Testing

We may love God and have big dreams in our hearts that He Himself has placed there, but if we don't have God's character, then we won't get very far. That's why He allows us to go through tests on the way from the dream to the destiny—tests that root out sin and prepare us to succeed when we get there.

I am not the first person to find myself seemingly sidetracked from a God-given dream. Thousands of years ago, a young man named Joseph also received a dream from God. And it wasn't long before he found himself in the middle of an unexpected test—a test that probably didn't seem to line up at all with the dream God had given him.

That test was only the beginning of a long season of testing for Joseph. In fact, he went on to experience ten distinct character tests on the way to his destiny. After passing those tests, he stepped into his destiny—the glorious fulfillment of God's dream. Walking out the fullness of that dream was not only a great blessing to Joseph but also to millions of people who came after him.

Every one of us will encounter these same ten tests on the way from our dreams to our destinies. And like Joseph, we will have to pass these tests in order to see our dreams fulfilled. That's why I'm so glad God doesn't flunk any of us on our tests. I saw a lot of "Fs" on my school papers growing up, and I'm sure there were many times God could have written a big "F" on the pages of my life! But instead, each time we fail one of these character tests, He graciously writes "Retake" and allows us to keep retaking the test until we pass it. Why? Because it's only when we pass the test that we're able to step into the destiny God has planned for us.

The Pride Test: Revealing the Pride Within

Interestingly enough, Joseph's first test was the same one I found myself facing that day at the prayer center. It's what I call the Pride Test, and it's a very important one. Joseph experienced it. I experienced it. And I'm convinced every one of us will have to pass this test before we can move from our dreams to our destinies.

Genesis 37 describes how Joseph first received his dream from God and how he handled it.

Joseph, being seventeen years old, was feeding the flock with his brothers. And the lad was with the sons of Bilhah and the sons of Zilpah, his father's wives; and Joseph brought a bad report of them to his father.

Now Israel loved Joseph more than all his children, because he was the son of his old age. Also he made him a tunic of many colors. But when his brothers saw that their father loved him more than all his brothers, they hated him and could not speak peaceably to him.

Now Joseph had a dream, and he told it to his brothers; and they hated him even more. So he said to them, "Please hear this dream which I have dreamed: There we were, binding sheaves in the field. Then behold, my sheaf arose and also stood upright; and indeed your sheaves stood all around and bowed down to my sheaf."

And his brothers said to him, "Shall you indeed reign over us? Or shall you indeed have dominion over us?" So they hated him even more for his dreams and for his words.

Then he dreamed still another dream and told it to his brothers, and said, "Look, I have dreamed another dream. And this time, the sun, the moon, and the eleven stars bowed down to me."

So he told it to his father and his brothers; and his father rebuked him and said to him, "What is this dream that you have dreamed? Shall your mother and I and your brothers indeed come to bow down to the earth before you?" And his brothers envied him, but his father kept the matter in mind. (Genesis 37:2-11)

We have to marvel at the fact that Joseph shared his first dream so enthusiastically with his older, stronger, bigger brothers—especially when the Bible tells us that his brothers already "hated him and could not speak peaceably to him" (Genesis 37:4). Notice it says the brothers didn't just dislike him—they *hated* him. Clearly Joseph didn't get the hint, and when he had his second dream, he did it again! Not a brilliant move on Joseph's part. I'm not sure about you, but I did a lot of stupid things when I was seventeen years old, and apparently Joseph did too. So it's no surprise that his brothers' response was less than enthusiastic.

Little did Joseph know what would happen between these dreams and his destiny. Although he was seventeen years old when he received his dreams from God, it wasn't until he was thirty years old that he began to fulfill them (see Genesis 41:46). Thirteen long years went by before Joseph began to walk in the first steps of his destiny. What could explain the long lag-time between the dreams and their fulfillment?

After all, it seemed obvious from the dreams that Joseph was destined for great power and influence. Indeed, his brothers were envious after hearing the dreams—although they had mocked them to his face. Joseph's father didn't discount the dreams entirely either. The Bible says his father rebuked him about them, but then he "kept the matter in mind" (Genesis 37:11).

But there was a test on the horizon for Joseph. Something was standing in the way of Joseph moving toward the destiny God had shown him, and Joseph was about to have an opportunity to face that obstacle and deal with it. The reason for this test was really quite simple: Joseph had pride in his heart.

It's important to notice that Joseph had pride in his heart *before* he ever received the dreams from God. The Bible says Joseph was keeping the flock with his brothers, and he "brought a bad report of them to his father" (Genesis 37:2). Never mind what the bad report was about— eph was a bit of a tattletale! Perhaps his brothers weren't exactly perfect, and they may indeed have deserved some correction. But this verse reveals that Joseph thought of *himself* as someone qualified to make that type of judgment about them. He even took it upon himself to see that they were corrected, although they were older and more experienced. Any time we pass judgment on the behavior of others, it reveals a prideful attitude on our part. And it seems Joseph had a prideful attitude.

God knew Joseph was prideful, yet He still gave him the dreams. God had a big destiny in mind for Joseph, and He knew his prideful attitude would have to go if Joseph were to successfully reach his destiny.

Now, here's something important to note: these dreams were *not* Joseph's destiny. Joseph's purpose on earth was not to have his brothers bow down to him like he dreamed, although that would happen. His purpose was to save the lives of millions of people. God was preparing Joseph to be second in command of the greatest nation on earth and to store up grain during a seven-year famine so millions could escape starvation. *That* was his destiny.

So why didn't God give Joseph dreams about saving multitudes or storing up grain? I believe there are two reasons. First, immature people are not always motivated by helping others or excited about saving up grain during a worldwide famine. It's not exactly thrilling to think about that being your destiny. However, God knew seventeen-year-old Joseph would find the idea of his older brothers—especially ones who hated him—bowing down to him exciting! The thought of being well-known, powerful, and successful is *extremely* motivating. You also may have been given a dream about being great and successful, but that's not God's ultimate purpose for your life. Helping people is your God-given destiny. I've realized as I've matured in the Lord that God may give me influence, but it's always for His purposes—not my own. God may have given Joseph dreams about his brothers bowing to him to motivate him in ways that other parts of his true destiny may not have.

Second, in giving Joseph these specific dreams, God was helping him take the first necessary steps toward his destiny by revealing issues in Joseph's heart. You may have wondered why God would give such huge dreams to a man so young, especially when He knew Joseph already had pride in his heart. Why not wait until he was a little older, a little wiser, a little humbler, perhaps? The answer is really quite simple: God planned for Joseph to step into his destiny at the age of thirty, and He knew that could never happen until Joseph dealt with his pride. God allowed Joseph to see the big picture at the young age of seventeen so the pride in his heart could be exposed and dealt with before he moved closer to his destiny.

A different dream or the full picture of his destiny may not have revealed this sin and allowed him to start working on passing the test. Like Joseph, God may have given you a specific dream to work out some things in your life. But please hear me: your dream is often not the same as your destiny. Your dream is simply the catalyst for the character tests on the path toward your destiny, and God knows exactly the kind of dream He needs to give you to get you started.

Yes, Joseph failed the first test, but God knew he would fail it. Remember, although we may fail, we never actually flunk a test with God; we just keep taking it over and over again until we pass it.

Every one of us deals with pride, and every one of us must pass the Pride Test. You may have to go lower and lower before you finally pass it, but God will see to it that you pass. Never forget the truth of the promise found in Philippians 1:6: "Being confident of this very thing, that He who has begun a good work in you will complete it until the of Jesus Christ."

God has big destinies for all of us, just as He did for Joseph, and He will seek to get rid of anything that stands in the way.

God may have revealed glimpses of the big destiny He has planned for you, but if your character isn't ready for it, the destiny will destroy you. Your character is the foundation of your destiny. That's why you will never have a larger destiny than your character can support. You need to be ready to carry the responsibility of your destiny. If you can't handle the dream, you will never be able to handle the destiny.

Your character is the foundation of your destiny.

So, if you seem to be stuck on the way to your destiny, allow God to work in your heart. Ask Him if there's an area of your character He may be trying to shape or improve. The Bible talks about refining precious metals through fire so they are pure for their purpose (see Zechariah 13:9). God may have given you big dreams followed by big tests to reveal issues that were already there so you can deal with them and move on. He wants to get you to the place where He can lead you into your destiny.

Dealing with Pride

It shouldn't surprise us that pride is often the first and most frequent test we face. After all, pride is the original sin. It's the sin that caused Lucifer to fall (see Isaiah 14:12–13), and it was an appeal to pride that Satan used to tempt Adam and Eve to fall as well (see Genesis 3:5). Obviously, pride and falling are closely linked. In fact, King Solomon warned us about this when he wrote, "Pride goes before destruction, and a haughty spirit before a fall" (Proverbs 16:18).

If we're honest, we will all admit to having dealt with pride at some time or another. Even if we've passed the Pride Test several times already, we'll probably continue to take this test as long as we live. It's a bit like a foundational subject in school, such as math. We may pass it at the third-grade level, but then we need to pass it at the fourth-grade level. Once we've passed it at the fourth-grade level, we need to pass at the fifth-grade level, and so on.

The good news is that each time we pass a test with God, we receive a new level of responsibility in His kingdom. Of course, with each new level of responsibility, we face a new level of pride tests.

The Problem Is Your Tongue

Here's a simple guideline for everyone who wants to pass the Pride Test: when God gives you a dream, don't brag about it! Joseph made this mistake when he told his brothers his dreams. The Scriptures tell us that his brothers hated him "for his dreams *and for his words*" (Genesis 37:8, emphasis added). It wasn't just Joseph's dreams that offended his brothers—it was also the way he talked about his dreams and the way he talked about himself. The dream was from God, but Joseph's bragging certainly was not.

Now, bragging is a sign of immaturity, but we have to give Joseph a little bit of a break here. After all, he was only seventeen. But seventeen-year-olds aren't the only ones who brag. Sadly, many thirty-year-olds, fifty-year-olds, and sixty-year-olds brag as well. It seems each of us is susceptible to boasting and self-promotion, just as every one of us is eptible to pride and insecurity.

If we want to move toward our destinies, we're going to have to learn to control our tongues. Why? Because the Bible tells us that whoever can control their tongue is a "perfect" person and is able to control the rest of their body as well (see James 3:2). If you want to deal with the pride in your life, you're going to have to control your tongue. If you can't control your words, then you'll never reach God's destiny for you. forget those things... the past,

11-26-23 This applies not only to words of vanity but also to words of anger, criticism, or any other words contrary to God's words and ways. But the area of bragging is certainly a good place to start! So don't brag about the call of God on your life. Don't brag about the gifts you have. Don't brag about the things you've done for God or the things you're going to do for Him. shhh ---

I've noticed that as soon as we start talking about all the things God has done through us, it seems as though He immediately stops doing them. Now, there's a difference between sharing your testimony with others out of gratitude for all God has done and bragging about how God has moved through you. The main difference is who is getting the glory. God will not share His glory. When we begin to take the glory that is meant for God and bask in it ourselves, the anointing of the Holy Spirit leaves us. Let's keep the focus on God and all He has done—not on us. When the focus is on *us*, or even on what God has done through us, we are taking a stroll down the slippery slope of pride.

To get control of our bragging, some of us simply need to stop talking for a while because when we talk, we talk about ourselves. In other words, we brag! If that sounds harsh, let me say that I am sharing from experience. I feel like an expert because I've failed at this subject so many times. (or we complain)

I'm sure you know people who think *before* they talk, people who think *while* they talk, and people who think *after* they talk. Of course, there are also people who *never* think—they still don't know what they said after they said it! I've always been a person who thinks while he talks, although I wish I wasn't.

Years ago, after I'd come to know the Lord and was trying to work on being more Christ-like, I asked my wife, Debbie, to help me in this area. I was beginning to wonder if I had a tendency to talk too much, especially about myself. I begged her to be honest with me about it. At first, she was reluctant to give me an answer, but after a lot of coaxing, she confirmed my suspicions—and then some.

In her kind and loving way, Debbie let me know I was on the right track. So I enlisted her help in changing my behavior. I said to her, "When we're out to eat with people, will you nudge me if I'm talking too much? If I start talking about myself, give me a little kick under the table."

Well, my legs were black and blue for months! (Sadly, I usually didn't respond to the first two or three kicks!) But I really did want help growing in this area. I needed to control my tongue, and I'm so grateful Debbie was willing to help me.

The Real Problem Is in Your Heart

It's good to have control of your tongue, but there's another important element we need to understand. Bragging is not only a mouth problem—it's also a heart problem. The problem may seem to be mouth-centered, but it really begins in your heart.

I've had people say to me, "Well, Pastor, you don't know what's in my heart. You can't say I'm prideful." Yes, I can! Jesus even addressed this in Matthew 12:34 when He said, "For out of the abundance of the heart the mouth speaks." Later, in Matthew 15:18, He said, "But those things which proceed out of the mouth come from the heart, and they defile a man." I may not know everything in your heart, but if you've been talking for an hour about yourself and saying prideful statements, then I have a pretty good idea that pride is in your heart.

The Bible makes it clear: if you have a problem with what is coming out of your mouth, then you need to take a good look inside your heart. Because whatever is in your heart will eventually come out of your mouth.

If you have a problem with what is coming out of your mouth, then you need to take a good look inside your heart.

Have you ever noticed that pride always has to be heard? Pride has to give its opinion every time, whether an opinion has been asked for or not. Pride has to have a voice. Pride has to tell everybody who he is, what he's done, and all the things he is going to do. Pride interrupts people. Pride can never just be quiet. Wow!

It's good to bridle the tongue, and we all need discipline in this area. But if pride is in your heart, it will eventually find its way out of your mouth, no matter how much self-discipline you apply (or how many kicks under the table you receive).

What really needs to happen is for God to do a work in your heart, because when God gets inside your heart, He can start to deal with the root of pride.

The Root of Pride

One reason pride tends to keep popping up is that we often try to deal with the "fruit" of it rather than getting to the "root." When we see the fruit of pride in our lives, we like to get out our pruning shears and snip away at the leaves—perhaps even lop off a few branches here and there. But if we don't deal with the root of pride, it will just keep sprouting up in our lives, prolonging our testing and delaying our destiny.

The root of pride must be removed, or we will continue to struggle in this area. When I first preached this sermon series and published this book, I made a strong statement: "The root of pride is insecurity." Now, this statement is still true, but over the years I've added two more words to help us better understand the root of pride: inferiority and inadequacy. There are times in our lives when we may not relate to being insecure, but most of us can relate to feelings of inadequacy or inferiority, such as when starting a new job or experiencing an imposing boss.

If you know a prideful person, then you know a person who struggles with insecurity, inferiority, or inadequacy. He or she may try to mask it with big, pompous-sounding words (which certainly look and sound like pride), but it's really their way of trying to appear more confident.

To put it another way, pride is the fruit the world sees because of what comes out of our mouths. But what they don't see is the root of insecurity in our hearts, and this insecurity is the cause of the problem. This is the reason why we'll never be able to overcome pride until we deal with the root. Our own sense of insecurity and the accompanying feelings of inferiority or inadequacy fuel our prideful behavior.

When Gateway Church was just a few years old, the congregation began growing exponentially. It was incredible to see, but it also meant

I was now being recognized at restaurants and grocery stores. It was strange, but I have to admit that I really liked it at first. You see, my sister was popular in high school. She was a cheerleader, and she was voted the "friendliest student" in school. However, my high school experience was very different. I hung out with the wrong crowd, did drugs, and was a troublemaker. I was the opposite of the popular kid. But now *I* was the popular one! I relished the fame for a season and became prideful over "my success," not fully recognizing it was rooted in an insecurity from my past. It eventually caught up with me, though, and I began to hate the weight popularity placed upon me. It took me a few years and a great therapist to work through the enemy's lies about my identity.

With every new season or position come new insecurities, inferiorities, and inadequacies. You will continue to be tested in this area as you grow and move forward in your destiny. It's a test I went through again not too long ago.

Debbie and I recently held a reunion at our home for the elders of Shady Grove Church, where I served before founding Gateway. We were having a wonderful time together that night, sharing memories and honoring Pastor Olen Griffing and his wife, Syble, who are a spiritual father and mother to me and many others. They have had such an impact on our lives and ministries, and as proof, I began spouting off how many viewers watch me on TV. I had just received the ratings back from my TV ministry, and they were rather impressive—the numbers were in the millions! But this group of people already knew how well our ministry was doing; I didn't have to tell them. I wasn't intentionally trying to brag, but afterward, I felt horrible because I realized how prideful and arrogant I sounded.

Later that night, I asked the Lord, "Why did I feel the need to do that? Why am I still trying to impress people after all these years?"

The Lord gently reminded me, "Because your identity cannot be found in what you do or who you are. Your identity can only be found in *Me*."

Like Joseph, I was looking for affirmation from these friends I had known for years. In truth, part of me was saying, "I want you all to know that I made it!" Pride was what came out of my mouth, but the root was something deeper.

There may be times we feel as if we have to let everyone know who we are and what we've accomplished. We try to build ourselves up and become confident in ourselves instead of resting in our status as God's children. That's one reason pride so often manifests itself in bragging. Bragging is really a way of trying to achieve a sense of security and acceptance by making sure everyone knows exactly how "special" we really are. Eventually, we begin to believe our own rhetoric, and pride takes root.

If pride is in your heart, then insecurity, inferiority, or inadequacy is in your soul (your mind, will, and emotions). Essentially, your thoughts, decisions, and feelings are the building blocks of your soul, and when insecurity, inferiority, or inadequacy becomes the driving force behind what you think, do, and feel, pride has a chance to infiltrate your heart.

If we take a closer look, we can see something lying behind this sense of insecurity, inferiority, or inadequacy. It's fear—fear that people won't accept us or value us unless they know how great we are. Fear that we won't live up to what's expected of us. Fear that people will discover how much we lack. So we talk about ourselves, hoping to be considered worthy of acceptance by others.

However, there is a fatal flaw in our logic. Our accomplishments, no matter how impressive, are not what make us valuable. Even our dreams from God, as wonderful and awe-inspiring as they might be, are not *who* we are.

As born-again believers, we are blood-washed sons and daughters of the King. *That* is our true identity. That is who we are. We must become comfortable and secure in that identity because once we are, pride no longer has power over us.

I don't know if you've noticed this, but the president of the United States does not feel the need to tell people he is the president. Think about it. Can you imagine the president walking into a room and announcing, "Pay attention everyone because I am the president! Commander-in-Chief! Leader of the free world! Yes, sir, 'Mr. President' is what they call me." No, he *knows* he is the president, and he doesn't have to tell anyone.

Do you realize Jesus didn't have to tell anybody who He was either? Jesus knew exactly who He was. But when Satan tempted Jesus in the wilderness, the first thing the enemy did was try to create insecurity about Jesus' identity (see Matthew 4:1–3). Satan said, "*If* You are the Son of God" (Matthew 4:3, emphasis added), and then he tried to tempt Jesus to prove something. But Jesus never even dignified that challenge with a direct answer. He simply replied, "It is written . . . It is written . . . it is written . . ." (Matthew 4:4, 7, 10).

Jesus could have said, "Oh, yes, I am the Son of God! Wait just a minute here, Satan! Let me tell you a thing or two about my Son-of-God-ness!" Instead, though, He set a beautiful example of security. Jesus rested in the simple truth of *His Father's words,* and that's all He expects us to do. When we are tempted with feelings of insecurity, inferiority, or inadequacy, we must go back to what God our Father has said about us and rest in that truth.

Let's explore some of what He has declared about who we are.

Your Identity in Christ

It's vital to understand that the ultimate key to your victory over pride is knowing who you are in Christ.

Jesus knew who He was in His relationship with the Father, so He didn't have to prove anything about Himself. In the same way, you must come to the place where your identity is in Christ and in your relationship *with* Him—not in what you do *for* Him. If your identity is in what you do or the name you've built for yourself, then you are failing the Pride Test.

So how can you root out insecurity, inferiority, and inadequacy and prevent pride from thriving in your life? With two powerful weapons: knowing who you *are* and remembering who you *were*.

The first weapon is to know who you are: a child of the King, beloved and cherished by the mighty and sovereign Creator of the universe.

It's easy to be secure when you know your heavenly Father loves you. And it really doesn't matter whether others know it or not. We don't need to brag or tell anyone about it, because we know in our hearts we're His children, and *that* is what is most important.

Knowing this—really *knowing* it—is the death of insecurity. But what about pride? How can we be sure we aren't prideful again?

The second weapon against pride is to remind yourself of who you used to be and remember you were adopted. Here's a beautiful illustration that will help you understand your identity in Christ:

> There once was a prince who lived in a castle. One day he looked out the window and saw a beautiful woman. He thought, I have to meet her! So he disguised himself by growing a beard, putting on ragged clothes, and taking a common job in the town.

As the prince, he could easily have ordered this woman to be his wife, but he wanted her to fall in love with him. He wanted to meet her where she lived, spend time with her, and get to know her.

Over the course of several years, he fell in love with her, and she fell in love with him. He proposed, and she accepted. But then he said to her, "I need you to know who I really am. I'm the prince."

She was shocked! But she was in love, so they went ahead with the wedding ceremony and returned to live in the palace.

The prince introduced his new wife to the king, and she officially became a daughter of the royal family. She knew she was born a pauper, but she could rest secure in the knowledge that her husband knew her and loved her. Her new father, the king, loved her as his daughter. She was adopted into the royal family through love.

You see, we all are the young woman in the story. We weren't born into royalty—we were born sinful and lowly. But Jesus, our Prince, looked out the window of His castle in heaven and fell in love with us. Then He came to live as a pauper on earth to win our hearts. With our acceptance of Him, we were adopted into His royal family. Through His extravagant, sacrificial, and unconditional love, we can now live as sons and daughters of the King!

Yes, we are secure in God. We don't have to tell anyone who we are, because we *know* we are the King's beloved children, and we can be secure in His love for all eternity. Knowing I'm a child of the King takes care of my insecurity. Remembering I was adopted takes care of my pride!

**We are the King's beloved children,
and we can be secure in His love for all eternity.**

Without God, we are nothing. Jesus declared this to us in John 15:5 when He said, "Apart from me you can do nothing" (NIV). There is a wonderful sense of security in knowing this truth. It's liberating to be in a room full of strangers and not feel the need to tell them what you've done or who you are.

When we pass the Pride Test, we can be a "nobody" or do "nothing" and still be confident, content, and at peace because the greatest joy in life comes from knowing Him.

If God continues to use us to do grand things, that's great! And if He uses someone else to a greater degree, that's wonderful, too, because being a follower of Christ is not about proving what we can do for God—*it's about receiving all He has already done for us*. It's about knowing Him and allowing Him to work in our lives, helping us fulfill the roles He has given us.

Humble Yourself

When I was a young man, I was asked to speak at a really large conference. I was the youngest speaker there, and my spiritual fathers were sitting on the front row. It was a big moment for me, and I definitely thought it would go to my head.

So I prayed beforehand, "God, please help me to be humble today."

The Lord responded, "I can't do anything about that. You either are, or you aren't. I can't help you to be humble."

I was a little shocked! But as I thought about it, I realized the Bible never tells us to pray for humility. It simply tells us to humble ourselves. First Peter 5:6 says, "Therefore *humble yourselves* under the mighty hand of God, that He may exalt you in due time" (emphasis added).

So how do you humble yourself? I have found a very easy method: spend time with God every day.

It's easy to be humble when you've spent time in the presence of a holy God. If you sit down to meet with God, it's very difficult to walk away puffed up with pride! The longer you stay out of God's presence, the more you get filled with your own presence. But when you have an encounter with the Creator and Sustainer of the universe, you see how big, wonderful, and awesome He is, and you see yourself as you really are. You are reminded of the fact that it's only because of His grace that you have come this far. You walk out of that meeting knowing exactly who you are and Whose you are.

I make sure to set aside time every day to read my Bible and pray. I also schedule an extended time of worship at least once a week, usually on my Sabbath day. I've found that having an hour or two simply to worship in His presence reorients my heart toward God and creates a space for Him to lovingly address certain things in my life. This is different than worshipping at church on Sunday mornings—it's intimate, individual time for me and God. I think everyone needs time like this with the Lord.

I also think everyone needs someone like Debbie—someone close to you who can honestly speak into your life. There have been so many times when Debbie has approached me about how something I said came across as prideful. It may not have been my intention, but she'll address it with me. I have also invited some good friends to keep me accountable in humility, just like Terry did all those years ago at the Prayer Center, and they share with me when they see something prideful sneaking into my life.

As you spend time with God, He will show you who you really are in Him. He will help you understand the security you have as His son or daughter. This is how you stay humble and pass the Pride Test. Then you can move forward on the path to discovering the wondrous destiny He has prepared for you.

CHAPTER TWO

The Pit Test

I heard a story once about a guy who worked the late shift at his job. It was always dark when he got off work, and he would cut across the cemetery on his way home. One moonless night he couldn't see very well, and he happened to fall into a grave that had been dug the previous day. Try as he might, he couldn't get himself out of that hole. So he began to shout and throw dirt and rocks, hoping someone would come and rescue him. But it was the middle of the night, and no one was around to hear his cries for help. Finally, he decided to just wait until morning, when someone was bound to come by and help him. So he just sat down quietly in the corner of the grave.

Later that night a drunk was walking across the cemetery, and he happened to fall into the same freshly dug grave. Try as he might, he couldn't get himself out of that hole. So, like the first man, he began to shout for help and throw rocks—but all was dark and quiet, and he received no response. Suddenly, a hand reached out from the darkness and touched him on the shoulder. A voice said, "Hey, buddy, there's no getting out of here."

But strangely enough—he did!

My kids tell me this is a "dad joke," but it demonstrates what we can accomplish if we're properly motivated. And when you find yourself in "the pits" of life, it's good to know how to get yourself out.

The Pit Test: Finding Your Way Out

Like it or not, all of us will go through times when we feel as if we are in a pit. We may not be sure how we got there and even less sure how to get ourselves out. But one thing is certain: we won't move into our destiny unless we get out of the pit!

Joseph didn't just *feel* like he was in a pit; he was literally in one! He had just received those glorious dreams from God, and the future seemed bright and wonderful. Then suddenly he was stuck in a pit (see Genesis 37:24), and it began to seem like his dreams of honor and authority were just some kind of cruel joke.

What caused Joseph to end up there? What lessons would he have to learn before he could get out? Like Joseph, it's important for us to understand the lessons of the Pit Test, so we can pass the test and move on.

Let's take a look at his story in Genesis 37:12–24.

Then his brothers went to feed their father's flock in Shechem. And Israel said to Joseph, "Are not your brothers feeding the flock in Shechem? Come, I will send you to them."

So he said to him, "Here I am."

Then he said to him, "Please go and see if it is well with your brothers and well with the flocks, and bring back word to me." So he sent him out of the Valley of Hebron, and he went to Shechem.

Now a certain man found him, and there he was, wandering in the field. And the man asked him, saying, "What are you seeking?"

So he said, "I am seeking my brothers. Please tell me where they are feeding their flocks."

And the man said, "They have departed from here, for I heard them say, 'Let us go to Dothan.'" So Joseph went after his brothers and found them in Dothan.

Now when they saw him afar off, even before he came near them, they conspired against him to kill him. Then they said to one another, "Look, this dreamer is coming! Come therefore, let us now kill him and cast him into some pit; and we shall say, 'Some wild beast has devoured him.' We shall see what will become of his dreams!"

But Reuben heard it, and he delivered him out of their hands, and said, "Let us not kill him." And Reuben said to them, "Shed no blood, but cast him into this pit which is in the wilderness, and do not lay a hand on him"—that he might deliver him out of their hands, and bring him back to his father.

So it came to pass, when Joseph had come to his brothers, that they stripped Joseph of his tunic, the tunic of many colors that was on him. Then they took him and cast him into a pit. And the pit was empty; there was no water in it.

I find it amusing that Joseph was sent out to find his brothers, but he ended up "wandering in the field" (Genesis 37:15). We know his brothers called him a "dreamer" (Genesis 37:19), and now it appears he may have been a daydreamer as well. After all, he didn't find the man—the man found him. Now Joseph was only seventeen, so we have to give him a little grace for his wandering and dreaming. But whatever Joseph was dreaming about that day, I have a feeling he wasn't imagining what was about to happen.

What a shock it must have been for him! From Joseph's point of view, everything had been going so well. He had recently let his father know that the older brothers could use a little improvement in their behavior, and now his father was sending him on a mission to go check on them. He was even wearing the beautiful coat that marked him as his father's favored son. It might have seemed to Joseph like his dream of leading his family was already being fulfilled. But before he knew what was happening, he was thrown into a pit! His father was nowhere in sight, and the beautiful coat his father had given him had been taken away and dipped in goat's blood. Joseph didn't have food or water, and even worse, there seemed to be no way out of the pit. He knew he might very well die there.

In that moment, it seemed as though his dreams would never come to pass. Joseph was going through the Pit Test—a test all of us will endure at one time or another.

You know you're experiencing the Pit Test when nothing in your life seems to be going right. Things may have been going smoothly, but then everything goes very wrong all at once. It's easy to get discouraged and depressed because you're in a pit, and it appears there's no way out.

Every one of us will fall into a pit at some point in our lives. The question is, *Are we going to stay in the pit forever, or are we going to pass the Pit Test and move on toward our destiny?*

If you want to know how to get out of the pits of life, it's important to understand how you fall into them.

Reasons You Find Yourself in the Pit

First, we need to recognize that some pits are simply a part of life. In John 16:33, Jesus said, "In the world you *will* have tribulation [or trouble]" (emphasis added).

Jesus understood we would have trouble because He knew we would be living in a world contaminated by the effects of sin. This fallen world is full of trouble, and pits are simply a byproduct of sin.

Now, we can (and often do) invite trouble upon ourselves, or trouble just decides to show up uninvited. Sometimes we are shoved into a pit, and it's not our fault we're there. Either way, in the course of life, we can expect to encounter some trials and tribulations. As long as we're on this earth, we will go through difficult situations and challenging times.

When we find ourselves in a pit, we tend to think we had very little to do with how we got there. But if we look inward, we usually find that we have played at least some part in getting ourselves into a pit. Now, I'm not talking about condemnation. I'm talking about soul searching. King David wrote, "Search me, O God, and know my heart; try me, and know my anxieties; and see if there is any wicked way in me" (Psalm 139:23-24). In other words, "God, did I do anything to cause this situation in my life? What got me in this place? What do You want me to learn from it so I can grow?"

All too often we don't recognize our own responsibility. In difficult times, it's much easier to blame others than it is to take a good, hard look at ourselves. And because the world is full of sin, there's certainly never a shortage of other people to blame!

It's very prevalent in our society today to adopt a victim mentality and blame all our problems on other people, such as our parents, spouse, or even the government.

For instance, you may be in a financial pit. It's easy to spend, spend, spend until all of a sudden, you're in a deep pit. I've known many people who go from financial pit to financial pit, and they tend to blame the economy, their salary, or their education. They don't think about whether they're stewarding their money well or tithing or budgeting. Instead of doing the soul-searching work of trying to find out their part in why they're in the pit, they simply blame everyone else.

In difficult times, it's much easier to blame others than it is to take a good, hard look at ourselves.

Back in the eighties, it was really trendy to own a Chevy Suburban. Before that, Suburbans were used as flower delivery trucks or for carrying caskets. But all of a sudden, they became cool, and my friends started buying these nice, roomy vehicles. And of course, I wanted one too!

So I asked the Lord, "Can I buy a Suburban?"

He quickly replied, "Nope."

And I, in all my great wisdom, started arguing with the Lord: "Well, it's in my budget. We are okay financially, and I know we can afford it. So can we buy one?"

Again, He said, "Nope."

I persisted, "Well, is there a reason?"

And He said, "Because I said so." (Just like parents do sometimes.)

I gave up arguing with Him for a couple months, but one spring day I thought, *Everyone's getting Suburbans. It's not like a Suburban is a sin. I must have misheard what the Lord said.* So I started looking and found a *great* deal on one. (I'm sure you know where I'm going with this. Don't judge me—I know I'm not the only person to think that something was God's will because it was a good deal!) So I drove to the car dealership, and as I was taking the exit, the song "Turn Your Heart Toward Home" came on the radio.

Immediately the Lord said to me, "Turn your heart toward home. This is not Me. You know this is not what I want for you." So I turned off the radio. I *really* wanted that Suburban.

I got to the dealership, and the Suburban looked great! And it was the exact price I could afford. I told the car salesman I'd buy it, and he asked me to come back in a few hours to trade in my old car and finalize the sale.

As I made my way back to the dealership later that day and started to exit, the same song, "Turn Your Heart Toward Home," came on the radio. Again, I ignored it.

I got to the dealership and found out the car wasn't ready yet, so Debbie and I went to dinner. On the way back, I took the same exit, and wouldn't you know it? The same song came on the radio! So obviously, being a godly man, you know what I did? I turned off the radio and bought the Suburban anyway!

Well, let me tell you, nothing was as I thought it would be. The gas gauge broke soon after I bought it, and it ran out of gas, stranding my whole family on the side of the road. Every tire went flat at a different time. Then the air conditioner broke. In June. In *Texas.* And I couldn't afford to fix it until October. Then, are you ready for this one? The engine had a small oil leak, ran out of oil, and blew up!

Finally, I said to the Lord, "I get the message!"

I put a new engine in the Suburban and sold it. I lost thousands of dollars.

Debbie asked why we were selling it if it had a new engine, and I said, "Because God told me not to buy it in the first place! I'm getting rid of this thing!"

A week later, a friend of mine called me and said, "Hey, my wife and I bought a new Suburban. Ours is only about three years old, and we want to give it to you. We were going to donate it last spring, but there were some details to work out, and the Lord told me to wait until the fall."

Pride and disobedience put me in a pit. I could've blamed the car dealership for selling me a bad car. I could have blamed God for not trying harder to stop me. I could have blamed Chevy for suddenly making Suburbans cool so I'd want one. I could even have blamed my friend for not telling me earlier about his desire to give me his car. But it was *my* mistake, *my* pride, and *my* disobedience. I needed to take responsibility and be obedient to God in order to get out of the pit. And God delivered me.

I don't wish to sound cruel or insensitive, but if you're forty-eight years old and still blaming your parents for where you are in life, you probably need to get over it. They may have done awful things to you, but at some point, you need to stop blaming them, work to find healing, and move on. You have been adopted by a new Father who loves you and is good to you. I realize I am using harsh language here, but I'm trying to make an important point: even if you did nothing wrong and the sins of others have put you into a pit, you can take responsibility to get out of it. Now, that doesn't mean you have to do it yourself. Truthfully, you may need the help of a counselor or someone to walk you through inner healing. If so, I really want to encourage you to seek help. But the truth is, God is ultimately the only One who can get you out of a pit. And you will never get out until you stop blaming other people for the difficulties you encounter in life.

Joseph had the perfect opportunity to develop a victim mentality. After all, he was just trying to obey his father when his brothers threw him into the pit. We know his brothers did it out of jealousy and hatred because the Scriptures clearly state his brothers not only envied him but hated him as well (see Genesis 37:4, 11). So it would have been easy for Joseph to put all the blame onto his brothers for being in the pit. It would have been easy for him to focus only on their sins and never take a good look at his own pride. It's true that Joseph's brothers had an evil attitude, but Joseph also had a sinful attitude of pride, which contributed to the problem.

In Genesis 37:18, it says: "Now when they saw him afar off, even before he came near them, they conspired against him to kill him." Think about that for a moment. How do you suppose they were able to see it was Joseph from such a great distance? It's simple: he was wearing that blasted coat! It may have been orange, green, yellow, and purple for all we know. Whatever it looked like, it was probably visible from very far away.

I'm sure Joseph loved that coat and wore it everywhere he went. His father had given it to him as a sign of his favor, so it's understandable that the coat was special to him. But since we know Joseph had a problem with pride, it's quite possible he wore the coat with an *attitude* of pride, maybe even with a haughty walk, causing his brothers to feel even more envious. His brothers were out in the wilderness taking care of the sheep and working hard for their father, and they could see that coat coming from a mile away. This may have made them angry, especially if they felt like Joseph was always showing off. Perhaps Joseph was constantly projecting the attitude, "I'm my father's favorite. I'm the best one. I'm better than all of you!"

Also, if you think about it, Joseph was old enough to be working in the field alongside his brothers. So why were they all working in the field together while he stayed home? Many theologians believe his father had to separate the brothers because they hated Joseph so much. His bragging created too much conflict and animosity. Since it's not likely that Jacob really wanted Joseph to check on his brothers' well-being, he may have sent Joseph with the hope that some reconciliation could take place. After all, they were ten grown men, all professionals, and all significantly older than Joseph. Eight of them were probably in their twenties and thirties. Reuben and Simeon, the two oldest, were in their forties. They knew how to take care of their sheep. They didn't need a seventeen-year-old kid to come check on them. Jacob probably knew his sons were doing okay—he was most likely trying to help a relationship develop between Joseph and his brothers. But Joseph was such a braggart that his relationship with his brothers had become terribly strained.

Joseph definitely shared some responsibility for creating the strained relationship and making it worse. He may have looked like an innocent victim in that pit, but he contributed to the events that put him there.

I've heard similar stories from individuals who believe their problems are strictly the result of the attitudes of others. "People are just jealous of me," they will say. "I'm not the one who has a problem. It's not the way that I act. It's not the way that I talk. It's not the way that I present myself. Everyone else has the problem!"

When we find ourselves in a pit, we first need to take a good look at ourselves. We need to humble ourselves and consider that we might be part of the problem and the reason we're in the pit. It's true that Joseph's brothers had an envy problem, but Joseph's pride was the real reason he ended up in the pit. Sometimes the source of our problems is within our own hearts.

We can learn a lot about the Pit Test by seeing ourselves in Joseph. He was a son who had his father's favor. In the same way, we are sons and daughters of the King, and we too have the favor of our heavenly Father. Because favor means grace, it signifies that God's grace is on us. Psalm 5:12 says, "For You, O LORD, will bless the righteous; with favor You will surround him as with a shield." God's favor—His grace—surrounds us.

Joseph's father, out of his great love for him, gave him a gift. But here's the problem: Joseph became proud of the gift his father gave him, and he showed it off every chance he got. He started to find his identity in the *gift* that identified him as the favored son, rather than in the *relationship* that made him the favored son. He ended up losing his gift as a result. Our relationship w/God is a Gift

In much the same way, our Father has given us gifts, but sometimes we can become caught up in them. We can become proud and show them off. We can start to find our identity or sense of worth in that gift, rather than in the One who gave it. I've had people come up to me and try to slip into conversation that they have a certain spiritual gift. But I just think, *Why do you have to tell me? Just use your gift instead of bragging about it and showing it off!* Our gifts aren't for showing off. They're for helping people.

Please understand this: the Giver of the gift is *so* much better than the gift. We need to be in love with the Giver. Because when we love the gift more than the Giver, we become prideful, and we risk losing the gift.

I want to clarify something important. Joseph's father gave him the gift, but it was not his father who took it away from him. Joseph lost his coat of many colors through his own actions. He lost it because he was prideful about it and what it represented.

When God gives us gifts, He doesn't take them back. The Bible tells us the gifts and callings of God are irrevocable; the King James Version says they are "without repentance" (Romans 11:29). This means God does not take back the gifts He has given us, but we can lose them ourselves. We've seen a lot of high-profile pastors and leaders over the years poorly steward their gifts because of pride and a lack of integrity. I wonder how many people have a gift from God but have misappropriated it or aren't able to use it because pride got in the way.

You may be thinking, *What if this happens to me? What if I lose the gift of God through my own actions? Is there any hope of getting it back?* To answer, I want you to think about the end of Joseph's story. Joseph ended up becoming the governor of Egypt, the second most powerful man in the world. As a result, he also became the second richest man in the world. He probably had hundreds of coats of many colors, as many coats as his heart could desire and his closet could hold. He may have even had a motorized coat rack that rotated his coats in front of him! The point is God restored all he had lost.

But Joseph got back something much more important than some nice clothes. He got back his relationship with his father. For years, he didn't have fellowship with his father—he wasn't even sure if he was alive. Once Joseph learned to walk in humility, God restored his

but that coat was gone.—

relationship with his father and his brothers as well as everything else he had lost. While the Bible doesn't tell us what happened to Joseph's bloody coat, personally, I don't think his father threw it away. It's possible Joseph might have received his beloved coat back. And perhaps he looked at it and thought, *Thank You, God. Thank You for the pit You delivered me out of and what You've done in my life.*

When you find yourself in a pit, you may feel that all is lost. But if you cry out to God in humility of heart, He is eager to restore you. The Bible says that if you humble yourself, you will be exalted (see 1 Peter 5:6).

Whatever you have lost, God can restore it if you repent and walk in humility.

Lies of the Pit

We've learned it's dangerous to walk in pride because you can end up in a pit. But we need to understand the pit itself can also be a dangerous place. That's because of what I call the lies of the pit.

Be assured, any time you fall into a pit you will encounter the lies of the enemy—lies of accusation, lies of hopelessness, and even fabricated evidence. And if you believe his lies, you could stay in the pit indefinitely. If you want to get out, you will have to learn to discern the enemy's lies and resist them with the truth.

The first truth we must keep in mind to overcome the lies of the pit is this: it's Satan who accuses us, not God. Revelation 12:10 identifies Satan as "the *accuser* of our brethren" (emphasis added). So *any* time you have an accusatory thought about yourself or someone else, know it's a lie from Satan. He is a slanderer and a liar. In fact, he's the father of all lies. In other words, if his lips are moving, he's lying.

I once heard a pastor share a story about a man who was serving communion at his church, and he accidentally bumped the communion table and spilled a little cup of grape juice. He glanced up and saw his pastor looking right at him. For two weeks, he was overcome with shame and guilt. He knew the look his pastor gave him meant he was mad at him for mishandling the Lord's Supper. He couldn't sleep or concentrate because he kept beating himself up over the incident. So the next time he saw his pastor, he started apologizing and explaining how it was an accident.

His pastor was puzzled and asked, "What are you talking about?"

The man tried to explain again: "Well, when I was serving communion a couple weeks ago, I bumped the table, and some of the juice spilled—you know, the blood of Christ. And you were looking right at me! I knew you were upset with what you saw."

The pastor smiled and responded, "I must have been thinking about something else because I don't remember this ever happening!"

This man had been obsessing about this situation every day for *two weeks*—beating himself up and living in shame and guilt—for something that wasn't even an issue! He had created a mental pit for himself, and the enemy was having a heyday with it.

I am sure he's not the only person who has ever overthought a situation into oblivion, giving the enemy free rein with their thoughts. How many hours and days of mental energy have you spent ruminating on slanderous lies the enemy introduces to you about yourself or someone else? How many times have you seen a post from a friend or acquaintance on social media that prompts a mental frenzy that takes weeks to unravel? Not all pits are Joseph-level, real-life holes in the ground. Some pits are ones you dig for yourself in your mind.

What's important to understand is that when you fall into a pit, whether it's one you imagine or one that's real, the devil will immediately begin to accuse you. You'll hear his accusations in your mind. *See, you're no good, or you wouldn't be in this pit. What's more, you'll never be any good! You'll never do anything for God. You'll never get your life straightened out.* Every time you hear condemning thoughts like this, remind yourself of the source, because it's Satan who accuses us, *not* God, and we are commanded to resist him (see James 4:7).

There's a difference between being accused by the enemy and being convicted by the Holy Spirit. But how can you tell the difference? It's one of the most frequent questions people ask me, and the answer is simple: if it's convicting, it's the Holy Spirit. If it's condemning, it's Satan. You can recognize conviction of the Holy Spirit because the Spirit always offers hope. Conviction says, "You shouldn't have spoken to your wife that way, but if you repent to Me and apologize to her, I'll make it right and help you overcome it." Conviction is specific and helpful. Condemnation is general and hurtful. It says, "You always do things wrong. You're a bad person. You'll never do anything right! You're stupid. You'll never get better. Things will never work out for you." Condemnation is not from God.

I feel such a burden for you to truly know God's character, so let me repeat this: God will *never* condemn you. John 3:17 says, "For God *did not* send His Son into the world to condemn the world, but that the world through Him might be saved" (emphasis added). God doesn't condemn us—He sent His Son to do the very opposite! Condemnation is always from the enemy.

When Joseph was in the pit, I'm sure he was accused by the enemy and tempted to believe his lies. Satan probably came to Joseph and said, "It's over, man. Those dreams you had are *never* going to come to pass. You've blown it too many times with that pride thing, and now it's simply too late. You're going to die in this pit! There is no reason to call out to God now. And why should you trust God anyway? After all, look what God let happen to you. He doesn't really care about you. Actually, He never did."

This is what the enemy does. Every time we're in a pit, he is right there to accuse us and lie to us. Satan is a pit professional! And he doesn't stop there. He accuses God as well. He says, "Look at what God did to you. Look at what God let happen to you. God is not faithful to you. If He were faithful, this never would have happened!"

Like Joseph, we must fight against the lies of the enemy. We know God is faithful. We know His words are true. But when we are in the pit, the enemy will try to get us to focus on our circumstances rather than on God's faithfulness. The enemy will even manipulate those circumstances to try to make his lies look like the truth. So if we let circumstances determine what we believe, we will get caught in the lies of the pit.

When we are in the pit, the enemy will try to get us to focus on our circumstances rather than on God's faithfulness.

It's important to understand this because the enemy is *very* deceptive. He will not only tell you a lie; he will also fabricate evidence to support his lies. This is how he was able to get Joseph's father to believe the lie that Joseph was dead.

So they took Joseph's tunic, killed a kid of the goats, and dipped the tunic in the blood. Then they sent the tunic of many colors, and they brought it to their father and said, "We have found this. Do you know whether it is your son's tunic or not?"

And he recognized it and said, "It is my son's tunic. A wild beast has devoured him. Without doubt Joseph is torn to pieces." (Genesis 37:31–33)

The brothers didn't actually tell their father that Joseph had been devoured by wild animals. Instead, they created false evidence and asked a misleading question: "Is this your son's coat?" Jacob believed the evidence, and he jumped to the conclusion that his son was dead. Out of his own mouth, Jacob said, "My son has been killed by wild animals." But it was a lie—a lie he would believe for more than two decades!

Think about it. For twenty-two years, Jacob believed his son was dead. For twenty-two years, he probably cried himself to sleep at night and had nightmares about a lion killing his son, ripping him limb from limb. The Bible says Jacob was so full of grief that he refused to be comforted, and he said, "For I shall go down into the grave to my son in mourning" (Genesis 37:35). But Joseph was not dead. Jacob had concluded it was the truth based on fabricated evidence.

Notice the callousness of Joseph's brothers. It makes me a little mad, actually. They heard their father's wailing and saw his grief. For twenty-two years, they never went to him with the truth that would have ended his grieving. They could have taken away their father's suffering in an instant by telling him, "Listen, Dad, it's not true. Joseph wasn't really torn apart by wild beasts. He's alive! We just fabricated the bloody coat." But they never refuted the lie they had so cleverly planted. Do you see the hardness of their hearts? That's the hardness of sin. This is how deceptive the enemy is.

We live in a sin-hardened world, and like Jacob, we will be tempted to believe fabricated evidence. When we allow the lies of the pit to determine what we believe, we suffer unnecessary grief.

This is something my son Josh experienced when he preached a weekend message for the first time at Gateway Church. A few days later, a lady from our church wrote a lot of negative and hateful things on social media, but the main point of her post was that the only reason Josh was preaching at Gateway was because of who his father was. Josh was really hurt when he read this. As a pastor's kid, he had some experience with mean things being written and said about me and our family, but this one really stung because he knew there was some truth to it. His dad *had* founded Gateway and asked him to preach that weekend.

Josh had been in California for a guys' trip that week when a friend texted him about the post. By the time he found it and finished reading it, his plane was taking off for the three-hour flight home. He didn't have Internet access on the plane, so he was left to sit and think about what this lady wrote about him. The more he thought about it, the more feelings of inadequacy and dejection began to creep in.

After some time, he finally said to the Lord, "I can't stop thinking about what that lady said about me. Is it true?"

And the Lord said, "It *is* true."

Josh instantly felt defeated, but then the Lord continued, "The only reason you preached at Gateway is because of who your *Father* is."

The truth is God was the One who had given Josh this opportunity. Satan had fabricated evidence and Josh believed it, but once he had an encounter with truth, the lie lost its power. No one—not even someone posting malicious opinions on social media—could tell him otherwise!

If you want to get out of the pit, you must learn to discern the lies of the enemy. You are especially vulnerable when you're in the pit. Your circumstances usually don't look very favorable, and that's precisely when Satan will manipulate those circumstances, even using half-truths, to deceive you. He wants you to jump to the wrong conclusion, so he will hold up those circumstances before you as evidence that you should believe him rather than have faith in God. But fabricated evidence, even if it looks convincing, is not the truth.

If you want to overcome the lies of the pit, you must learn to focus on what God says. When you are in the pit, you must remember that nothing is too hard for God, no matter what evidence the enemy might produce.

Let's say you're going through some challenges. Satan will say, "You're never going to be healed. Look at that report!" or "Your business is not going to make it—look at this Wall Street Journal article!" And here's a huge lie Satan tells us: "You're married to the wrong person." Then he will fabricate evidence to convince you it's true. There are so many compatibility tests available today, and some might even show that certain personality types aren't compatible and should not be married to each other. You might look at the test results and say, "Goodness gracious, I'm the opposite of my wife! I guess I'm married to the wrong person." Of course you're the opposite of your wife—that's why she's called the opposite sex! And that's probably what originally attracted you to her. You like what's different about her. Debbie and I have been married for more than forty-three years, and she still surprises me! It makes life with her fun. You wouldn't want to marry someone like you—if you were married to you, you'd go crazy!

The truth is when two people who are opposites come together, God can do a beautiful thing, because together they look like Jesus. This is God's plan for marriage. Yet when things get uncomfortable or difficult, Satan is right there to lie about your marriage.

Even worse than Satan's false evidence is his biggest lie: "You've messed up too much. It's too late for you. You've messed up so badly you will never fulfill God's destiny for your life."

Do you realize the Bible is a book entirely about restoration? It's filled with stories about people who messed up so badly it seemed even God couldn't do anything about it—yet He restored every one of them. Nothing is impossible for God! As long as you have breath, it's never too late to call out to God. It doesn't matter what pit you're in. If you call out to God, He can fix it.

The Purpose of the Pit

We can gain some important insights from another man in the Bible who messed up and got thrown into a pit. His name was Jonah. Remember him? God had a big destiny in mind for Jonah and gave him an assignment to save an entire city from destruction (see Jonah 1:2). But when God commanded him to go to Nineveh, Jonah decided to go in the opposite direction (see Jonah 1:3). Incidentally, this is always a bad strategy!

Jonah ended up in the maritime version of a pit—the belly of a fish. "Then Jonah prayed to the LORD his God from the fish's belly. And he said: 'I cried out to the LORD because of my affliction, and He answered me. Out of the belly of Sheol I cried, and You heard my voice'" (Jonah 2:1–2).

Sheol is simply an Old Testament word for "the pit." It shouldn't surprise us that Jonah ended up there. He messed up pretty badly. God had given Jonah a very important assignment, and he refused to do it. He ran away from God's plans, and as a result, he ended up in a pit. But from the bottom of that pit, Jonah cried out to God. And God heard his voice and delivered him.

That is the real purpose of the pit: to get you to cry out to God so He can deliver you and bring you back into relationship with Him. It's to get you in a place that is so far down you can't see a way out of it—a place where you can't do it on your own. Because the truth is you actually can't do *anything* on your own. Every breath comes from God! And once you realize this, you will cry out to God, and He will deliver you.

Several years ago, I was on vacation with Debbie in Colorado. It was a beautiful location, and we were having a great time, but I was feeling overwhelmed. The church was growing so quickly, and I knew I was inadequate to lead it. I was spiraling into a mental pit. So I told Debbie I needed to take a walk and spend time with the Lord. I went outside and sat on a rock overlooking an incredible vista of mountains and trees. I couldn't enjoy it, though, because I was torn up inside.

The Lord asked, "What is wrong with you?" (He obviously already knew what was going on, but He knew I needed to talk through it.)

"It's too big. What You've called me to do, it's too big for me. I can't do it," I said.

And He said, "Son, everything you've ever done was too big. It's always, always been too big for you. You know what the problem is? You actually thought you could do this on your own. Well, you couldn't even do this when the church was small. It's not about what you can do, it's about what I can do through you. It's not about your adequacy, it's about Mine."

I cried out to God, and He rescued me from my mental pit. He reminded me that I need Him *every day*. My pit of self-doubt and inadequacy actually saved me from striving to somehow make my destiny happen on my own. Doing that surely would have killed me. Similarly, both Jonah and Joseph were in pits that saved their lives. Jonah would have drowned if not for that fish. And Joseph's brothers were going to kill him. Even though Joseph was sold into slavery afterward, the pit still saved his life.

No matter what pit you're in—even if you dug it yourself—God is big enough to get you out of it!

No matter what pit you're in—even if you dug it yourself—God is big enough to get you out of it!

It's not hard for God to get you out of a pit. He is a redeeming God, and He delights in getting His children out of trouble. It doesn't matter how many pits you might be in. You could even be in several pits at the same time. You might be in a Pit Test with your finances, a Pit Test with your marriage, and a Pit Test with your job. God can deliver you out of every one of them if you'll just call out to Him.

The most important question is not whether God can deliver you out of the pit. The most important question is whether you are going to call out to God in humility. Are you going to ask God what He's trying to do in your life? Or are you going to wallow in the pit and gripe, murmur, and complain?

If we're being honest, much of what we like to call "prayer" is nothing more than complaining. If we are "talking" to God, we think of it as prayer, but it really isn't talking to God as though He is our loving Father. It's griping to Him about everything we don't like and want Him to change.

I wonder what the first few hours in that pit were like for Joseph. It's not hard to imagine him pacing back and forth, murmuring to God about how unfair it all was: "God, why would You let this happen to me? I'm such a good and upright guy. And I just want to remind You, God, that You have a big destiny for my life. My brothers are supposed to be bowing to me! I can't believe You would let this happen to me!"

But after some time, Joseph's perspective must have shifted. Somewhere in the pit, he must have cried out to God in true humility. He must have taken responsibility for his own sins and failures, fallen to his knees, and said, "I see it all now, God. I need You to forgive me. I admit that I'm a prideful, arrogant person, and I ask You to do a work in my heart."

When he cried out to God, his situation began to change! Although it wasn't apparent at the time, circumstances began to line up in the direction of his destiny. I think the moment Joseph repented, his brother Judah got the idea to sell Joseph to Midianite traders, rather than leave him in the pit to die (see Genesis 37:26–28). Then those Midianite traders brought Joseph to Egypt and sold him to Potiphar (see Genesis 37:36). Now being sold as a slave might not seem like a great alternative to the pit, but it was better than certain death, and Joseph certainly would have died if he had been left there.

Before Joseph ever got into that pit, God had a plan to get him out and bring him into his destiny. So when Joseph cried out to God, God began working through his situation, because being sold as a slave in

Egypt brought Joseph one step closer to his destiny. Joseph's brothers meant it for evil, but God meant it for good (see Genesis 50:20).

After Joseph's experience in the pit, he was a changed man. He may have failed the Pride Test, but he passed the Pit Test. He then went on to take and pass eight more tests in his life. It's amazing to see how Joseph did the right thing each time he was faced with challenges and temptations.

Redemption from the Pit

God always has a plan. No matter what pit we might be in, God has a plan to get us out of it. And if we dig a little deeper in this story, we can see some types and shadows of God's master plan of redemption. His ultimate plan was to redeem us through His Son, Jesus Christ, and there are types, or images, of Jesus all throughout Joseph's story.

Remember, Joseph's brothers hadn't really wanted to throw him into a pit. Their original plan was to kill him! But Joseph's oldest brother Reuben intervened.

> And Reuben said to them, "Shed no blood, but cast him into this pit which is in the wilderness, and do not lay a hand on him"—that he might deliver him out of their hands, and bring him back to his father. (Genesis 37:22)

Now if anyone had a right to be jealous of Joseph, it was Reuben. He was the firstborn son, and the firstborn was the one on whom the honor should have rested. But Reuben gave up that honor for Joseph's sake. In this situation with Joseph, Reuben had two purposes as the firstborn son: he wanted to deliver Joseph, and he wanted to bring him back to his father.

In this way, Reuben was a type of the Lord Jesus Christ. Jesus is the firstborn Son of God, the One on whom God's favor rests. But Jesus gave up all those rights and privileges so you and I could become God's favored sons and daughters. Jesus left the glories of heaven with a twofold purpose: to deliver us and to bring us back to His Father. So Reuben is a type of Christ.

Joseph is also a type of Christ.

- Joseph was stripped of his robe of many colors (see Genesis 37:23). Jesus was stripped of His robe, and soldiers gambled for it (see Matthew 27:28, 35).

- Joseph was sold for twenty pieces of silver to the Midianite traders (see Genesis 37:26–28), but they took him to Egypt and sold him at a profit. The price of a slave at that time was thirty pieces of silver. So history indicates that Joseph was ultimately sold for thirty pieces of silver.[1] Jesus was sold for thirty pieces of silver (see Matthew 26:14–15).

- Joseph was betrayed by Judah (see Genesis 37:26–27). Jesus was betrayed by Judas (see Matthew 26:25). "Judah" and "Judas" are the same word in Hebrew.

- The Midianite traders who brought Joseph to Egypt were carrying spices, balm, and myrrh (see Genesis 37:25). The disciple Nicodemus brought myrrh and aloes to the tomb to embalm the body of Jesus (see John 19:39).

- Joseph was thrown into a pit, and then God delivered him out of that pit. Jesus was in the grave for three days, and then God raised Him up and delivered Him out of that pit.

But there is a very important difference between Jesus and Joseph: *Jesus didn't do anything to deserve being thrown into a pit.*

Rather, we are the ones who deserve to be thrown into the pit. We are sinners, and we should be thrown into the pit for all eternity. Instead, Jesus Christ went to the pit for us, so we would never have to go there. He spent three days in *Sheol*—in hell—so we wouldn't have to spend eternity there. Jesus did it willingly for you and for me, but God didn't leave Him there.

Psalm 16:10 says, "For You will not leave my soul in Sheol, nor will You allow Your Holy One to see corruption." This was a Messianic prophecy about Jesus—a prophecy that was fulfilled.

God did not leave His only begotten Son in a pit. And I promise you He will not leave you in one either. If you are in a pit right now, and it looks like there is no way out, I have good news: Jesus Christ has been there before you. Our Lord and Savior went to the pit for you, and then God raised Him up and delivered Him.

Jesus Christ died to deliver you from *every* pit, whether you fell into it, were pushed into it, or dug it for yourself. He died so you could have eternal life. He came to deliver you and bring you back into relationship with the Father. Don't let the enemy's lies distract you. Receive what Jesus did for you.

You may have lost the gift God gave you by walking in pride, but God can restore it. Just do what Joseph did. Do what Jonah did. Cry out to God! Say, "God, I'm sorry. I can't get out of this pit on my own. But You can get me out!"

When you humble yourself and cry out to God, He will deliver you out of every pit. He will promote you beyond the pit, and He will exalt you so you can walk in the destiny He has planned.

CHAPTER THREE

The Palace Test

My tires screeched as I hurried my car around a tight corner in the airport parking garage. Debbie and I were running late, and there wasn't a moment to lose if we were going to catch our flight.

I breathed a little prayer of thanks as I spotted an open parking space. As I tried to back the car into the spot, I forgot to take into account a trailer hitch we had just put on the week before. It was sticking out just the "wrong" amount, and as I backed up, it hit the bumper on the car behind me. Just what we didn't need at that moment! I jumped out to investigate, only to see that the impact had barely damaged the plastic on the other vehicle's bumper.

Now I had to choose what to do next. The right thing was to leave a note, but taking the time to do so would definitely cause us to miss our flight. I hate to admit this, but I couldn't help noticing the car was old and had quite a few dings, dents, and scratches. *The dented plastic would hardly be noticeable*, I rationalized. I was in a dilemma and needed to make a decision. I told myself the damaged plastic probably wouldn't have any effect on the owner of the car, but missing our flight would certainly have a big effect on us and our plans.

"We've got to get on that plane!" I declared, and we began to head toward the terminal. We hadn't gotten very far when I heard a still, small voice speak to me.

"Is it really worth it?" the Voice asked. "Is catching a plane so important that it's worth forfeiting the favor of God?"

I stopped in my tracks, turned to Debbie, and said, "I'm sorry, Sugar. I have to go back and leave a note."

"I know," Debbie said, her voice a mixture of pride and relief. "I knew you would."

"We're probably going to miss our flight, you know."

"I know," she replied, without a hint of misgiving.

So we went back, and I wrote a note with my phone number and apologies and left it on the damaged car. We ended up missing our flight, but we were able to book a later one. So we went to lunch, enjoyed each other's company for a while, and took the later flight.

The Palace Test: Learning Good Stewardship

What seemed so important at the time was really a temporary inconvenience. In retrospect, it's ridiculous that I could have considered that inconvenience to be more serious than the consequences of *not* doing the right thing. Jesus said if I am unfaithful in a small thing, or that which is "least," then He will rightly assume that I will also be unfaithful in "much." And a person whom God cannot trust with much is a person who will have to wait a long time to enter into his or her destiny.

Jesus talked about this in Luke 16:10–12:

> He who is faithful in what is least is faithful also in much; and he who
> is unjust in what is least is unjust also in much. Therefore if you have
> not been faithful in the unrighteous mammon, who will commit to
> your trust the true riches? And if you have not been faithful in what is
> another man's, who will give you what is your own?

What are you going to do with another man's belongings? What are
you going to do with those things God has entrusted to you? Are you
going to be faithful and obedient regardless of your situation? What will
you do with the job He has given you? With the boss He has given you?
This is the Palace Test, also known as the test of stewardship, and it's
the first test Joseph encountered after he was delivered out of the pit.

Every one of us would like to move into our glorious destiny, but as
we've already seen, every great destiny carries with it great responsibility. God is watching to see whether we can be trusted with little things
before He will give us the great things He has in store for us. Until we
pass this test, we will never move on into our destiny.

In the book of Colossians, God speaks to us about this.

> Bondservants, obey in all things your masters according to the flesh, not
> with eyeservice, as men-pleasers, but in sincerity of heart, fearing God.
> And whatever you do, do it heartily, as to the Lord and not to men,
> knowing that from the Lord you will receive the reward of the inheri-
> tance; for you serve the Lord Christ. But he who does wrong will be repaid
> for what he has done, and there is no partiality. (Colossians 3:22–25)

God is saying that He wants us to serve our earthly masters with
all our hearts, just as if we were serving Him. And He reminds us that
He is the One who will reward us, since it's really Christ Jesus we are
serving (see v. 24). So even if you are a "bondservant" (v. 22), even

if you are serving an unbelieving boss, God wants you to serve that boss from your heart with all sincerity because when you do, you are serving "the Lord Christ" (v. 24).

Can you serve someone as though you were serving the Lord? Do you work with unbelievers? Do you work with people who have a different political viewpoint? Can you have a right attitude toward them? If you can't serve those around you well, even if you don't like them or agree with them, then you will never pass the Palace Test.

There are a lot of people who say, "When I get a better job and I work for a better person, I'll work harder." Well, you're not going to get a better job, because if you're not faithful where you are, why would God give you more? God has placed you in that situation as His servant, and He is watching to see if you will faithfully represent Him.

Whatever your job may be, you must understand that you not only work for your employer—you also work for God. And because you work for God, He will reward you. He will promote you and put His blessing on all you do.

This is the reason Joseph was promoted everywhere he went after he was sold into slavery. As Joseph's story progresses, we see that he didn't only work for Potiphar, he didn't only work for the keeper of the prison, and he didn't only work for Pharaoh. Joseph always worked for the Lord (v. 23), whatever his circumstances and whoever his boss. And God blessed him.

It wasn't very long after Joseph was delivered out of the pit that he found himself living in a palace. Soon afterward, he was given rule over almost everything in the palace. Yet he had to remember that *nothing in the palace belonged to him.* Joseph was only a steward. (And this is why I like to call the Palace Test the test of stewardship!)

Genesis 39 tells the story.

Now Joseph had been taken down to Egypt. And Potiphar, an officer of Pharaoh, captain of the guard, an Egyptian, bought him from the Ishmaelites who had taken him down there. The LORD was with Joseph, and he was a successful man; and he was in the house of his master the Egyptian. And his master saw that the LORD was with him and that the LORD made all he did to prosper in his hand. So Joseph found favor in his sight, and served him. Then he made him overseer of his house, and all that he had he put under his authority. So it was, from the time that he had made him overseer of his house and all that he had, that the LORD blessed the Egyptian's house for Joseph's sake; and the blessing of the LORD was on all that he had in the house and in the field. Thus he left all that he had in Joseph's hand, and he did not know what he had except for the bread which he ate. (vv. 1–6)

Joseph went from the pit to the palace pretty quickly. That might sound wonderful, but don't forget that Joseph was still a slave. Although he was put in charge of all of Potiphar's belongings, he had no promise of a natural reward for doing a good job—not even the minimum wage! Joseph was a slave, and as a slave he had no rights of any kind. Yet Joseph proved himself a faithful guardian of Potiphar's business and passed this critical test. How do we know?

Look at verse 2 again: "The LORD was with Joseph" and His presence caused Joseph to be "a successful man." Egyptians during this time were polytheistic, so they believed in many gods. They didn't know that the God of Abraham, Isaac, and Jacob was the *one true* God. But the presence of God was so obvious on Joseph's life that even his Egyptian master knew that "the LORD was with him" (v. 3). The tangible presence of God in Joseph's life caused him to have favor with his master. But Joseph didn't try to take advantage of his favored status with Potiphar. Rather, Scripture tells us that Joseph "served him" (v. 4).

In other words, Joseph had the right attitude toward his job, even his job as a slave. He could have easily done the bare minimum, grumbling all the while, and no one would have second-guessed it. He had been a favored son, but now he was a slave. He could have taken some of Potiphar's things for himself. Who would know? But Joseph took a different approach. He didn't allow the injustice of his situation to prevent him from serving his master faithfully. Because of this, Potiphar made Joseph the "overseer of his house and all that he had" (Genesis 39:4). This Hebrew word for "overseer" is translated in the Septuagint as the same Greek word used in 1 Timothy and Titus to refer to an elder of the church.[1] So Joseph's master actually gave him the position of an "elder" in his house—a pretty high honor to bestow upon a slave. Not only that, in verse 5, we see that Potiphar "did not know what he had except for the bread which he ate." He didn't even know what was in his bank account! He didn't just name Joseph an elder in his home—he also trusted that Joseph would act like one as well.

If you look further in the chapter, you can see that Joseph carried this same attitude with him when he was sent to prison. (We'll talk later about why he was sent to prison and the tests he faced there.) But we see a similar situation with his time in prison: "The keeper of the prison did not look into anything that was under Joseph's authority, because the LORD was with him; and whatever he did, the LORD made it prosper" (Genesis 39:23).

Once again, Joseph did not allow the injustice of his situation to prevent him from being a faithful worker. As a result, "the LORD was with him" (v. 23) in the prison, just as He had been in the palace, and Joseph was made the overseer of the prison. How did Joseph pass the Palace Test? He passed it by being faithful with another man's resources; by being faithful to do the right thing, even when there seemed to be no reward for doing so. He obeyed the Lord's commands and statutes no matter how bleak his situation seemed. And because of that, God was with Joseph and prospered the work of his hands.

Think about this for a moment. Whatever Joseph did, the Lord made it prosper. Even the labor he did as a slave was so blessed by the Lord that it caused the house of his master to prosper—just for Joseph's sake!

Would it be okay if that happened to you? Would it be okay if the Lord made whatever you touched prosper? Would you mind if He made your marriage prosper? If He made your children prosper? If He made your job, your health, and your relationships prosper? If, like Joseph, He made you prosper in everything you did? I think most of us would say, "Sign me up for that!"

The wonderful news is that you *can* be like Joseph. You can learn the keys to being a faithful steward. When you learn these keys, the Lord will be with you as He was with Joseph, and the Lord will cause you to prosper in all you do.

"Prosper" Is Not a Bad Word

Let's settle something right at the start: "Prosper" is not a bad word! Yet it seems every time God restores a truth to the Church, Satan tries to twist it. In other words, when God reveals a truth to us, Satan tries to make us abuse that truth and take it too far. I believe God was restoring the truth about biblical prosperity to the Church, but then Satan tempted some people to get greedy in this area. Sadly, there is a hyper-prosperity teaching in the Church right now that's not accurate or biblical. The enemy has tempted some influential people in ministry to get out of balance and say that God wants everyone to have a Rolex and a Mercedes. Please hear me: they are misusing this word. "Prosperity Doctrine" and "Prosperity Gospel" have become labels for an incorrect theology, and because of that, we have pulled back from the biblical view of prosperity as well.

God wants you to prosper; He wants you to succeed.

The word "prosper" is a biblical word, not a bad one! Do not look at the excesses of a few and back away from what the Bible says is true. The Bible says that God wants you to prosper; He wants you to succeed. Why would it bother you to know God wants you to prosper? Why would it bother you to know that a good and loving God wants your marriage to prosper, wants your relationship with your children to prosper, wants you to be blessed and to be a blessing? There are so many Scripture passages about prospering that I can't share all of them here, but let me show you a few.

Take a look at Genesis 26:12–13:

> Then Isaac sowed in that land, and reaped in the same year a hundredfold; and the LORD blessed him. The man began to *prosper*, and continued *prospering* until he became very *prosperous*. (emphasis added)

Did you notice the Lord uses the word "prosper" three times in this verse about Isaac (who, incidentally, is Joseph's grandfather)? I think God is trying to say something here! Remember, these are not the words of man; the words in the Bible have been spoken by God Himself. And He is not afraid to use the words "prosper" or "prospered" or even "prosperity." Other examples include Deuteronomy 29:9, which says, "Therefore keep the words of this covenant, and do them, that you may *prosper* in all that you do" (emphasis added). And 2 Kings 18:7 says, "The LORD was with him; he *prospered* wherever he went." (emphasis added). I could go on and on. In fact, the Old Testament uses some variation of the word "prospering" 63 times!

Consider these words from the New Testament:

> Beloved, I pray that you may *prosper* in all things and be in health, just as your soul *prospers.* (3 John 2, emphasis added)

The Lord has no problem using this word. And here's why: the Hebrew word for "prospering" means "to push forward," or to make progress, and the Greek word for "prospering" means "to help on the road."[2] In other words, if you "prosper" other people, you help them along the road. If you "prosper" others, you push them forward and help them get farther along than they were.

How would you like to have God "push you forward" in your marriage? How would you like to have God "push you forward" in your job? How would you like to say, "No, no, God! Quit pushing! That's enough! I have already been so blessed!" But then God just keeps pushing you forward. Wouldn't that be wonderful?!

The great news is God does want to push you forward, and He wants to help you make progress. We need to look beyond the hyper-materialistic teaching about prosperity and really believe what God's Word says. He wants to prosper you in everything you do, just as He prospered Joseph. But it's really up to us whether we will walk in the blessing and favor of God as Joseph did.

So what are the four keys that caused Joseph to prosper in the palace? Let's find out!

The Key to Prosperity:
The Presence of the Lord

The first key to prospering is quite simply this: the presence of the Lord. If God is with you, you are going to prosper because God prospers in everything He does. Do you realize that God's ventures are always successful? He has never failed at anything He has done. It doesn't mean everything will always go right for you or that you'll never go through a storm. We've already established that we will have trouble in this world. But if God is with you, no matter the situation, you are going to be successful! He will take you through the storm. If God is with you, He is always going to be pushing you forward. If God is with you, you cannot help but be blessed. So the key to prospering is having the presence of the Lord in your life.

Joseph had the presence of the Lord in his life in a tangible way. It's amazing to me that Potiphar, who did not know the Lord, was still able to recognize that God was with Joseph: "[Potiphar] saw that the LORD was with him and that the LORD made all he did to prosper in his hand" (Genesis 39:3). Potiphar realized God's favor rested upon Joseph.

Does your boss, who may be an unbeliever, recognize that God is with you? Does he recognize that his company is being blessed because you are an employee? Because if God is with you, He will prosper everything you do.

The phrase "The Lord was with him" is found throughout the Bible and is used to describe many other people of faith. It's not unusual for the Lord to bless His faithful servants with His presence. The Lord wants to bless you with His presence, too. And this is the key to prospering—to have the presence of the Lord with you at all times. But that prompts another question.

What is the key to the presence of the Lord?

The Key to the Presence of the Lord: Obedience

Let's face it, most of us don't like the word "obedience." (Oddly enough, we seem to want *other* people to like it, though.) Whether or not we like this word is not the issue. We cannot escape this simple truth: obedience is the key to having the presence of God in our lives. If we don't obey God, He can't walk with us. Because of His holy and righteous nature, God only walks with obedient servants.

We see this link in 2 Chronicles 17:3-4:

> Now the LORD was with Jehoshaphat, because he walked in the former ways of his father David; he did not seek the Baals, but sought the God of his father, and walked in His commandments and not according to the acts of Israel.

The Bible says God "was with Jehoshaphat" (v. 3). Why? Because he "walked in [God's] commandments" (v. 4)! The Lord was with Jehoshaphat because he walked in God's ways—because he obeyed. And we are told that Jehoshaphat followed the example of David, who had also lived in the presence of God.

> Now Saul was afraid of David, because the LORD was with him, but had departed from Saul. And David behaved wisely in all his ways, and the LORD was with him. (1 Samuel 18:12, 14)

The Lord was with David, but He had departed from Saul. Even Saul was aware of this. Was this because God was playing favorites?

No, the Bible states quite clearly the Lord was with David because "David behaved wisely in all his ways" (v. 14). In other words, David was obedient to the Lord, and because David was obedient to the Lord, "the LORD was with him" (v. 14).

Why did the Lord depart from Saul? In 1 Samuel 15, we read about how Saul failed to obey the Lord. God had spoken to Saul and given him specific instructions. But Saul refused to do what God said to do and then tried to justify his disobedience rather than repent. So the presence of the Lord departed from him. God does not require perfection, because we're all human, but He does not walk with the rebellious and disobedient. "'If you are willing and obedient, you shall eat the good of the land; but if you refuse and rebel, you shall be devoured by the sword'; for the mouth of the LORD has spoken" (Isaiah 1:19–20).

The Lord says in this passage that if you want to "eat the good of the land" (v. 19)—in other words, if you want to prosper—you must be willing and obedient. Then He also says that if you are *not* willing and obedient—but refuse and rebel—you will *not* prosper but will, in fact, be devoured. That seems pretty straightforward: Refuse to obey and expose yourself to the forces of destruction. Or obey and prosper!

Notice that God says we must be *willing* and *obedient* in order to prosper. Clearly our *attitudes* are just as important to God as our *actions*. He wants us to obey Him, and He wants us to do it with a willing heart. Is it possible to be obedient and yet not be willing? Just ask the parent of a teenager who has been told to clean her room before she is allowed to go out. If you've ever heard the angry stomping around that sometimes goes with the cleaning, you can imagine the way some of our "obedience" appears to the Lord.

God wants us to obey Him, but He wants us to do it with a willing heart because *our hearts are what He really wants*. This is precisely what we're told in 2 Chronicles: "For the eyes of the LORD move to and fro throughout the earth that He may strongly support those whose heart is completely His" (2 Chronicles 16:9 NASB).

The Lord wants *us*, not just some outward act. And if we want Him—if we want His presence in our lives—then we must obey Him wholeheartedly. It's a choice!

> Behold, I set before you today a blessing and a curse: the blessing, if you obey the commandments of the LORD your God which I command you today; and the curse, if you do not obey the commandments of the LORD your God, but turn aside from the way which I command you today, to go after other gods which you have not known. (Deuteronomy 11:26–28)

God has set before us a blessing and a curse. The choice is really very simple: "If you obey Me, you will be blessed. If you disobey Me, you will not be blessed."

Please understand, God is not talking about our salvation here. Salvation is not by works but by grace, which comes through faith in the atoning blood of Jesus Christ. But in these verses God is talking about *being blessed in this life*. He is letting us know that we can choose to be blessed or cursed during our time on this earth. And if we choose to obey His commands, we have chosen the blessing: "If they obey and serve Him, they shall spend their days in prosperity, and their years in pleasures. But if they do not obey, they shall perish by the sword, and they shall die without knowledge" (Job 36:11–12). When we walk away from God, there is death. Now, please hear me, God is not cursing us. We simply live in a cursed and fallen world. It doesn't mean God doesn't love us or that we don't have access to Him. But it does mean we won't enjoy the benefits of His presence in the same way.

Would you like to spend your days in prosperity and your years under God's protection enjoying good things? Then obey God and serve Him.

Let me emphasize again that this is not a doctrine of works. This is a doctrine of *obedience*. We know salvation is the free gift of God, but we must understand that the *blessing* of God comes through obedience. Our obedience to God is the best indication that our hearts truly belong to Him.

Jehoshaphat, David, and Joseph all walked in obedience to God. As a result, God was with them. They showed their love toward God by obeying Him with willing hearts, and He blessed their lives with His presence. Likewise, if we show God our love by obeying Him with willing hearts, God's presence will be with us!

I'm not talking about the omnipresence of God—His presence that is in every place at every time. Every person in this world—every believer and every nonbeliever—is in the omnipresence of God. Even the rocks and the stones are always in God's presence, since He is everywhere. That's not the kind of presence we want to settle for as believers, though. God has invited us to *true* intimacy with Him.

Nor am I talking about the inward presence of God. When you are born again, the Holy Spirit comes to live inside your heart by faith. This is the inner presence of God, and it's a wonderful thing to have the Holy Spirit of the living God come and dwell within you. But there is something *more*: the manifest presence of God. This is when God shows up in a tangible way and makes His presence known. I hope every believer has experienced the special sweetness that sometimes fills the atmosphere during times of worship and prayer. That is the manifest presence of God.

There are other times when God's presence manifests in unusual or unexpected ways. Many of us have experienced this. I remember this happening one time after I lost my grandmother. I was at the hospital with her when she passed away, and I went into the bathroom and began to cry. My grandmother had lived with us when I was growing up, and I loved her very much. As I knelt by the toilet in the little hospital bathroom and cried, all of a sudden it seemed like that room was filled with the presence of God. I felt as if Jesus were standing there with me, putting His hand on my shoulder. I sensed His presence in such a powerful, tangible way! As I think back to that moment, I'm reminded of how wonderful it is to experience the manifest presence of God.

Have you ever met someone who obviously has the presence of God on them? You can't help but notice it. Joseph was a person like that. Even Potiphar noticed it.

Here's my heart's desire: I want to be like that. I want to live in God's manifest presence every moment of every day. I hope you share my desire too. If you do, remember that the key to having His presence in your life is obedience.

**The key to having His presence
in your life is obedience.**

However, just as obedience will cause God's presence to manifest in your life, disobedience will cause His presence to leave.

Some of you may be remembering another Scripture and think what I've said here doesn't line up. Hebrews 13:5 says, "For He Himself has said, 'I will never leave you nor forsake you.'" Again, the Lord is omnipresent. It's true that He will never leave us. The problem is that we can leave Him.

Early on in my ministry, I became extremely busy. I was an associate pastor, and the needs of the church and the people we served were all-consuming. To appease my busy schedule, I began to skip my quiet time with the Lord. It was gradual, but it got to a point where during church services, I would run around doing work and wouldn't pause to enter into worship. I was doing good things, but I was no longer setting aside time with the Lord. Suddenly, all these things started going wrong in my life. It was one thing after another, and the hits just kept on coming. Finally, I said to the Lord, "Why did You leave me? I don't understand why all this is happening."

That's when He gave me a vision of a hailstorm. There were huge chunks of hail falling all over the place, but God had a steel umbrella. When I walked closely with Him and obeyed Him, He protected me. The hail couldn't get through the steel umbrella. But when I chose to disobey God and walk away from Him, I was left out in the storm, trying to dodge the hail.

I'm here to tell you, you can't dodge it! When we walk away from the presence of the Lord, we no longer get to enjoy the benefits of His presence.

The clearest biblical example of this occurred in the life of Cain. Genesis 4:16 says, "Then Cain went out from the presence of the LORD." Why did this happen? Simply put, Cain was disobedient. He first disobeyed God in the matter of his offerings, and then Cain killed his brother Abel. The Lord gave Cain a chance to confess what he had done. He asked, "Where is your brother?" Of course, God knew where Abel was. He didn't need Cain to tell Him. God was simply giving him an opportunity to repent of his sin. You see, God was not looking for sinless perfection in Cain—He was looking for a repentant heart.

Things could have turned out so differently for Cain. But instead of confessing his sin and saying "God, I'm sorry, I've done something I shouldn't have," Cain denied any responsibility for what he had done.

He sarcastically replied, "Am I my brother's keeper?"

So God said, "Your brother's blood is crying out to me from the ground."

In this way God was telling Cain, "I knew what you did all along. I just wanted you to confess it and acknowledge it as wrong."

Still Cain refused to confess and repent, so he "went out from the presence of the LORD." Because of disobedience, the presence of God no longer manifested in Cain's life.

Disobedience cost Adam and Eve the presence of God as well. They had enjoyed the manifest presence of God in the Garden of Eden. The Bible says God walked in the garden in the cool of the day (see Genesis 3:8). But after Adam and Eve sinned, they hid themselves from God's presence. God came to Adam and gave him a chance to repent, and God came to Eve and gave her a chance to repent. But sin caused them both to hide from the presence of God.

Perfectionism is not the goal—we all make mistakes. But Proverbs 28:13 says, "He who covers his sins will not prosper, but whoever confesses and forsakes them will have mercy." This verse doesn't say, "He who is perfect will have mercy." It says that those who forsake their sins and turn from them in repentance will have mercy. And those who cover up their sins will not prosper.

Let's look at King David again. David understood the manifest presence of God. He knew what it was like to have God's presence rest upon him. He was called a man after God's own heart! And yet he certainly failed to obey at times. He knew what it was like to lose God's presence through disobedience. But David also knew he could cry out to God in repentance for his sin, asking God to forgive him. In Psalm 51:11 David pleads, "Do not cast me away from Your presence, and do not take Your Holy Spirit from me."

When David repented, the Lord forgave him. In contrast to King Saul's lack of repentance, David returned to walking in obedience to God, and the presence of God was restored to his life. David prospered. Saul did not.

God's forgiveness is available to you too. If you've been disobedient or rebellious, it's never too late to repent and be welcomed back into the presence of our merciful God.

The presence of God is what makes you prosper in all you do. And obedience is the key to a life marked by the presence of God. This presents another question.

What is the key to obedience?

The Key to Obedience: Faith

I've actually heard people say, "I know that obedience is important, but I just can't seem to obey God in this certain area. I've tried and tried." You must understand that working out of your own strength—"trying hard"—is not the answer. The key to a life of obedience is simply faith. Because if you truly believe that a life of obedience will produce the blessings of God, you won't *try* to obey Him. You'll *want* to obey Him!

Think about it. If you really believe the consequences of a certain action are going to be bad for you, you will decide not to do it. If you really believe God is going to reward you for doing the right thing, then you will decide to do that. The critical phrase here is "if you believe," because faith is what produces obedience in our lives.

If you truly believe in something, you will do it. If you believe what God has said in His Word, you will do what He says. Let's look again at Colossians 3:22–24:

Bondservants, obey in all things your masters according to the flesh, not with eyeservice, as men-pleasers, but in sincerity of heart, fearing God. And whatever you do, do it heartily, as to the Lord and not to men, knowing that from the Lord you will receive the reward of the inheritance; for you serve the Lord Christ.

We are called to obey, "knowing"—not "guessing" or "figuring"— that the Lord will reward us. The Bible clearly states that the key to obedience is faith.

Faith is the reason a farmer plants crops. A farmer tills the ground and waters it because he *believes* a crop will grow from the seed he has planted. Faith is not as mysterious as we make it out to be.

Think about it. Every day you place your faith in a myriad of inanimate objects. When you get in your car and turn your key in the ignition, you have faith it's going to start. Sadly, many Christians have more faith in a hot water heater than they do in God! I don't know about you, but when I turn on the hot water faucet and the water feels cold, I don't immediately conclude that the hot water heater doesn't work.

Now, we did live in a house once where I think the hot water heater was located three houses down. We would turn on the hot water valve, go watch a movie, and come back to hot water! The point is we waited because we knew the water was eventually going to get hot. We had faith in it.

Some people turn on the faucet of prayer, and if it feels cold at the start, they turn it right back off. But when you turn the faucet of prayer on and *leave it on*, it's going to get hotter than you can imagine! That's what faith is—believing, even when the water is cold. It's leaving the faucet on, no matter what the circumstances say, because God has said that the hot water is coming, and you believe Him!

So why would we not believe that we will get a reward if we obey the Lord's commandments? It's so clear throughout the Bible. And that belief doesn't mean we think everything is always going to turn out perfectly. It means that when we look back over our lives, we will see God's provision and prosperity. If we truly believe this, we will obey, and if we obey, we will eat the "good of the land" (Isaiah 1:19). In other words, faith ultimately brings prosperity and the presence of God. So let's keep in mind these words from Exodus: "Now therefore, if you will indeed obey My voice and keep My covenant, then you shall be a special treasure to Me above all people; for all the earth is Mine" (Exodus 19:5). If we *believe* that, we will want to obey Him. We will want to be a special treasure to our Father.

Even children have a promise from God regarding obedience.

Children, obey your parents in the Lord, for this is right. "Honor your father and mother," which is the first commandment with promise: "that it may be well with you and you may live long on the earth." (Ephesians 6:1-3)

God says that if children honor their parents, they will live long on the earth, and even better, it will "be well" with them (see v. 3). (I don't even know if you want to live long if things aren't going well with you!) In other words, obedience to your parents will bring the blessing of God.

By the way, if things seem as if they have never gone well for you in your life, you may want to ask yourself whether you have failed to honor your parents. The Bible tells us this is "the first commandment with [a] promise" (v. 2). In other words, this is a good place to start applying the truths of obedience and blessings. This command does not say to honor your father and mother if they are good people. It does not say to honor your father and mother if they are Christians.

It simply says to honor your father and mother so that things "may be well with you" (v. 3).

I believe one of the reasons God's favor is on my life is because I made a commitment to honor my parents. They were not perfect—no one is—but they were my parents. I'm not going to speak negatively about them. I'm going to honor them, as God says I should. And if I honor them, things will go well with me.

How do children honor their parents? First and foremost by obeying them: "Children, obey your parents in the Lord, for this is right" (Ephesians 6:1). Do you know why children obey? Children obey because they believe that things will go well with them if they do. If a child believes he or she will get a reward by obeying, that belief will influence his or her behavior. If a child believes he or she will get a punishment for disobeying, that expectation will influence his or her behavior as well.

When our children were growing up, we rewarded good behavior and we disciplined for bad behavior. Our children believed if they did right, I would reward them. They also believed that if they disobeyed, they would get in trouble. Of course, I would much rather have rewarded them than punished them, and I'm sure our heavenly Father feels the same way. I loved to reward them with special gifts, because I wanted them to understand that if you do a good thing, God will reward you.

Some children disobey because they don't believe. They don't believe disobedience will cause anything to not "be well" with them. But it's amazing how quickly that lack of faith can be corrected with some parental discipline!

I realize books have been written that contradict what the Bible has to say about disciplining children. But godly discipline helps a child believe that obedience brings good results and disobedience brings painful ones! Our duty as parents is to prepare our children for the real world, and that includes consequences. Colossians 3:25 goes on to say, "But he who does wrong will be repaid for what he has done, and there is no partiality." If we teach children there aren't any consequences for disobedience, then they will grow up and make poor choices that hurt themselves and others. It will not "be well" with them.

As adults, we are not much different from children. We disobey God because we don't really *believe* we're going to suffer any consequences for our disobedience. And if we really *believed* God rewards us when we obey Him, we would *want* to obey. We obey because we believe. We disobey because we don't believe.

**We obey because we believe.
We disobey because we don't believe.**

God said that those who do not obey Him will not enter His rest. In other words, they will not enter the place in their destiny in which God will bless every aspect of their lives. "And to whom did He swear that [the Israelites] would not enter His rest, but to those who did not obey? So we see that they could not enter in because of unbelief" (Hebrews 3:18-19). We often assume the children of Israel did not enter into their destiny—the Promised Land—because they did not walk in obedience. But if we read verse 19, we see it was not really disobedience that prevented them from entering in—it was unbelief. If they had *believed* God's Words, they would have obeyed Him. And if they had obeyed Him, they would have entered into His rest.

I had a guy say to me one time, "Pastor Robert, I believe in tithing. I just don't do it."

That was absurd to me! So I responded, "Oh, I understand. I believe in bathing. I just don't do it!"

If you believe it, you do it. Belief is the key. If you believe what the Bible says about the rewards of tithing—that God will rebuke the enemy for your sake and open up the windows of heaven to bless you—you do it! If you don't, then you don't truly believe God's Word.

God wants every one of us to enter our promised land. Our promised land is a place where the blessing of God is on us, prospering us in everything we do. The key to having that blessing is having His presence in our lives. The key to His manifest presence is obedience to His commands, and in order to walk in obedience to His commands, we have to believe. We must have faith.

So what is the key to having faith?

The Key to Faith: Hearing the Word

The key to having faith is in hearing the Word of God. I want to emphasize this: the key to having faith is *not* in *obeying* the Word of God—the key to having faith is in *hearing* the Word of God. Now I believe in obeying the Word, and we must obey God if we want to have His blessing on our lives. But it's not obedience that produces faith. Rather, it's faith that produces obedience. And faith comes only by the Word of God. This is not my idea. God made this very plain in Romans 10:17 through the apostle Paul: "So then faith comes by hearing, and hearing by the word of God." This Scripture verse says that if I hear the Word of God, "faith comes." In other words, faith shows up. All I have to do is hear the Word of God. There is something about *hearing* the Word of God that produces faith.

Now I know the Bible says I must be a doer of the Word as well. James 1:22 says, "But be doers of the word, and not hearers only, deceiving yourselves." But it's *hearing* the Word that is the key to doing it! The more I hear the Word of God, the more faith I will have. And the more faith I have, the more I will want to obey God and live out His Word.

The reason a lot of people are not doers of the Word is because they don't really have faith. But the reason they don't have faith is that they haven't heard much of the Word. The Bible says the way faith comes to us is by *hearing the Word of God.*

Therefore, the more of the Word of God you have in you, the more faith you will have. The more faith you have, the more you will obey. The more you obey, the more the presence of God will manifest in your life. And the more you live in the presence of God, the more you will prosper and succeed wherever God has placed you, whether you're a servant in a palace, a manager in an office building, or a stay-at-home parent.

Every one of us can prosper, and every one of us can be successful. The way we begin is by hearing the Word of God. So start to make the Word of God part of your everyday life!

When my son James was a teenager, he knew he wanted to study business. So I asked my good friend Steve Dulin, a very successful businessman, to mentor him. Steve told James that he really needed to know the Word of God, and he challenged him to memorize four Scriptures a week. Then Steve encouraged James to buy the Bible on CD and listen to it every time he got in the car and even when he was sleeping at night. (Those were the days before smartphones and even iPods!) James went to the bookstore and found the audio Bible CD options on the shelf. He saw the New King James Version was $49.95, the NIV was $49.95, and the New American Standard was $49.95. Then he saw that the King James Version was *only* $9.95. Now, something you have to know about James is that he has always been naturally frugal, and as a student, he was also short on cash. So guess which version he bought and listened to every day? You guessed it! The King James Version!

After James had been listening to the CDs for a few weeks, I got a call from my other son, Josh, asking, "What's going on with James?"

I replied, "I don't know what you're talking about."

Josh said, "Well, I just got off the phone with him, but when he answered the phone, he said, 'Wherefore art thou, my brother? Hast thou been in the field with my father?'" That's when it dawned on me that James had been listening to the *old* King James Version of the Bible! So Debbie and I bought him the *New* King James Version.

After college, James went to work for a home building business and was very successful. Then in 2009, during a recession, James began to feel like he was going to get laid off. He went to lunch with the owner one day, and sure enough, he found out he would be laid off soon because of the economy. That same day, I had lunch with a business owner in our church. He asked how James was doing, and I mentioned to him that James may be getting laid off. This man said, "Well, I have an open position. The reason I asked about James is because I wanted to see if it would be all right with you if I talked to him about it."

The very same day at the very same time, James was getting laid off from one job and being offered another! That's what I call prosperity! It was the Lord prospering James and pushing him forward. James *knew* the Word of God, and God prospered him.

I encourage you to listen to God's Word whenever you can—while you're getting ready in the morning, while you're driving to work, or while you're washing the dishes. Bible apps make this so simple now.

Read the Bible daily. Memorize Scripture passages and meditate on them. Write verses on note cards and tape them on your mirror so you see them all the time. If you hear His Word consistently, faith will come naturally, just as God promised it would. As your faith increases, you will find yourself walking in obedience. As you walk in obedience, you're going to have the presence of God on your life. And if the presence of God is with you, you're going to succeed and prosper!

At Gateway, we have a phrase we say that influences the way we do ministry: "Hear. Believe. Obey." If you ever visit our church or watch our services online, you might hear it. We even have it printed on T-shirts and hats. And it comes straight from Romans 10:17, which says, "So then faith comes by hearing, and hearing by the word of God." We know that when we are faithful to the Word of God and hear what He says, believe it, and obey it, then God's presence will be with us and prosper us.

In 2008, the Gateway Church leadership was in negotiations to purchase land in Southlake, Texas, so we could build a larger building. We found 180 acres in a great location—right off a major freeway and across from the town square that had many shops and restaurants. We were originally quoted $25 million for the land, but we were able to work out a phenomenal deal for $12 million.

A few days before closing, the developer called us and said, "Our attorneys went over the contract and noticed the mineral rights were in the contract, but we're pulling them out. We are keeping the mineral rights."

That meant any oil or valuable mineral deposits within the land would not belong to us but to the developer. The pastor who was working through the negotiations called to tell me the news, and I let him know I needed to pray about it.

I went before the Lord and asked Him for a word.

He responded, "Read Deuteronomy 11."

Now, when we started Gateway Church, Deuteronomy 11 was one of the chapters the Lord gave me about the church. I had read it hundreds of times, so I grumbled a little and said, "I already know what Deuteronomy 11 says!"

The Lord responded, "I know what it says too."

So I opened up my Bible and started reading Deuteronomy 11. As I'm reading it, I'm thinking, *Yes, yes, I know. I've read this. Yes, yes.* But then I got to verses 11–14:

> The land which you cross over to possess is a land of hills and valleys, which drinks water from the rain of heaven, a land for which the LORD your God cares; the eyes of the LORD your God are always on it, from the beginning of the year to the very end of the year. And it shall be that if you earnestly obey My commandments which I command you today, to love the LORD your God and serve Him with all your heart and with all your soul, then I will give you the rain for your land in its season, the early rain and the latter rain, that you may gather in your grain, your new wine, and your *oil.* (emphasis added)

I felt the Lord say, "I am about to give you this land. The grain is yours, the wine is yours, and the oil is yours."

I called the pastor back and said, "Tell the developer the oil is ours, and it's a deal breaker." I knew we would be passing up 180 acres in a perfect spot if they said no, but I had a word from God, and I had to be obedient.

The developer called back a few hours later and said, "Okay, we'll give you the mineral rights."

Now, here's what's amazing. We went to the closing to sign all the paperwork, and a gentleman who worked for the developer looked at the contract and said, "May I ask you a question? How did you get the mineral rights?"

"Do you really want to know?" I asked, and he nodded.

"Well, I prayed, and God gave me a Bible verse and said the oil was ours. So we asked for the mineral rights back."

The guy responded, "I'm a Christian, so I understand what you're saying, but I need to tell you something. I've been doing closings for this developer for twenty-five years, and you have to know that this developer's parent company is a major oil conglomerate. This is the *first* time they've ever given away the mineral rights."

God's presence was truly in that negotiation, and since then, Gateway Church has prospered greatly from not only the land but also from retaining the mineral rights.

What if I hadn't taken time to pray after that phone call? What if I hadn't heard the Lord, believed what He said, and been obedient to His Word? What if I had simply given up? The money for the land wasn't mine. We were stewarding Gateway's money, and I'm so glad I was faithful to pause and hear from the Lord, believe His Word, and obey it. His presence didn't disappoint. (And it's worth mentioning that when the Lord tells you to read a Scripture, you do it, no matter how familiar you are with it!)

The Blessing of God's Presence

There are no words to describe the blessing of having God's presence in your life. Right now, I can feel the favor of God on my life, and it's a wonderful feeling. It's so wonderful that I don't want to do one single thing to mess it up! The favor of God makes you feel like nothing is impossible. The favor of God makes you feel like anything you attempt to do for God will succeed. Because when you sense that God is with you, you know your efforts on His behalf will not fail. What could possibly be worth losing the blessing, favor, and manifest presence of God?

I don't want to walk in disobedience, because I know if I disobey God, His presence will leave my life. And I don't want to lose His presence or His favor!

And I didn't want to lose it that day at the airport either. That's why, ultimately, it wasn't a hard decision to leave a note on the car I bumped, even though I knew we would miss our flight. It was easy to do the right thing once I remembered that God has called me to be faithful in small matters, as well as great, as I live out my destiny according to His will.

I want to walk in the destiny God has planned for me. And I know that if I am to be given more responsibility, I must first be found faithful in little things—even a small crack in a piece of plastic on an old car.

I eventually received a call from the lady whose vehicle I had damaged. I apologized for the accident and gave her our insurance information so she could get her bumper repaired. Before we got off the phone, she said, "I just have to ask you a question. I have shown your note to everyone in my office, and no one can believe you actually left it. It would have been so easy to just drive away. We don't know if you're a saint, a space alien, or what—but none of us can figure out why you left a note."

This woman was an unbeliever. Yet like Potiphar, she recognized there was something different about my behavior. I was able to explain to her the reason I had left the note. It opened the door for me to be able to share the gospel with her and tell her how Jesus Christ had changed my life and that He could change her life too.

"You said everyone in your office wants to know why I left that note," I said to her. "Be sure to tell them the reason is because Jesus Christ has changed my life, and He wants to do that for all of them too."

There is nothing on this earth that can compare to the joy of a moment like that—a moment when the presence of God rests upon you and you are able to do something very important for Him. But it all begins by being faithful in the smallest things—by being a faithful steward. If I had not been faithful to do the right thing when I bumped into that woman's car, I would never have had the opportunity to be God's messenger to the people in her office. I also would have risked losing the presence of God in my life—a blessing shared only with those who walk closely with Him in obedience.

Remember, faithfulness—good stewardship—is a precursor to God's presence. And His presence is what causes us to be successful in everything we do. It's what causes us to have the favor of God on our lives. I want all of us to have God's favor on our lives. And the wonderful truth is that God's favor and His presence are available to everyone and anyone!

Remember, faithfulness—good stewardship—is a precursor to God's presence. And His presence is what causes us to be successful in everything we do.

Like Joseph, you can live in the favor, blessing, and prosperity of God. God *can* bless you, and He *wants* to bless you.

So be faithful in little things. Be a good employee "as to the Lord" (Colossians 3:23) and a good steward of whatever He has given you.

Spend time in God's Word and watch your faith increase. As faith comes, obedience will naturally follow. Hear, believe, obey. And when you honor God and walk in obedience to Him—no matter your circumstances or position—He will honor you with His presence. Then His favor and blessings will rest on your life, and like Joseph, you will prosper in all you do.

And then you will know you've passed the Palace Test. You can look forward with joy to hearing Him say, "Well done, good and faithful servant; you were faithful over a few things, I will make you ruler over many things. Enter into the joy of your lord" (Matthew 25:21).

CHAPTER FOUR

The Purity Test

I t was unusually quiet as I preached that Sunday.

Admittedly, I don't pastor the most vocal congregation in the world. Nevertheless, on most occasions I can count on a steady scattering of "Amens" and "That's rights." But not this day. Throughout my sermon, though my preaching was often passionate, the congregation remained somber and silent.

The topic? Sexual purity.

Afterward, someone asked me an interesting question: "Why do you suppose there weren't very many 'Amens' today?"

"Why do *you* think?" was my only reply.

It's actually rather odd that the subject of sexuality would make any of us uncomfortable these days. After all, we live in a society that is saturated with sexuality and sensuality—one that seems bent on making us as comfortable as we can be about sex!

In the 1990s, our country endured a scandal involving immorality at the highest level of elected office. Some were genuinely appalled; others merely viewed the incident from a political standpoint. The majority, however, couldn't care less. What shocked me most about this very sad chapter in our history was the widely held idea that the president's private behavior had nothing to do with his leadership of our country. Nothing could be further from the truth.

Whatever your political views, you must understand there are certain truths that will never change, and God has spelled them out quite clearly for us in the Bible.

The Purity Test: Sexual Stewardship

Popular culture may declare that sexual morality has nothing to do with character, but God begs to differ. Sexual morality has *everything* to do with character, and character is very important to God. That's why if you want to walk in the destiny God has planned for you, you have to understand what He says about sexual purity.

Don't misunderstand what I'm saying here. God created us as sexual beings, and He wants each one of us to enjoy a wonderful, fulfilling sex life with our spouse. But just as with every other gift God has given us, we have a responsibility to steward this gift in a way that is pleasing to Him. God is watching to see if we will be faithful stewards in this area of our lives as well. Remember, if we are faithful in little things, God knows He can trust us with much. But if we are unfaithful in little things, God says we will also be unfaithful in much (see Luke 16:10).

It's very important to understand this because a person who is immoral in this area of his or her life will also be immoral in other areas. A person who cheats on his or her spouse will oftentimes also cheat his or her employer (or his or her country). This is not an idea I came up with; it's simply *what God has said in His Word*. Our sexual conduct really does matter to God, and that's why it's imperative to be faithful in this area of our lives.

Character is a foundational issue. As character goes, the rest of the house goes. If the foundation is bad, everything else will be bad. We can never "only" be sexually immoral because sexual immorality opens the door to a host of other sins. If we are sexually immoral, we will also lie and be deceptive because we have to cover up our sin. The Bible says that King David was "a man after [God's] own heart" (Acts 13:22). Yet sexual immorality drove him to lie and even murder in an attempt to cover up his sin.

Since the political scandal that happened in the 1990s, we've all heard stories of other great leaders, political and corporate, who have stumbled into sexual immorality and remained as trusted leaders in their professions. In fact, it's almost become the norm in our society today. I understand the need to give grace for mistakes, but I'm saddened to see that our culture has declined to the point that many would say a leader's sexual immorality has no bearing on his or her leadership ability. Appalling as this is, it's a sobering indication that our nation needs revival and repentance, and it ought to stir us to search our own hearts and pray. But whatever ideas popular culture may be promoting, only God's ideas really matter.

In God's kingdom, character has everything to do with fitness for leadership. We must understand that if we allow any compromise in this area, we are putting our God-given destinies at risk.

Of course, God is a redeemer by nature. If you've fallen in this area and sincerely repent before God, He will forgive and restore you. But if you *persist* in immorality, you will not step into your destiny. Why? Because God is looking for faithful stewards He can trust wholeheartedly.

This is the Purity Test, and in our hyper-sexualized society, each one of us faces this critical test on a daily basis. Thankfully, we can all draw inspiration and insight from the story of Joseph. When faced with great temptation, Joseph passed this test with flying colors! Genesis 39 tells the story.

> Now Joseph was handsome in form and appearance. And it came to pass after these things that his master's wife cast longing eyes on Joseph, and she said, "Lie with me."
>
> But he refused and said to his master's wife, "Look, my master does not know what is with me in the house, and he has committed all that he has to my hand. There is no one greater in this house than I, nor has he kept back anything from me but you, because you are his wife. How then can I do this great wickedness, and sin against God?"
>
> So it was, as she spoke to Joseph day by day, that he did not heed her, to lie with her or to be with her.
>
> But it happened about this time, when Joseph went into the house to do his work, and none of the men of the house was inside, that she caught him by his garment, saying, "Lie with me." But he left his garment in her hand, and fled and ran outside. (vv. 6–12)

The reason Joseph passed this test is very simple: when the temptation became too great for him to walk away—*he ran!* God advises us to follow Joseph's example and "flee sexual immorality" (1 Corinthians 6:18). The literal meaning of *flee* is "to run away.[1]" God doesn't say we should just walk away from immorality. He tells us to *run* from it! And that's exactly what Joseph did, even though he had to leave his garment in Potiphar's wife's hand so he could get away.

Notice what Joseph calls immorality: "great wickedness, and sin against God" (Genesis 39:9). Joseph ran away from temptation because he understood something our society seems to have forgotten: sexual immorality is evil and sinful. Joseph also knew the wrong done would not only be against his master Potiphar. He understood that sexual immorality would also be a wrong done against God and would harm his relationship with the Lord. So he ran.

In many ways, this is just another aspect of faithful stewardship, because in the Ten Commandments, God forbids us to covet anything that belongs to our neighbor, including our neighbor's wife (see Exodus 20:17). Potiphar's wife was deliberately tempting Joseph to covet her, so Joseph's stewardship was being tested in that area. Now, I'm not trying to shame this woman or put her down; the enemy was attacking Joseph through her. (Remember, our battle is not against flesh and blood.) And the question was no longer whether Joseph could steward another man's *belongings* faithfully. Now it was, could he exercise faithful stewardship of another man's *wife*?

But there is more to consider. Could Joseph steward his own body? Could he steward his own appetites and desires? Would Joseph serve God faithfully in this area of his life?

These are very important questions—ones each of us will have to face. We like to think we can discipline ourselves to walk with God, to spend time in the Word and in prayer. But many of us cannot even steward our physical appetites in a way that honors God. This is one of the first areas in which we must learn to discipline ourselves, because if we cannot bring our own bodies under control, how will we be faithful in any other area?

The apostle Paul understood this quite clearly. In 1 Corinthians 9:27, he wrote, "I discipline my body and bring it into subjection, lest, when

I have preached to others, I myself should become disqualified." If we don't want to be disqualified from our God-given destinies, we must learn to keep our physical body under control—and not only in the area of food. We must bring our sexual appetite under control as well.

Sexual temptation is an issue every person must confront. I was once speaking at a men's retreat, and I asked the question, "How many of you men have ever struggled with lust?" Around 90 percent of the men raised their hands. I reflected a bit and then said, "Well, it's obvious the other 10 percent of you struggle with lying!"

Let's get real. Dealing with sexual temptation is simply part of who we are because God created us as sexual beings, and He wants us to enjoy that aspect of our identity. As with everything else God created, He has a wonderful plan for this part of our lives. But are we going to follow His plan, as laid out in His Word, or are we going to follow the world's leading and walk in disobedience?

Dealing with sexual temptation is simply part of who we are because God created us as sexual beings.

Remember, the path of obedience is always the path of God's blessing and God's promotion. So if we want to fulfill His dream for our lives, we are going to have to bring this area under God's control.

I struggled with the Purity Test, but God showed me some keys that helped me pass this important test, and I believe they will help you, too. But first, let's talk about why it's imperative to remain pure.

Impurity Will Affect Your Family

If someone tells you that sexual impurity will not affect your family, that person is either a liar or is greatly deceived. If you allow impurity to become part of your life, it *will* affect your spouse, your children, and your grandchildren.

In 2 Samuel 11–13, we find one of the most famous illustrations of this reality. It all starts in chapter 11, when King David sees beautiful Bathsheba bathing on the roof. We know he lusted after her, committed adultery, and eventually murdered her husband. It's not until the prophet Nathan confronts David in chapter 12 that he repents. And then in chapter 13, we see the consequences of David's sin: his children begin to commit gross immorality.

After this Absalom the son of David had a lovely sister, whose name was Tamar; and Amnon the son of David loved her. Amnon was so distressed over his sister Tamar that he became sick; for she was a virgin. And it was improper for Amnon to do anything to her. But Amnon had a friend whose name was Jonadab the son of Shimeah, David's brother. Now Jonadab was a very crafty man. And he said to him, "Why are you, the king's son, becoming thinner day after day? Will you not tell me?"

Amnon said to him, "I love Tamar, my brother Absalom's sister."

So Jonadab said to him, "Lie down on your bed and pretend to be ill. And when your father comes to see you, say to him, 'Please let my sister Tamar come and give me food, and prepare the food in my sight, that I may see it and eat it from her hand.'" Then Amnon lay down and pretended to be ill; and when the king came to see him, Amnon said to the king, "Please let Tamar my sister come and make a couple of cakes for me in my sight, that I may eat from her hand." (2 Samuel 13:1–6)

Let me pause here and explain some things about this passage. You see, King David had eight wives who are mentioned by name in the Bible. It was possible he had more who are not named. During his time, kings would often take wives for military alliances. Absalom and Tamar were children from one wife, and Amnon was a son from a different wife. Thus, Amnon and Tamar were half-siblings. It sounds like a soap opera, I know. But some parts of the Bible *are* like soap operas because they involve humans. The Bible says Amnon was in love with his half-sister, which he knew was wrong and could never result in marriage because the law said, "Cursed is the one who lies with his sister, the daughter of his father or the daughter of his mother" (Deuteronomy 27:22).

Yet we see in 2 Samuel 13:3 how Amnon's friend Jonadab (who was also his cousin) started influencing Amnon to do something about his improper feelings toward Tamar. Jonadab is also described as "crafty" and "subtle," which are similar words used to describe Satan in the Bible. Like the enemy, Jonadab started influencing and tempting Amnon to do what he knew was wrong. (In my opinion, Amnon needed some better friends!)

Amnon went to his father, King David, who agreed to send Tamar to Amnon's house to make food and care for him. After Tamar made some cakes, he refused to eat. He then made everyone but Tamar leave the room. Let's pick up the story again here:

> Now when she had brought [the cakes] to him to eat, he took hold of her and said to her, "Come, lie with me, my sister."
>
> But she answered him, "No, my brother, do not force me, for no such thing should be done in Israel. Do not do this disgraceful thing! And I, where could I take my shame? And as for you, you would be like one of the fools in Israel. Now therefore, please speak to the king; for he will

not withhold me from you." However, he would not heed her voice; and being stronger than she, he forced her and lay with her.

Then Amnon hated her exceedingly, so that the hatred with which he hated her was greater than the love with which he had loved her. And Amnon said to her, "Arise, be gone!"

So she said to him, "No, indeed! This evil of sending me away is worse than the other that you did to me."

But he would not listen to her. Then he called his servant who attended him, and said, "Here! Put this woman out, away from me, and bolt the door behind her." (2 Samuel 13:11–17)

This story is disturbing on many levels. Amnon's love for Tamar turned to lust, and when his lust was fulfilled, it turned to hate. Listen, rape is *never* done out of love.

So *why* am I telling you this troubling story? Two reasons. First, to remind you that the enemy is cruel. He wants to ruin your life. He knows what sexual impurity does to a relationship. He knows it turns love to hate. When sexual impurity is introduced into a relationship, respect can be lost, and there is no love without respect. The second reason I'm sharing this story is because I believe David had a chance to stop the sins of his children. I mean, how did he not see Amnon's request for what it was? He could have seen through that and said "What? You want her to come to your bedroom and feed you? You're not fooling me!" But the reason David didn't see it was because impurity had been in his own life. Yes, he repented of his impurity with Bathsheba, and God forgave him, but sin still has consequences. David had a blind spot to his kids' impurity because he had the same weakness.

You can bring your kids to church and teach them everything they need to know about God, but if you have sexual immorality in your life, your family will reap the consequences. You're leaving the enemy with a door open to your family.

I know this seems harsh, but don't let anyone deceive you. Immorality in your own life will always have a negative impact on the lives of your children. The Bible even tells us that the iniquity of the fathers is passed down to the children.

> God . . . keeping mercy for thousands, forgiving iniquity and transgression and sin, by no means clearing the guilty, visiting the iniquity of the fathers upon the children and the children's children to the third and the fourth generation. (Exodus 34:6–7)

If we do not deal with iniquity in our own lives, we will see it repeated in the lives of our children. But notice this passage does not say that the *sins* of the fathers are passed down to the children (even though it's frequently quoted this way). Rather, it speaks of the *iniquity* that is passed down.

There is an important difference between sin and iniquity. Sin is the outward movement; iniquity is the inward motivation. Sin is the action; iniquity is the attitude. Sin is in the hand; iniquity is in the heart.

If iniquity is in the heart, the hand will follow accordingly. If the attitude is in the heart, then the action will follow. Therefore, if we want to overcome our struggles in the area of sexual purity, we must deal with the inward motivation. We have to deal with the iniquity because the hidden things of the heart are what our children will inherit from us.

The word *sin* means to "trespass, to transgress, or to step over the line."[2] If you step onto another person's property, and a Private Property sign is posted, you're trespassing. That's transgression, and that's what sin is. Sin is going where you're not supposed to go or stepping over a line you're not supposed to cross.

When God says, "Don't step over this line," and we step over it, that's sin. That's transgression. But the heart attitude behind the action is iniquity. For example, adultery is sin, but lust is iniquity. Adultery is the outward movement, but lust is the inward motivation. We need to understand that lust is an iniquity, and iniquity is in the heart.

I've heard some men say, "Well, I know I deal with this stuff, but I've never actually done anything. I've never put that lust into action. Sure, I look at pornography and struggle with lust. But I've always been faithful to my wife."

Such a person needs to understand that it's not the *sins* of the parents that are passed down to the children; it's the *iniquities*. If we allow lust to stay in our hearts, we are going to see it in our children, because God said He would visit the *iniquities* of the fathers on the children to the third and fourth generation (see Exodus 20:5). John Wesley, a theologian from the 1700s, is often attributed with saying, "What one generation tolerates, the next generation will embrace." If lust is in the heart of one generation, it may be acted upon in the hands of the next.

Here's the great news: God has made a way for us to be free from both our sins and our iniquities. Isaiah 53:5 says, "But He was wounded for our transgressions, He was bruised for our iniquities." (Remember, *transgressions* are outward and relate to our sins or trespasses. *Iniquities* are inward and have to do with our heart.) Jesus was wounded outwardly for our outward sins. And He was bruised inwardly for our inward iniquities.

In other words, everything we need to be set free from sin and iniquity has been done in Jesus Christ through His extraordinary sacrifice. Jesus has set us free from sin and iniquity by His atoning work on the cross. But if we don't allow Him to set us free from iniquity, we will give our children an inheritance we don't want them to have.

Impurity Is Always Lust, Not Love

I've often said to people, "If you're dating someone and they say, 'If you love me, you'll do it,' that's a lie." Impurity is *always* lust, *never* love! If you're in an adulterous relationship, it's not love; it's lust. Potiphar's wife did not love Joseph—she lusted after him. If she loved him, she would not have lied about him and allowed him to sit in prison for years.

Most sin is born of selfishness, and lust is the most selfish sin there is. Lust does not want gratification for anyone but self. Lust doesn't care whether the spouse gets hurt. Lust doesn't care if the kids get hurt. If you allow it, lust will take over, and it will affect not only you but also your current and future family as well.

I want to speak directly to single people right now. I know you are under tremendous pressure from the world to compromise your sexual purity. Our current culture is extremely sexualized. But you need to understand the truth. Satan is a liar, and sexual immorality has consequences (and they are not the same consequences that love produces). These consequences bring great pain and heartache. Sometimes, out of awkwardness with the topic, parents and leaders don't adequately explain why God says, "Don't step over that line." God is not a prude who doesn't want you to have fun. He warns you not to step over that line of sin because He knows pain and death are on the other side. It's like when a dad tells his children to not play in the street. It's not because he doesn't want them to have fun; it's because he doesn't want them to be hit by a car! God loves you, and He doesn't want you on the road to destruction.

Our world is filled with broken and hurting people, and we wonder why. Could it be because purity has become a joke? Pop culture has made virginity a problem to be solved instead of something to be protected and treasured.

God loves you, and He doesn't want you on the road to destruction.

I was once asked by a young couple, "If we love each other and we're going to get married anyway, what difference does a piece of paper make?"

The way they phrased this question let me know the enemy was telling them to focus on the marriage license, not their action. The enemy is crafty!

"None," was my reply. "The piece of paper makes no difference at all. I'll tell you what does make a difference, though—the blessing of God. It makes all the difference in the world!"

Who would not want the blessing of God on their sexual relationship with their spouse? When we walk in obedience to God, we have His blessing. But when we walk in disobedience to God, we invite destruction into that area of our lives. The only way to close the door is through repentance.

Here's what Debbie and I did with our kids. You may not have the same conviction or capacity, but we told our kids that if they met the right person—a godly person whom we confirmed as being their future spouse as well—and they were still in college, we would continue to pay for their education after they got married. We didn't want to hold their education hostage and force them to wait until after they graduated to get married if the temptation to be impure before marriage was too great. We told them, "We would rather you enter into marriage poor and pure than educated and impure." I knew firsthand the trouble that comes with impurity before marriage, and I was willing to put my money where my mouth was. It was *that* important to us that our kids remain pure.

Some couples who have been married for years also need to understand this because they may have opened the door to destruction before they got married and don't know how to shut it. If that's you, please keep reading—I can help you shut that door.

I have observed that premarital sex can open the door to dissatisfaction with sex after the wedding vows have been spoken, because if you are going to have premarital sex, you have to sneak around to do it. If a young couple is going to be impure, they won't just come right out and say it. If their parents ask, "What are you doing on your date tonight?" they're typically not going to respond with, "We're going to have sex. Be home by 11!" No, they will probably lie.

All impurity involves deception. So if you had premarital sex, you had to do some sneaking around, and that developed an appetite for "sneaking around sex"—an appetite God never intended you to develop. By compromising in this way, you set your marriage up for failure.

I know that may seem like a strong statement, but I have witnessed the sad results of this all too often. When I counsel couples who have gone through adultery, I have learned to ask them about this: "I'm not trying to pry, but I need to know so we can shut a door. Did the two of you have premarital sex?" In nearly every case, the answer is "Yes."

Here's how it happens. When you have premarital sex, you sneak around and get butterflies in your stomach. You get an adrenaline rush because you're doing something that's forbidden and exciting. But after you get married, you don't have to sneak around anymore, and the adrenaline rush is gone. Then one of you will say, "It's just not the same." You might begin to watch X-rated videos and pornography because you're trying to satisfy an appetite that was created by sin.

That is why a man will begin talking to or flirting with a female co-worker at his office—he's trying to satisfy an appetite for the forbidden that was aroused in him by premarital sex. Then he will begin to engage in an extramarital affair with her. In order to do that, what will he have to do? That's right—sneak around, cover it up, be deceptive. He'll get the same adrenaline rush with her that he had with his wife before they got married. He associates that feeling with love, so he'll begin to think he loves his co-worker and not his wife. Then he'll divorce his wife and marry his co-worker.

Now what happens? He doesn't have to sneak around anymore, and now the cycle of sin and deception is ready to repeat itself. This is why some people have been divorced three, four, and five times. I don't want to say this about everyone who has had multiple marriages, because this is not always the reason, but there are some people who have created an appetite that can never be satisfied outside of an illicit relationship. Other people subconsciously realize this and don't want to get married at all because they fear marriage might "ruin" what they have. They just continue in a life of sin, which is exactly what the enemy wants.

Please know that this scenario doesn't just happen with men. Women can also establish an unhealthy appetite for the romance or emotional intimacy associated with sneaking around. This is not a "man" problem or a "woman" problem—this is a *human* problem. We are trying to satisfy an appetite God never intended us to have—an appetite that was created by lust, not love.

If you want to close the door that premarital sex has created, you do so the same way you close it with any other sin: you confess it and repent. Confess it to God and to someone you both trust. Unfortunately, many Christian couples who have had premarital sex don't want to admit it. They want to just gloss it over, pretending to others and to themselves that it never happened. But it did happen, and until they repent of that sin, it will continue to affect them.

If this is you, I am not trying to condemn you, and I am not saying you have to broadcast your failings to the world. You don't have to post it on social media and tag me in it. But if you want to shut that door, you cannot just gloss over the fact that you had premarital sex. You have to deal with it as sin. You have to go to your spouse and ask forgiveness for having violated God's commandments. You have to call sin "sin" and repent to one another and to God. Have a trusted friend or pastor pray over the two of you. Repent and pray for forgiveness together, because if you don't deal with it as sin, you will leave an open door for the enemy into your marriage. It's very important to close that door. If you don't, it will affect your marriage, your family, and your children.

Impurity Will Affect Your Relationship with God

Your family relationships are not the only relationships affected by immorality. Immorality will negatively impact your relationship with God as well. Why? Because immorality brings with it great deception, and God is a God of truth. There is no falseness or deception in Him.

Immorality always involves deception and manipulation, because in order to be involved in sin, you will have to sneak around and lie. Any person who is involved in immorality is a deceptive liar. That's the bottom line. Now I realize this is a strong statement, and I promise I'm not looking down on anyone. I am simply describing the way I used to be. I know what I'm talking about because I used to be a very immoral person. (In other words, I speak from experience!)

Immoral people must cover up things, so they become deceptive in every area of their lives. By doing so, they eventually learn to be deceptive not only with their spouse or their parents but also with God.

Please don't misunderstand me—God cannot be deceived! He knows exactly what you and I are doing. But when you open your life to impurity, you open yourself to demonic spirits. And those spirits will tell you that no one sees what you're doing—not even God.

You can't be involved in impurity and also have an open and transparent relationship with God. You may go to church and raise your hands in worship, but you cover your heart. You learn how to pray without dealing with sin. But what does God say about those kinds of prayers?

Psalm 66:18 says, "If I regard iniquity in my heart, the Lord will not hear [me]." And Proverbs 28:9 tells us, "One who turns away his ear from hearing the law, even his prayer is an abomination."

Please don't be deceived. If you are involved in an immoral relationship, it will stand between you and true fellowship with God. When deception takes over, you can convince yourself that sin doesn't matter and you can still hear from God. But you may not really be hearing from God. You may hear a spirit talking to you, but it may not be the Holy Spirit!

One couple involved in an immoral relationship went so far as to tell me they prayed together. I am going to admit that those words made me feel sick because that is the height of deception. They may be talking to a spirit with such prayers, but the spirit they are talking to is *not* holy! They start to believe that spirit is God, but it's actually a demonic spirit masquerading as an angel of light. Those who are involved in immorality become blinded to the point that they can't even see their sin. And they come to believe that God does not see it either.

You cannot have an open relationship with God if you're walking in impurity. If you persist in immorality, your lying and deception will become a way of life. You will learn how to be a religious person rather than a godly person. You will learn how to go to church and put a "face" on. You will learn how to pray with a "face" on. Eventually, you will even learn how to go to God with a "face" on. But God is not fooled by that "face."

In the end, you also will have learned how to tune out the voice of the Holy Spirit. Because you know the Holy Spirit is saying to you over and over again, "Turn away from sin. Turn back to God. Turn back to what is right." The reason He is pleading with you is because He sees the end of the road that is filled with death and destruction—a broken family, a broken marriage, and a broken life. He sees all of that. Yet He loves you, which is why He's pleading with you to come back.

If you allow lust to stay in your heart, you will learn how to walk in a rebellious relationship with the Holy Spirit. You will learn how to say "no" to the Holy Spirit over and over again. You will learn to tune out the voice of God and grieve the Holy Spirit.

Do not be deceived. Immorality *will* affect your relationship with God. If you believe you can keep immorality in your heart and still have a pure relationship with God, you have been deceived.

This is precisely why the apostle James wrote this to the Church:

> But each one is tempted when he is drawn away by his own desires and enticed. Then, when desire has conceived, it gives birth to sin; and sin, when it is full-grown, brings forth death. Do not be deceived, my beloved brethren. (James 1:14–16)

James is wondering, *How in the world could you go back to your sinful ways now? How could you allow that lust to draw you away from the truth? You must have been deceived because you know that lust will turn into sin, and that sin will result in death.*

James is pleading with believers to not be deceived but to let God do a work in this area of their lives. If you're deceived, God is pleading with you to repent because that's the only way you can have a relationship with Him. You must come to God on His terms, not yours. Repent, renounce your sin, and tell God you want to come back to Him.

Repentance is vital. This is a strong statement, but we all need to hear it: if you allow sin to thrive in this area of your life, you will *not* fulfill your destiny.

Impurity Will Affect Your Future

Satan will try to persuade you that immorality has no real impact on you, your family, or your future. And he can present a pretty convincing case.

It would be hard to find a case that looked more convincing than Joseph's. After all, Joseph was a slave. He had no rights. He had no future. He could never get married. He could never have a family of his own. Even if he was allowed to marry, his wife would also be a slave—the property of another man. His future held no promise of any kind of sexual fulfillment. So what did he really have to lose by yielding to temptation?

The truth is that Joseph had everything to lose. Sinning against God would have cost him his fellowship and communion with God. He would have lost God's blessing and the key to his destiny. He would have lost what God had planned for his future if he had not passed this test.

Joseph had everything to lose, and so do you. But that's not what the enemy will tell you in a moment of temptation. Satan will tell you there are no real consequences to immorality. He will tell you that no one will ever know. But I can tell you two people who will *definitely* know: God and you.

King Solomon talks about this in Proverbs 7 when he tells the story about an immoral woman who brings young men into her home when her husband goes out of town. She says to one young man:

Come, let us take our fill of love until morning;
Let us delight ourselves with love.
For my husband is not at home;
He has gone on a long journey;
He has taken a bag of money with him,
And will come home on the appointed day.
With her enticing speech she caused him to yield,
With her flattering lips she seduced him.
Immediately he went after her, as an ox goes to the slaughter,

Or as a fool to the correction of the stocks,

Till an arrow struck his liver.

As a bird hastens to the snare,

He did not know it would cost his life. (Proverbs 7:18–23, emphasis added)

I don't know how much clearer this can be! Like an ox that goes to slaughter (v. 22) is the man or woman who pursues sexual immorality. It *will* affect your future.

Immorality is disobedience toward God, and such disobedience will cause His favor and blessing to leave your life. You might live to be 105 years old, but you won't have lived the amazing life God had planned for you. Impurity will cost you the presence of God in your life, and it will cost you your destiny.

So how do we protect ourselves against impurity? First, we need to know where impurity starts.

Impurity Begins in the Eye, Not in the Heart

Since lust is in the heart, it might be easy to assume that impurity begins there too. But it doesn't. Impurity actually begins in the eye. It begins with looking.

Notice the Scripture passage says Potiphar's wife "cast longing eyes on Joseph" (Genesis 39:7). The Bible tells us Joseph was a handsome man (v. 6), so I suppose it's only natural that she would notice he was attractive. But at some point, she began to not only notice Joseph but also to really *look* at him. After she started looking at Joseph, it was only a matter of time before looking turned into longing—or lust, to put it bluntly. When noticing turned into looking with desire, lust was stirred up. The impurity began in her eyes when she began looking at Joseph longingly.

Here's some advice that will go a long way toward steering clear of immorality: don't *look*! Don't allow yourself to look or continue looking, because if you allow yourself to continue to look, you're inviting lust into your life. Look away!

King David's sin of adultery began when he wandered out onto the roof and happened to see Bathsheba bathing (see 2 Samuel 11:2), but how long did he look? Instead of dwelling, David could have turned and looked the other way. He could have walked back into his house and cried out to the Lord for help. But instead, he continued to look, and lust was inevitably stirred up.

When I was a teenager, my youth pastor tried to help us in this area, and he told us, "The second look is lust." Unfortunately, that advice didn't seem to help me very much. I just took one *very long* first look!

When you think about it, Joseph probably had a lot of opportunities to look. He was the steward of the house and was in charge of everything in it. He probably knew when his master's wife bathed and when she dressed—and she was most likely a beautiful woman! It wouldn't have been difficult for Joseph to look. But if Joseph had allowed himself to look, he would have given lust an opportunity to invade his heart, and he probably would have fallen into sin when temptation came. But the reason Joseph didn't fall when temptation came was because lust was not in his heart, and lust was not in his heart because he had not allowed it into his eyes.

"Don't look" should become a motto for us all. Don't look at pornography. Don't look at inappropriate websites. Don't look at provocative pictures on social media. Don't look at sexually explicit movies. Don't

look at seductive television programs. If you see someone attractive who is not dressed appropriately, the first thought that should come to your mind ought to be, *Don't look!* Because when you look, lust is the next step, and after lust comes immorality.

Let me pause here. Since I first preached this series two decades ago, a lot of things have changed. Pornography itself is not new, but our access to it has increased dramatically. To view pornography years ago, you had to get in your car and show your face in an adult bookstore. Now many of us have personal computers and phones in our pockets with the ability to access anything at any time, in record time. With just a few clicks, anyone can easily find porn. Not only that, but you might be on social media scrolling through pictures of your cousin's birthday party or a friend's new car, and then, bam! An ad pops up with an explicit photo. And a choice has to be made. The enemy is constantly luring men and women alike to just take a *look*.

In fact, in recent years, the Barna Group did a sobering study about pornography[3] in America, polling both Christians and non-Christians. The study is a dire call to action for the Church. I like numbers, so let me share a few statistics to help prove the enormity of our porn problem. The results stated that one out of three Americans seek out porn at least once a month.[4] A different study reported that an estimated 91.5 percent of men and 60.2 percent of women (ages 18 to 73) consumed porn in the past month.[5] Approximately 72 percent of non-Christian men (ages 13 to 24) use porn on a monthly basis,[6] and 20 percent of men come across porn on a daily basis.[7] There has also been a rise in women viewing pornography: 36 percent of non-Christian women (ages 13 to 24) view porn on a regular basis.[8] This isn't just a "man" problem. And although the statistics among practicing Christians are not as high, they are not zero—41 percent of Christian males (ages 13 to 24) and 13 percent of Christian females (ages 13 to 24) seek out porn at least once or twice a month.[9]

And it's not only young people who struggle with this. I want to highlight another very sobering statistic: one in five youth pastors and one in seven senior pastors use porn on a regular basis. This adds up to more than fifty thousand US church leaders using porn.[10] And for Christians, there is still great shame and guilt wrapped around porn usage, so it's very possible these numbers could actually be much higher. This is a true moral crisis within our country and the Church.

Over the years, the idea of watching porn has not only become normalized in our society, but porn itself has also become "more explicit, violent, and racist."[11] Producers have tried to compete with an overinflated industry and desensitized masses by making their content even more demeaning and harsh. Watching pornography is more common and encouraged than ever before, especially among teens and young adults who think that everyone looks at porn occasionally. Essentially, very few young people think porn is a bad thing. In fact, when asked to rank "bad things" in order of severity, most people placed viewing porn pretty low on the list. And you won't believe this: teens and young adults rank "not recycling" and "overeating" as significantly more immoral than viewing porn.[12] And young people aren't only viewing it, but they are also *participating* in it. The majority of teens and young adults, both males and females, report having "received a nude image [from someone] via text, email, social media or app."[13] And 40 percent report having *sent* images like this to someone.[14]

So why is porn use a problem? Why are these statistics so disturbing? Because people don't want to acknowledge the serious damage porn does. The enemy has flooded our culture with immorality and coated it with lies about empowerment and freedom. Yet, the allegations connecting pornography and human trafficking cannot be ignored.[15] Reports indicate that "thousands of trafficked children and young adults have been forced to make pornographic films"[16] without their consent. Nonconsensual content and abuse are commonplace within the porn industry, and it's almost impossible to know what content is or isn't consensual.[17]

If all of that doesn't make you pause, know this: viewing porn has severe consequences to your soul and your relationship with God and others. Research states that the effects of porn usage can contribute to sexless marriages, infidelity, paying for sex, a decreased desire for marriage or children,[18] and poorer mental health.[19] One study says that regular porn use "dramatically reduces [a person's] capacity to love"[20] or experience healthy affection and intimacy in marriage. Scientists have found that regular porn use can literally affect the brain the same way drugs can, causing compulsive cravings, impaired decision making, and addictive behavior.[21] Studies are also looking into claims that porn usage is linked to an increase in sexual violence, exploitation, and other sex crimes.[22] Don't let the enemy fool you! Pornography is an addictive, damaging, and pervasive problem in our society.

We've all heard this convenient lie: "I'll just look, but I won't do anything." You know how well that works? Have you ever heard someone say, "I'm just going to look; I'm not going to buy"? It doesn't work! If you look, you will buy because looking gets your desire stirred up. If you start looking for homes, you're going to buy a new house. If you start looking for cars, you *will* buy a new car. Auto dealers call it "new car fever."

We bought a new home a while back, and for some reason I started looking at these new stainless steel barbecue grills. They were so bright and shiny. Of course, I already had a perfectly good barbecue grill. It worked just fine, but it was black. It wasn't shiny like the new ones. Somehow, I started looking at the new ones, and every time we went into a store, I'd say to Debbie, "I'm going to look at the barbecue grills."

But as I began to really think and pray about it, just as I pray over every financial decision, I heard the Lord say, "You don't need a new barbecue grill. Stop looking!" If I had continued looking, I would have eventually bought one. So I had to stop looking.

Here's my point: if you're not going to buy a new barbecue grill, don't go to the store where they're sold. If you're not in the market for adultery, don't look!

Let me show you what a thoroughly biblical principle this is. Psalm 101:3 says, "I will set nothing wicked before my eyes." What if we purposed to do that—to set nothing wicked before our eyes? Think about how that would affect us. Every time we go to a movie, watch a TV show, read a magazine, or open up our phones, we are setting something before our eyes, so we should be careful.

Debbie and I love watching movies together, but we're careful about which ones we choose to watch. Debbie has a sensitivity to violence—it disturbs her and keeps her up at night. I don't have that same sensitivity, but I will not watch a movie with nudity in it. I just won't do it. It would be like bringing an alcoholic to a bar. I used to be in bondage in this area, and I can't have one look because it can stir up something in me. But the choice to keep my eyes pure is worth it. And I have had victory in this area for more than thirty-five years. Listen to me: resolve to set *nothing* before your eyes that could stir up temptation.

Research the reasons for movie or TV show ratings before you watch. Place accountability safeguards on your digital devices to prevent you from going to certain sites or allowing certain ads to pop up.

Proverbs 27:20 says, "Hell and Destruction are never full; so the eyes of man are never satisfied." The Bible says the *eyes* are never satisfied. The eyes have a lust of their own. This is also described in 1 John 2:16 as "the lust of the flesh, the lust of the eyes, and the pride of life." So there is lust of the eyes, or to put it another way, a lust of looking.

In Matthew 5:28-29, Jesus tells us, "But I say to you that whoever *looks* at a woman to *lust* for her has already committed *adultery* with her in her heart. If your right eye causes you to sin, pluck it out and cast it from you" (emphasis added). Jesus is showing us a progression here. He is telling us that the *eye* can cause us to sin. He is talking about the sin of looking. The progression He describes involves first looking, then lusting, and finally immorality. So, implicitly, He's giving us some real wisdom here: stop looking!

Jesus tells us more about the eyes in Matthew 6:22-23: "The lamp of the body is the eye. If therefore your eye is good, your whole body will be full of light. But if your eye is bad, your whole body will be full of darkness." Jesus is saying that what we set before our eyes is what will eventually end up in our hearts and affect our entire bodies. If we continue to set darkness before our eyes, our bodies will end up full of that darkness. If we look at things that stir up lust, our bodies will end up full of that lust. So we must set before our eyes what is good and wholesome. If we set what is "light" before our eyes, our entire being will be affected by that light.

Job said, "I have made a covenant with my eyes; Why then should I look upon a young woman?" (Job 31:1). This is a good Scripture passage for everyone, especially men, to memorize! Job made a covenant with his eyes, and you should too. Make a covenant with your eyes and with God at the same time. Say to God, "I will not look! If I see something I know is seductive, I will look away. I will not look a second time. I will not look a long time. I will look away."

I know only too well that the eyes can open the door to darkness. For many years this was a difficult struggle for me, and the Lord has really dealt with me in this area. If you wrestle with this as well, there is hope. God knew we would live in these times, and His Word is timeless and still applicable. The Bible says, "No temptation has overtaken you except such as is common to man; but God is faithful, who will not allow you to be tempted beyond what you are able, but with the temptation will also make the way of escape, that you may be able to bear it" (1 Corinthians 10:13). Temptation can *always* be overcome, and God will *always* provide an escape. We just need to remain close to Him every day. We *can* control our looking!

If you are failing in this area, you have not forfeited your destiny, but there are steps you must take to pass this test.

The Importance of Honesty and Accountability

One thing you need to understand is that Satan works in the darkness. So if you have difficulty with sexual purity, you need to expose it and uncover it. Because the more you keep it hidden, the more power you give to Satan.

A man who struggles with lust is often afraid to come clean with his wife about it, because he's afraid she will reject him. He needs to understand that it's actually his deception that destroys his wife's trust, not the lust. It's the lying and covering up that causes his wife to reject him or lose respect for him.

I have talked to many couples who have suffered in this area of their marriage. In every case, it was the deception and resulting loss of trust that hurt the spouse the most, far more deeply than the immorality.

If you struggle in this area, run *to* your spouse, not away from him or her. Go to your spouse and say, "I love you. I want only you. But sexual temptation is so pervasive in our society, and I've developed some unhealthy appetites. I don't want to do these things anymore, and I want to make myself accountable." It will help you immeasurably if you'll just be honest and open and make yourself accountable to someone. Years ago, I made the decision to be accountable not only to Debbie but also to my friends. Being accountable has not always been easy, but it has proved to be a good and healthy thing.

Just a few months ago, one of the elders of our church checked on me, and it didn't offend me at all.

He asked me, "How are you doing in this area?"

I said, "Thank you for asking. Debbie and I are doing great, and I'm doing very well."

"Great," he said. "I know God is blessing us as a church. And I just want you to know that I'll help you if this area should become a problem. If the enemy attacks you, I want you to know you've got a brother who will help you."

I appreciated that. It's a good thing! It's healthy!

But arriving at the decision to be accountable is not always easy or comfortable. When I decided to make myself accountable to Debbie, we had been married about seven years. We sat down, and I said to her, "I need to come clean with you about my past. You know I have an immoral past, but I want to tell you *everything*." Then I told her everything.

I have a very bad past, and I thought she would be shocked. I was actually afraid she would say, "You're a pervert!" and then leave. That's really what I thought. But despite my fears, I knew I needed to bring my struggle out into the open. So I said to her, "That's it. There's the truth. This is who you really married."

But God had a surprise for me. Instead of rejecting me, Debbie said, "I knew you were bad when I married you, but I love you anyway. One thing I really love about you is that you're not dishonest about it. You know when you've been bad, you tell God when you've been bad, and you allow God to work in your life. That's the best thing you can do."

After this conversation, I told her I had a habit I needed to break—a habit of looking. I expected her to be shocked, but do you know what she said? With a hint of sarcasm, she said, "You think?!" She already knew! Guys, *they already know.* Nevertheless, I asked for her help anyway. I made myself accountable to her.

"I don't want to look, but I need some help. Will you help me?" I asked. "If you see me looking, I want you to pray for me. I want you to talk to me about it. And I want you to call me on it."

I had no idea how quickly my request would be answered. Soon after, we took a vacation and were at the swimming pool. Needless to say, the pool is a very hard place not to look! Sure enough, a lady walked by me, and I took a long look at her. The next thing I knew, Debbie reached over and pinched me right where no person should ever be pinched—on the back of my arm. She grabbed my skin in a very painful squeeze and twist, looked into my eyes, and asked with great seriousness in her voice, "Do I need to pray for you?!"

Believe me, after several pinches like that, I quit looking! If you struggle with looking and with lust—and *many* people do—I want to encourage you to become accountable to your spouse and to someone you trust. Ask a trusted friend or a leader at your church or find an accountability group you can attend. If you're married, *run to* your spouse, not away.

And if your spouse comes to you with a conversation like I did with Debbie, please do not condemn him or her. I know people who have talked to their spouses about having this problem, and the spouse went bonkers because they felt insecure. I completely understand this, but you need to know that Satan works in darkness. If your spouse can't talk with you about his or her struggle, you're encouraging them to keep it covered. Please do not feel insecure or threatened. They're not saying they're not attracted to you. And they're not saying they don't love you. Lust is not love. Lust is like an unhealthy appetite that's never satisfied and only wants more. The best thing that someone can do is bring it into the light and talk about it.

This is far from an exact analogy, but a problem with lust is like an unhealthy appetite for sugar. Imagine you're driving with your spouse, and you pass the local Krispy Kreme doughnut shop. The sign is lit up outside, which indicates the doughnuts are hot and fresh, and you suddenly hear, "Pull over *right now*! We *have to* stop at Krispy Kreme! Please, I just need one . . . dozen!" Your spouse has developed an appetite that's difficult to control, and it takes understanding, healing, discipline, and accountability to overcome.

Obviously, doughnuts and sexual impurity are not the same—the severity and consequences for your soul, family, and future are vastly different. This is just an oversimplified illustration. But what I'm saying is that lust is simply an appetite.

I want you to remember these two words: *struggle together.* If you're married, be honest. If you're on the receiving end of one of these conversations, support your spouse and struggle through it together. I understand you might need some marriage counseling. I understand you might want to kill the other person. But struggle together. If you're single, find a friend, a sibling, or someone you trust with whom you can go through the struggle of this test. It has helped me, and it will help you too.

Bringing your struggles into the light is a good and healthy thing.

What Is the Answer?

What is the answer to overcoming the temptations that surround us? How can we pass the Purity Test on a continuing basis and be counted faithful to walk in our destiny? We can see the answer by looking once again at the way Joseph passed this test.

The Bible says Potiphar's wife spoke to Joseph "day by day" (Genesis 39:10). Joseph had to deal with this temptation on a daily basis. Every day this woman tried to get Joseph to sin. Every day Joseph had to lean on God for strength to resist. Every day Joseph had to trust in God to help him.

Joseph had many opportunities to sin. If lust had been in his heart, eventually he would have fallen. But when the temptation became too great, he ran away. The reason he had the strength to run away is that he had not allowed lust a place in his heart. He had kept lust *out* of his heart by allowing God a place *in* his heart, each and every day. Joseph had learned the secret of walking with God day by day.

Like Joseph, you will encounter temptations on a daily basis. And like Joseph, you must deal with those temptations by trusting in God *day by day*. This is the answer to gaining victory in this area.

The enemy does not take a day off from attacking you. In fact, he will often attack you when you're at your weakest. He will set temptation before you day by day. So you can't take a day off either. You have to rely on God day by day.

Day by day you have to pray.

Day by day you have to fill your mind with the Word of God.

Day by day you must choose not to "look."

Day by day you must trust God to help you.

The secret to victory in the area of purity is simply *trusting in God every single day*. If you go to God every day and ask for His help, He will strengthen you to resist temptation. He will give you the ability to walk in purity and obedience to Him.

The secret to victory in the area of purity is simply *trusting in God every single day*.

If you are in bondage, I encourage you to turn to God. Don't run away from Him—run *to* Him! He's not condemning you. He is pleading with you to come to Him for help. If you've messed up, go to God. He is your answer! If you just lean on Him day by day, He will be there to help you. And day by day you will start to gain the victory in this area of your life.

It's amazing to me how often people who have fallen in this area are so filled with shame that they don't want to confess it before God.

Guess what? He already knows! And long before you sinned, Jesus Christ had already paid the price to set you free. Satan is the one who doesn't want you to confess your sin. He wants to keep your sin in the dark so he can continue to have power over you. If you want to be free from sin, the very best thing you can do is confess it. Because when you bring sin out into the light, you immediately take away Satan's power.

No matter what the enemy may say, disobedience in the area of purity *will* delay or derail you on the road to your destiny. It's crucial to bring these matters before God and allow Him to work in your life.

If you've fallen into sin, I want you to know there is hope. You can get back on the road to your destiny. Our God is a God of grace and mercy. He gave His only Son to make a way for you to be forgiven and set free. If you repent and turn away from sin with your whole heart, then He will forgive and restore you. I can tell you from personal experience that He is faithful. I am a restored person currently walking in my destiny. But it required deep brokenness and complete repentance. Turn away from sin and turn to God in transparency and humility.

On the other hand, you may not be struggling in this area right now. Perhaps you have learned to trust in God every day, to run away from immorality, and to look away from temptation. That is a wonderful thing, and you ought to give praise and thanks to God for His grace and redeeming power in your life.

Still, I believe there is wisdom for everyone in the words Paul shares with us: "Therefore let him who thinks he stands take heed lest he fall" (1 Corinthians 10:12). We live in a sexual and sensual society, a culture that will constantly tempt us to compromise and sin. Every one of us must "take heed" to pass the Purity Test. We must cry out to God to help us be a pure people, a holy people. We must lean on Him every day for the grace to walk in purity before Him and run like Joseph did when we're tempted. Because our God has commanded us, "You shall be holy, for I the LORD your God am holy" (Leviticus 19:2).

It's only when we're found faithful in the test of purity that God's presence and blessing can rest upon our lives. It's only then that we will be able to walk in the fullness of the destiny God has planned for each of us.

CHAPTER FIVE

The Prison Test

S hortly after Debbie and I got married, I started working for a local ministry. My primary role was speaking at youth retreats and small churches. When I preached at churches, the congregation often took up an offering for me. I always gave the money from these offerings to the ministry, which helped to offset my salary.

My employer was a great guy, but at that time he was working through some personal difficulties. It soon became clear I couldn't work for him anymore, so I decided to quit my job and start ministering on my own. When I told him I was leaving, he asked me how much the offering was from the last church where I spoke. I let him know we received $400, and he said, "Why don't you keep it, and that will help you get started."

About a week or two after I quit, the pastor of the church where I spoke last called me and said, "We saw so many young people get saved when you were here, and we heard you're on your own now. We had some extra funds, so we'd like to double the offering we gave you! We're going to send you another $400." It was a huge blessing to Debbie and me!

During this time, I had a friend who was often jealous of me and the opportunities I received. He felt like I was always in the right place at the right time, and conversely, he wasn't. He believed I got all the breaks, and he didn't. So when he heard about the extra gift I received, he didn't see it as a blessing. Instead, he told my former employer that the church gave me an extra offering and that I had kept it. They both felt like I had been dishonest and stolen from the ministry.

Truthfully, it hadn't even crossed my mind to tell my former employer about the gift because the church called me *after* I left. I knew in my heart I hadn't done anything wrong. Yet at the same time, the Holy Spirit was prompting me to send him the full $800, so that's what I did. It wasn't an easy decision, and it didn't feel fair, especially since I was lied about and falsely accused. But I had to obey what God was leading me to do.

While Joseph's dilemma isn't about money, at this point in his story, he has a similar decision to make. He passed the Purity Test with flying colors. In spite of the fact that he was a slave and it looked like he had nothing to lose, Joseph chose to do the right thing. When the temptation became too great, he ran away rather than take the chance that he might yield to sin. He chose to honor God and honor his responsibility as the steward of his master's household (see Genesis 39:7–12).

Here's a question, though: since Joseph made the decision to walk in obedience, no matter the price, he should expect God's blessing on his life, right?

Let's look at what happened next.

> And so it was, when she saw that he had left his garment in her hand and fled outside, that she called to the men of her house and spoke to

them, saying, "See, he has brought in to us a Hebrew to mock us. He came in to me to lie with me, and I cried out with a loud voice. And it happened, when he heard that I lifted my voice and cried out, that he left his garment with me, and fled and went outside."

So she kept his garment with her until his master came home. Then she spoke to him with words like these, saying, "The Hebrew servant whom you brought to us came in to me to mock me; so it happened, as I lifted my voice and cried out, that he left his garment with me and fled outside."

So it was, when his master heard the words which his wife spoke to him, saying, "Your servant did to me after this manner," that his anger was aroused. Then Joseph's master took him and put him into the prison, a place where the king's prisoners were confined. And he was there in the prison. (Genesis 39:13–20)

Yes, Joseph chose to do the right thing. But the immediate reward he got for it was to be lied about, falsely accused, and thrown into prison! Not exactly the results you would expect to see from such a God-honoring decision.

The Prison Test: Persevering

Sadly, this part of Joseph's story simply reflects what can and does happen in the fallen world in which we live. Yes, we must obey God if we want to walk in His blessings, but obedience is no guarantee that bad things will never happen to us! Just like Joseph, we must choose to do the right thing if we want to have the presence of God in our lives. But sometimes, just like Joseph, we will do the right thing and still get bad results. When this happens, we are going through what I call the Prison Test.

The Prison Test is about continuing to honor the Lord in your circumstances, even if they're unjust. It could also be called the Perseverance Test because this is the longest of all the tests and can last for years. Every one of us will go through it at some point in our lives, and it's within the Prison Test that we learn to persevere.

We must choose to do the right thing if we want to have the presence of God in our lives.

Perhaps you've heard the sarcastic saying, "No good deed goes unpunished." Have you ever done the right thing, but instead of receiving blessings, you suffered consequences? Have you ever chosen to obey God's Word, but the results made it look as though His promises were not true? Have you ever been accused of something you didn't do? Has anyone ever lied about you or spread a false rumor about you, and people believed it? I don't really need to ask these questions, because I'm sure we all could answer, "Yes!"

This is what happened to Joseph too, except he ended up in prison—for *years!* He went through a long and very painful period when it looked as though there were no rewards for serving God.

But God had a big destiny in mind for Joseph, and big destinies must be supported by big character. In order to walk in his destiny, Joseph was going to need to build his character through perseverance. And it was during the Prison Test that God gave Joseph the grace to persevere.

Remember, Jesus told us, "In the world you *will* have tribulation" (John 16:33, emphasis added). He didn't say you *might* have tribulation. He didn't say that some would have tribulation and others would not. No, Jesus said that as long as you are in this world—as long as you are breathing—you *will* have tribulation. So you might as well get used to it.

You're probably familiar with Jesus' parable of the two houses in Matthew 7:24-27. We used to sing about it when I was a kid in Sunday School: "The wise man built his house upon the rock! . . . The foolish man built his house upon the sand!" Well, there's something many people overlook about this parable: The storm came to *both* houses! Both the foolish man (the one who did not obey the words of Jesus) and the wise man (the one who listened to and acted upon Jesus' words) experienced the same storm. It rains on the just and the unjust alike. The underlying truth in this parable is this: life is stormy because we live in a fallen world.

Whether you're saved or lost, righteous or wicked, saintly or sinful, the storms of life are going to come. Tribulation and trials will batter the house of your life from time to time. The question is, *Will you allow them to do the work God intends for them to accomplish in your life?*

Joseph was in the middle of some serious tribulation. He had run away from sin, only to end up in a dungeon. Prison was probably a horrible place, but the penalty for attempted rape in Egypt was death, so it was actually by the grace of God that Joseph ended up in prison rather than an early grave.

I personally believe that Potiphar suspected his wife was lying. He was probably well aware of her true character, and he also knew the character of Joseph. He wanted to spare Joseph's life, but he had to do something to save face, so he had Joseph thrown into prison.

The prison was under Potiphar's authority, since he was the captain of the guard. I like to believe he put in a good word for Joseph, telling the keeper of the prison what a good servant Joseph was. But more than anything else, the choices Joseph made in prison caused him to be promoted there.

Although Joseph was suffering unjustly, he continued to do the right thing. While he didn't deserve to be in that dungeon, he didn't let it stop him from doing his work "heartily, as to the Lord" (Colossians 3:23). We know this is true because the Bible tells us Joseph was such a good steward that he ended up being promoted, and soon he was in charge of the whole prison (see Genesis 39:22). The Lord was with Joseph, making everything he did there prosper (see Genesis 39:23).

Here's the wonderful thing about Joseph. He didn't allow the injustice of his situation to stop the work of God in his life. No matter how difficult or unfair his circumstances seemed to be, Joseph allowed God to continue to use him. It's absolutely essential we learn to do that also. I have observed some people waiting for God to deliver them out of their unjust circumstances before they will do anything for Him. But if we are waiting for God to deliver us *before* we serve Him, we will never do anything for God!

When God called me to plant Gateway Church, I was still on staff at Shady Grove Church. So I made sure to talk with Pastor Olen and the elders before moving forward. I wanted their blessing, and they readily gave it. They were very supportive and released me in a godly way to start a new church. But somehow a rumor got started within the congregation that I left the wrong way—that I didn't approach leadership first and that I was going out on my own without their blessing.

This rumor caught on like wildfire, and it left a dark cloud on what was supposed to be an incredible new season. I knew I hadn't done anything wrong and that this was an attack from the enemy. I also knew I wasn't supposed to defend myself—that would just add fuel to the fire. And I couldn't wait for God to convince everyone the rumor wasn't true before I obeyed what He was calling me to do.

So I continued to move forward and start the church, trusting that He would be my defender. And God's blessing has been on Gateway from the very beginning. I'm so thankful I didn't wait until God delivered me before I obeyed.

We must allow God to use us *now*, whatever our circumstances might be, and trust in Him for the final outcome.

No one likes the idea of experiencing tribulation, but if we look at the fifth chapter of Romans, we see that God has some interesting things to say about it.

> And not only that, but we also *glory in tribulations*, knowing that tribulation produces perseverance; and perseverance, character; and character, hope. Now hope does not disappoint, because the love of God has been poured out in our hearts by the Holy Spirit who was given to us. (vv. 3–5, emphasis added)

We're going to talk about this passage a lot in this chapter, but let's start with verse 3 where Paul says we "*glory* in tribulations." What does he mean by the word "glory"? The typical Greek word for "glory" is *doxa*. It means "shine, brightness, majesty, or splendor." But the Greek word for "glory" in this verse is different and only used a few times in the New Testament. It can be translated as "rejoice."[1] This Scripture passage is saying we *rejoice* in tribulation. That's right. We *rejoice* in it!

But if we go deeper in the Greek word origins, we find even more of what God has to say about tribulation. The root of the Greek word translated as "glory" here is a word that essentially means "to wish or desire."[2] So this verse is not only telling us to rejoice in tribulation, but it's also saying to *desire* it! I don't know about you, but I don't pray for tribulation. I don't desire tribulation. And my first inclination is not to rejoice in tribulation!

So how do we reach the point where we actually *wish* for tribulation and rejoice in it when it comes? I believe the answer can be found in understanding what God says about the way tribulation works in our lives. According to the Bible, tribulation produces good things in us. So the reason we can rejoice in tribulation—and even wish for it—is because we know what it produces.

Tribulation Produces Perseverance

I've searched high and low in the Bible to find all the ways we can obtain perseverance. But in all my searching, I have discovered only *one*. That one thing is tribulation.

Romans 5:3 tells us, "Tribulation produces perseverance." According to the Bible, there is no other way to get it. So why not allow tribulation to produce perseverance, as God says it will? Why not allow tribulation to do a valuable work of God in our lives?

In John 15, Jesus talks about two vines. One vine produces fruit, and the other vine does not. The vine that doesn't produce fruit gets cut off, while the vine that does produce fruit gets pruned, or "cut on." There doesn't seem to be a whole lot of difference, does there? Both vines end up getting cut (see John 15:1–2).

Of course, if I had to choose, I would much rather be pruned than cut off entirely. The point is that in either case, you can expect to be cut. If you do badly, you'll be cut off, or disciplined. If you do well, you'll be cut on, or pruned back, so you can bear more fruit.

So whether we do the right thing or the wrong thing, we're going to experience some "cutting." That's what happened to Joseph. He made the right decision, and he ended up being "pruned." But God had a plan for the pruning. God's plan was that Joseph would one day bear more fruit.

The book of James says it this way: "My brethren, count it all joy when you fall into various trials, knowing that the testing of your faith produces patience" (James 1:2–3).

If there's one thing we all know about patience, it's this: We all want it. And we want it now! But patience doesn't come just because we want it. The only way to get patience is through "the testing of our faith." That's why we can "count it all joy" when we're going through a trial. We can actually rejoice when we're being pruned. We can say, "Thank You, Lord, for this time of pruning and this time of testing. You have said this is going to produce something good in me. You have said this will produce patience. So when I come out of this trial, I am going to have more of the fruit of the Spirit, and I am going to look more like Jesus."

Now, it's important for us to understand the difference between patience and perseverance. Trials produce patience, while tribulation produces perseverance. Trials are short. Tribulations are long.

Patience can be described as waiting with contentment. The key words here are "with contentment." Patience is different from simply waiting because we all know it's possible to wait and not be content.

To illustrate what I'm talking about, I immediately think of how I feel when my computer is operating slowly. You know the spinning wheel that pops up when you're waiting for a program to open? I don't know what it's actually called, but I call it the "spiral of death." I hate it! I can't understand why my computer can't go as fast as I can. It's supposed to be a brilliant machine, but then the spiral of death pops up, and I just have to sit there and watch it spin and spin and spin! This small thing has a unique way of exasperating me to no end.

God and I are still working on "waiting with contentment"! That fruit of the Spirit is still being developed in my life, because when patience has had its perfect work in me, I will not only wait, but I will wait "with contentment."

Perseverance is similar to patience, in that perseverance also involves waiting. But perseverance involves more than just waiting with contentment. It involves *fighting a battle* while waiting with contentment. It demands that you fight the good fight of faith while you wait.

Perseverance takes longer than patience. You're not going to get perseverance in a week. The only way you get perseverance is by going through a long, difficult season. You can have patience for five minutes while the spiral of death spins. You can have patience for a week or for a month. But when a trial goes on for a long time—when months turn into years and still you must stand in faith while the enemy attacks you with thoughts of doubt and hopelessness—it takes more than patience to endure. It takes perseverance.

Joseph's tribulation lasted thirteen long years. For thirteen years it looked as though God had forgotten him. For thirteen years he had to battle his negative thoughts and keep his focus on God. For thirteen years he had to keep believing what God had said was true. He had to have enormous patience while his troubles went on year after year. But he had to do more than just wait with contentment. He had to wait with an earnest faith in God. *That* is perseverance.

Joseph was not the only Bible character who had to persevere. David was anointed as the king of Israel, but it was thirteen years before he assumed the throne. Paul was anointed as an apostle, but it was thirteen years before his first missionary journey. Once, when I preached on this subject, a woman came up to me after the service to tell me she, too, had waited thirteen years to have a child. She said, "I couldn't believe my ears when you said, 'thirteen years'!"

If thirteen years sounds like a long time, remember that Abraham had to wait twenty-five years for the son God promised him. And Moses waited forty years before he stepped into his destiny and led the Israelites out of Egypt.

All this to say, Joseph could have become bitter toward his brothers, he could have become bitter toward the Egyptians, and he could have become bitter toward God. But instead, he kept his heart right and his focus on God. He persevered. And Joseph's perseverance resulted in character.

Perseverance Produces Character

According to the formula in Romans 5:3, tribulation produces perseverance, and perseverance produces character. Character is defined as moral excellence. For Christians, it's whether we act or react the way Jesus would.

Character can only be developed through perseverance. Just as I could find nothing in the Bible other than tribulation that produces perseverance, I've searched high and low and can find nothing other than perseverance that produces character. (If you find it, let me know!)

Now, I would love it if I could simply go to someone who has godly character, have him or her lay hands on me in prayer, and then instantly receive character. Or I wish the Bible said, "Ice cream produces character." Wouldn't that be great? But it doesn't work that way. You can't get character by having someone pray for you or lay hands on you. Character must be *developed* on the inside. Character is only developed through perseverance. And perseverance only comes by enduring tribulation.

Isn't this an encouraging message? Perhaps not to our flesh.

But it's an important message because character is absolutely essential in supporting the destiny God has for you. And in order to develop that character, you're going to have to go through difficulties. (And the truth is you'll go through them whether you learn this or not.)

God will not allow you to step into your destiny until you have a certain level of character because when you step into your destiny, the spiritual warfare against you is going to increase. Your responsibilities will increase. Your influence will increase. You will need strong character to endure, persevere, and walk your destiny out to the end. Without character, you will never succeed in the destiny God has for you.

We all like the idea of instant rewards. But one of the worst things someone could do for us would be to promote us before we have the character needed to handle that responsibility or deliver us out of a trial before God has achieved His goals in our character through it. Of course, none of us likes to go through a trial. But if you want to step into your destiny, you will have to go through it and allow God to develop His character in you.

Sometimes when we see someone going through a hard time, we want to rush right in and deliver him or her out of it. This is especially true of well-meaning Christians. Don't get me wrong—quite often we are simply responding in love and compassion. But there are times when God is trying to use a situation to teach His children something important, something they need to know for their destiny. It could have to do with managing their finances, or possibly even their relationships. And if a good, well-meaning Christian comes along and delivers them out of that difficulty, they might never learn the lesson God wants them to learn. Then they eventually end up right back in that same crisis situation, and they have to keep retaking that test until they pass it!

Please hear me, this doesn't mean we shouldn't help people. Because of my position, I often have the ability to promote people or help people financially, and I love to do it. But I am always careful. I typically ask God, "Do you want me to do this? You've given me these resources and this authority, but what are You doing in this person's life? I don't want to circumvent what You're trying to do with them. That's much more important."

Even Jesus had to learn by going through trials! Hebrews 5:8 says this: "Though He was a Son, yet he learned obedience by the things which He suffered." People often wonder about the meaning of this Scripture. After all, we know Jesus is the Son of God. And since Jesus is God, He is omniscient. That means He knows everything. But this verse says Jesus, the Son of God, "learned obedience." How could Jesus, who knows everything, *learn* anything? And how could Jesus, who never sinned, learn *obedience*?

We must remember that although Jesus is the Son of God, He came to earth as a man. As a man, He suffered just like we do. As a man, He was tempted in every way we are. And as a man, He learned obedience through the things He suffered.

The Bible tells us, "He Himself has suffered, being tempted" (Hebrews 2:18). It also says He "was in all points tempted as we are, yet without sin" (Hebrews 4:15).

You see, when He was in heaven, Jesus didn't have to learn obedience. He was the Son of God, and He was perfect. There was no fleshly body to tempt Him to sin. But as a man on earth, He had to go through trials. As a man, He was tempted to sin, and He had to overcome those temptations.

I'm not saying Jesus wasn't perfect when He was on earth. He was. He was fully God, but it's important to remember that He was also fully man. As a man, He had to suffer. *And as He suffered, He learned obedience.*

Obedience is a character issue, and character can only be learned. It cannot be imparted. We are not born with character. We are born with a sin nature. But character is developed as we are subjected to adversity. And this verse shows us that even Jesus Christ Himself developed character as a man and learned through the things He suffered.

The closer we get to reaching the destiny God has for us, the more character will be required, and the only way character is produced is through even more difficult trials. A person who has weak character has only been through relatively minor trials. A person who has unshakeable character has been through significant, life-altering trials and tribulations.

Now, please don't become fearful and start wondering what awful trials or tribulations God has up His sleeve. God is not going to send bad things your way—they are just going to happen in the natural process of life. Remember, Jesus said, "In the world you *will* have tribulation" (John 16:33, emphasis added). As long as you are on Earth, trouble will happen. That's just part of life. So make the most of it, and allow whatever trial or tribulation you're going through right now to produce godly character in you.

One way challenging seasons work in our lives is by causing deep character flaws to emerge. We can see this happening in Joseph's situation. Why do you suppose Joseph had to go through such a long and difficult tribulation? I believe God wanted to work through part of Joseph's character. Not only was he a man with God's blessing and favor upon his life, but he also had tremendous God-given leadership ability. If you look at Joseph's life, you can see that he rose to a position of authority in every situation, whether as a slave, as a prisoner, or as the second-in-command over all Egypt. Obviously, Joseph had a special ability to make whatever he was involved with a success, and people trusted him. While it was the favor of God that made Joseph the acting ruler of Egypt, it was the natural ability God had given him that equipped him to do the job! God had given Joseph a special gift, and when you have a special gift, it's easy to lean on that gift rather than on God.

While Joseph was in prison, he used God's gift to interpret dreams for a butler and a baker who were in prison with him. Then when the butler returned to Pharaoh's court, Joseph asked him to remember him (Genesis 40:8–15). But the butler forgot Joseph, and it took two more years before Joseph was delivered out of prison (Genesis 40:23; 41:1).

Why did it take two more years? Let's read the story.

> And Joseph said to him, "This is the interpretation of it: The three branches are three days. Now within three days Pharaoh will lift up your head and restore you to your place, and you will put Pharaoh's cup in his hand according to the former manner, when you were his butler. But remember me when it is well with you, and please show kindness to me; make mention of me to Pharaoh, and get me out of this house. For indeed I was stolen away from the land of the Hebrews; and also I have done nothing here that they should put me into the dungeon." (Genesis 40:12–15)

Do you know why the butler forgot Joseph? I believe God made the butler forget because Joseph was trying to manipulate his circumstances. God moved through Joseph, giving him the interpretation of the dreams for the butler and the baker. But then Joseph jumped in with his own concerns and added, "Hey, put in a good word for me when you get out of here." Let's see how many times Joseph says "me" in verse 14: "Remember *me* when it is well with you, and please show kindness to *me*; make mention of *me* to Pharaoh, and get *me* out of this house" (emphasis added). I believe God could have released him from prison right then, but when Joseph did that, God said, "Nope! He's not quite ready."

As the story continues, we learn that "two full years" pass before Pharaoh has a dream (Genesis 41:1), and the butler suddenly remembers Joseph. It was through interpreting Pharaoh's dreams that Joseph is finally delivered from the prison to the palace. Now, we know God gave Pharaoh those dreams to show him what was about to happen. But why didn't God give Pharaoh the dreams two years earlier? Why would God allow Joseph to endure two more years in that dungeon?

Joseph did a lot of things right in his life, but he was definitely human. And I believe there was a deep character flaw in Joseph, and God wanted it to emerge. The character flaw in Joseph was a tendency to be prideful and trust in his own abilities. I believe God said, "If I reward you now, you'll think the way to get ahead is to drop hints and manipulate the situation. If I deliver you now, you'll think that man promoted you and got you out of prison. So I'll let you wait two more years. Then you'll know I am the One who delivered you."

Listen to me: God *never* rewards manipulation.

God planned for Joseph to become the second-in-command over all Egypt and the instrument of His provision during the famine. But in order for Joseph to rule as God's chosen vessel, he had to learn to lean totally on God—not on his own wisdom or ability. Pride, self-reliance, and self-sufficiency all had to be dealt with before Joseph could step into his destiny. In the midst of that long and difficult season, Joseph learned that his own abilities were not enough.

God is the *only* one who can promote us and deliver us.

It's the same lesson many of us have to learn. God is the *only* one who can promote us and deliver us. We have to stop trying to manipulate situations and instead let God work through our surrender, obedience, and reliance on Him. It's only during trials and tribulation that we start to see things from God's perspective. We come to a deeper understanding of who we really are and of who God is. We learn to respond correctly when troubles come. This is the way perseverance produces character in our lives.

Everyone experiences hardship and injustice. But the hard times and unjust situations we experience are not the deciding factors in our lives. The most important issue in our lives is *the way we respond* to trials when they come. When we respond to them in the right way, character is being developed in our lives. *And character is simply doing the right thing, no matter your circumstances.*

As character is developed, something wonderful happens: we begin to have hope.

Character Produces Hope

When you respond the right way in a tough or unjust situation, something happens to your perspective. You start to see the bigger picture—what God has in mind for your life. Suddenly, God looks much bigger than your trial or problem. This is how character works to produce hope. Hope sees things from God's perspective, no matter how the circumstances might look.

More than once, Joseph did the right thing and suffered the wrong results. Because of Satan, he often ended up on the receiving end of some injustice. But did you notice that Satan never had any new tricks? He used the same tactics on Joseph more than once.

First, he used Joseph's coat to fabricate evidence that Joseph had been killed by wild animals (see Genesis 37:31-32). Later, he used Joseph's coat to fabricate evidence that Joseph had attempted to rape Potiphar's wife (see Genesis 39:12-15). I don't know about you, but if I were Joseph, I'm not sure I would ever wear another coat! It could be freezing out, but if someone offered me a coat, I'd say, "Get behind me, Satan. I don't want a coat!"

As a young man, Joseph was just trying to do a good job for his father, Jacob, and he ended up being thrown into a pit (see Genesis 37:13-14, 23-24). Later, he was just trying to be a faithful steward for Potiphar, and he was thrown into prison (see Genesis 39:20).

Joseph interpreted his dreams for his brothers, and they sold him into slavery and forgot about him (see Genesis 37:6-10, 24-30). Years later he interpreted a dream for the butler, but the butler went back to the palace and forgot about him (see Genesis 40:23).

Here's the reason I'm saying all this: Once Satan finds out that something works, he'll use it again and again. He doesn't have to invent anything new—he already knows how he can get to you! For example, you can't imagine how many people have told me, "I got offended by something that happened at church, and I didn't go back for five years." And I think, *Well, have you ever been offended at the grocery store? Have you ever been offended at a restaurant? Yet you keep going back to those places?* Satan knows that with some people he can continue to bring up offenses within the church and keep them away from corporate worship, the teaching of the Word, and the fellowship of believers. Then, when they are isolated, he can tempt and pursue them even more.

Despite Satan's tricks, Joseph continued wearing coats (I think!). He continued doing a good job and stewarding what was in front of him. And he continued interpreting dreams, which opened the door for him to step into his destiny.

Have you noticed that most of the tests so far have to do with stewardship—how well could Joseph steward his actions, another man's belongings, his own body, and now his attitude? Please understand, you will not fulfill your God-given destiny if you're not a good steward. We must be good stewards.

Due to his circumstances, there were many times Joseph could have become bitter. And maybe he had a few slipups and allowed bitterness into his heart for a time during those thirteen years of waiting. We don't know. In the end, though, he kept his heart right before God and responded in the right way to those wrong situations. He kept his focus on God, and he persevered. That perseverance developed character in Joseph, which helped him to see things from God's perspective. And seeing things from God's perspective produced hope in Joseph's heart.

And here's the great thing: *Joseph didn't allow his hope to turn to disappointment.* His tribulation lasted for thirteen long years. After the first eleven years had gone by, he interpreted the butler's dream, and when the dream came true, Joseph probably thought his deliverance had finally come. I'm sure he was looking forward to being released from prison any day. But then days turned into weeks, and weeks turned into months—and months turned into two more years! Joseph had a perfect opportunity to become disappointed, but he kept his hope in God.

Now, I need to tell you something about hope. Hope is not that God will deliver you *from* your circumstances. Hope is the knowledge that God will walk with you *through* your circumstances.

There's a popular verse about hope that is often misapplied. It says, "Hope deferred makes the heart sick" (Proverbs 13:12), and while this is true, we often miss the context and misinterpret the real meaning. You see, Proverbs 13 is a chapter of contrast. For instance, verse 11 says that wealth gained by dishonesty will be diminished. So it doesn't say there is anything wrong with wealth itself. But if you gain it dishonestly, you will lose it. It's a contrast. With that in mind, here's what I believe verse 12 would be better translated as: "*Misplaced* hope makes the heart sick." It's not that hope itself makes the heart sick, because Romans 5:5 says, "Hope does not disappoint," and the Bible cannot contradict itself. We just have to look at *where* our hope is placed. Essentially, if your hope is placed in your circumstances changing, and then they don't, your heart will get sick. But if your hope is in God, who never changes, you will never have a sick heart.

Deferred hope is misplaced hope. And when you're going through a long and difficult trial, it can very easily turn into disappointment. You must not allow that to happen. You must keep trusting God and hoping in Him. For those of us who have walked through long tribulations, this is sometimes easier said than done. But you must persevere and allow Him to show you His perspective. Realign where your hope lies. Because if your hope is misplaced and turns into disappointment, you will end up heartsick.

Joseph fought against this for thirteen long years. If he had allowed those unjust situations and all the waiting to rob him of his hope in God, he would have had a sick heart. Such a malady could have caused him to die before reaching his destiny. But Joseph kept his hope and trust in God's everyday provision and presence, not in when his future outside of the prison would start.

I don't know what this looks like in your own life—whether you're hoping for a better job, you need physical healing, or you want to have a child. It's so tempting to hope that your circumstances will change. But when you place your hope in God instead of your need, everything changes.

You see, hope is not just for the future. Hope is for the present! No matter what trial you might be going through right now, even if you're in a dungeon, hope says God is right there with you. God is with you now.

I've noticed there's a tendency in some churches to continually preach about a move of God that is still to come. This bothers me because they're not really preaching hope. They seem to have overlooked the reality that we're currently living in a move of God.

People must know we don't have to wait for a move of God in the future. We are in a move of God right now! We have been in a move of God since Jesus Christ came to the earth. *Right now* you can have deliverance! *Right now* you can have healing! *Right now* you can have the gifts of the Holy Spirit! You don't have to wait for some move of God in the future. God is moving in the earth right now!

I know there are times of special outpourings of the Holy Spirit. But we need to thank God for what His Spirit is pouring out in our lives *right now*. If we continually look to the future or to our circumstances changing, our hearts will become frail and sickly in the waiting.

Hope is *right now*!

Hope is believing God is working everything for our good *right now*.

Hope is believing God loves us and is going to take care of us *right now*.

Hope is believing we're in the center of God's will so we can have peace and joy *right now*.

Hope is believing God is with us *right now*, no matter what trial or tribulation we might be going through.

That is biblical hope, not deferred or misplaced hope. And character produces a godly kind of hope.

And guess what hope produces?

Hope Produces Appointments

Romans 5:5 tells us what hope does *not* do: *"Hope does not disappoint"* (emphasis added).

Let's look at that word "disappoint." The prefix "dis" means "not." Therefore, "dis-appoint" is the opposite of "appoint." So the word "disappointment" means that an appointment has been missed. If you say, "I was disappointed," it means that you missed an appointment with something you were hoping would happen.

If "hope does not disappoint," then what does it do? That's easy—hope appoints! Because I love grammar, let me take a moment and show you something amazing. Knowing that "dis" means "not," we can see that the phrase "hope does not disappoint" has a double negative. If we break it down, it really says, "Hope does *not not* appoint." The two "nots" cancel each other out, and we end up with "hope does appoint!"

Hope produces appointments for you. And the appointments hope produces are *divine appointments*. They are moments for you to minister to others and see their lives change, as well as your own. But without hope, you could become caught up in the trial you're going through and miss those divine appointments.

Joseph could have had a pity party for himself. After all, he was in a very unjust situation, and it didn't look as if there were a way out. But instead of feeling sorry for himself, he kept his head up and his eyes on God. He didn't let a hopeless situation prevent him from looking for divine appointments right there in the prison. He chose to reach out and minister to the needs of others. How do we know this? "And Joseph came in to them in the morning and looked at them, and saw that they were sad. So he asked Pharaoh's officers who were with him in the custody of his lord's house, saying, 'Why do you look so sad today?'" (Genesis 40:6–7).

Joseph was able to notice the butler and the baker were sad because he had not allowed his own problems to consume him. In spite of his troubles, Joseph persevered and allowed character to produce godly hope in his heart. Joseph could have easily missed this moment if he had been focusing on himself. But he wasn't. He was looking outward, not inward. He was looking to see how he could minister to someone else. I don't think it was a coincidence that his ministry to one of his fellow prisoners was eventually the key to Joseph's deliverance! What led to Joseph's deliverance wasn't him sulking about being in prison— it was ministering to other people!

What led to Joseph's deliverance wasn't him sulking about being in prison— it was ministering to other people!

Like Joseph, you must keep your hope in God no matter what you're going through, and remember He has divine appointments for you every day. There are people all around you who need God, and God wants you to minister to those people. But if your focus is on your own problems and trials, you'll walk right past opportunities to minister to the needs of others. You'll miss appointments that are important to God. And if you miss an appointment that's important to God, you may miss an appointment that's important to your destiny.

Joseph's brothers tried to thwart his destiny. Potiphar's wife tried to thwart his destiny. Then the butler messed it up. All of these people did things that seemed certain to thwart God's plan for Joseph and prevent him from entering into his destiny. But in spite of what they did, Joseph kept doing the right thing. And because he kept doing the right thing, Joseph didn't miss his divine appointment.

You must understand this truth. There is only one person who can thwart your destiny. There is only one person who can hinder you from reaching your destiny. There is only one person who can delay your destiny. Want to take a wild guess who it is? You're right! It's *you.* You are the only one who can thwart, hinder, or delay your destiny.

I have accepted the fact that I'm the only one who can mess up my destiny. Just like you, I've had others do things to me and say things about me that are wrong and hurtful. And I realize that if I don't respond in the right way to those injustices, I can mess up God's plan for my life. This doesn't have to do with God's sovereignty. It has to do with the fact that God is not going to let me step into a destiny I cannot handle because He knows what will happen. But if I make a mistake and come to Him with a repentant heart, He will restore and reaffirm His destiny for me. And if I choose to do what is right, there is nothing anyone can say or do that will interfere with the plans God has for me! And if you choose to do what is right, no one else can stop the destiny God has for you.

In the same way, no one else could interfere with Joseph's God-given destiny. Without a doubt, Joseph is a wonderful example for us of how we can persevere and come through tribulation with character and hope.

We see again here how Joseph is also a type of Christ.

- Joseph went to prison for something he didn't do. Christ suffered for something he didn't do.

- Joseph was numbered with the criminals in the prison. Jesus "was numbered with the transgressors" (Isaiah 53:12).

- Joseph was jailed with two prisoners. One was set free, and one was condemned (see Genesis 40:21-22). Jesus was crucified between two thieves. One received forgiveness, and one did not (see Luke 23:33, 39-43).

- Joseph said to the butler, "Remember me when it is well with you, and please show kindness to me; make mention of me to Pharoah, and get me out of this house" (Genesis 40:14), but the butler forgot about him. The thief said to Jesus, "Remember me when You come into Your kingdom" (Luke 23:42), but Jesus did not forget about him. Jesus remembered him that very day, and that day he was with Jesus in heaven (see Luke 23:43).

Here's my word for you: Even if other people don't keep their word, even if other people forget you, God never will. God will always keep His Word, and He will always remember you.

So when you're going through a long and difficult trial, allow it to produce perseverance in you. Keep fighting the good fight of faith as you wait with contentment for God's deliverance.

I told you the story about quitting my job and giving my former employer $800. After that, I continued to preach wherever I was invited. But those opportunities didn't provide a consistent source of income, and we didn't have health insurance. So Debbie went to a temp agency to find employment. She had to take an aptitude test to see what her skill set was for certain jobs, and she scored great in every area, except math. (This was not a surprise to either one of us—she will tell you herself that numbers are a necessary evil in her world.) The woman at the temp agency told her there wasn't anything available for her particular skill set at the moment. But then she added, "You know what? I saw a word this morning I've never seen before, but I think I heard you say it. What did you tell me your husband is?"

Debbie responded, "He's an evangelist."

The lady pulled out a folder titled "James Robison Evangelistic Association" and asked if that was the same thing.

Debbie nodded, and the lady replied, "Well, they have an opening, and I'd like to at least send you for a job interview."

At that time, James' ministry had six hundred employees, and the only opening was in payroll. Debbie was not happy about working with numbers, but she interviewed anyway. At the end of her interview, the manager told Debbie, "I've interviewed three other people who are more qualified for this job, but God is telling me to give it to you."

Debbie started the job, which gave us more income and enabled us to receive health insurance—and it couldn't have come at a better time! She got pregnant with our son Josh, and we didn't have to pay out of pocket for her doctor's appointments or his delivery. This was a huge financial blessing for us! But it wasn't all God had in mind.

One day, I stopped by Debbie's office to take her to lunch, and as I was standing in the parking lot, a car pulled up. I watched the window roll down, and inside was James Robison.

"Hey, I've been hearing about all these kids getting saved at school assemblies and events where you're preaching," he said. "I'm going to Corpus Christi next week to do a crusade. Would you like to go with me? I'd like you to do some school assemblies and invite the kids to the crusade."

Before I knew it, I was meeting with the principal of the largest high school in Corpus Christi. I gave him recommendation letters from other principals and shared with him what I would talk about at the assembly. He said that he couldn't call a full-school assembly, but I could speak in their health classes about resisting drugs and alcohol. I spoke in several classes that day, inserting humor and the gospel, and it went so well that the principal called the other schools in the area and had me do assemblies with them too! I invited everyone I met to the crusade, and when the night finally came later that week, *six hundred kids got saved*!

It all started with me standing in a parking lot waiting to take my wife to lunch. That one divine appointment, prefaced by other divine appointments, opened up even more opportunities to minister alongside James Robison, and eventually see thousands and thousands of people saved. You might think I was just in the right place at the right time, but it was God's place at God's time. He orchestrated the divine appointments that paved the way for my destiny.

The Prison Test is about doing the right thing even when you're falsely accused, even when you're thrown in prison, even when you're waiting a long time for your circumstances to change.

I understand this waiting period can feel like an eternity. You may even start to wonder, "Is God really faithful?" I know because I've been there. More than once! I don't have all the answers, but I do know this: God *is* faithful. And He will use the Prison Test to develop perseverance and His character in your life.

Ask the Holy Spirit to help you see things from God's perspective. Pray "Open my eyes, Lord, that I may see" (see 2 Kings 6:17). And then no matter how wrong your situation is, keep doing the right thing.

You may see things change quickly. Or it may take years. In some instances, you might not understand God's perspective until you see Him face to face in heaven. The apostle Paul wrote about the "eternal weight of glory" (2 Corinthians 4:17), and it's this perspective that always produces hope.

God's hope will not disappoint you. His hope will carry you to a divine appointment with your destiny!

CHAPTER SIX

The Prophetic Test

We know God created each one of us. He is the Creator of all things, which means He is also the Creator of our destinies. But have you ever thought about *how* He creates things? Does He just wave His mighty hand? Or does He dream about something, and then it automatically comes into being? The Bible tells us very plainly how God creates. When God wants to create something, He *speaks*.

In the very first chapter of Genesis, we read when God created the heavens and the earth, He *spoke* and said, "Let there be light" (Genesis 1:3). When God created the animals, He *spoke* and said, "Let the earth bring forth the living creature according to its kind" (Genesis 1:24). And when God created man, He *spoke* and said, "Let Us make man in Our image" (Genesis 1:26).

Hebrews 11:3 tells us, "The worlds were framed by the *word* of God, so that the things which are seen were not made of things which are visible" (emphasis added). Everything God created has been created by the words of His mouth. God brings things to pass by *speaking*.

In John chapter 1, God says: "In the beginning was the Word, and the Word was with God, and the Word was God. . . . All things were made through Him [the Word], and without Him [the Word] nothing was made that was made" (vv. 1, 3). In these verses, God tells us that He and His Word are one. The next thing He tells us is that "all things" were made through His Word (v. 3). (Obviously, "the Word" refers to His Son, Jesus. But notice, He calls His own Son "the Word.") Then, just in case that wasn't clear enough, God also lets us know that without His Word, "nothing was made that was made" (v. 3). This means everything that is made is made by God's words, and if it isn't made by God's words, it simply doesn't exist!

When God wants to make something, He *says* it. When God has a plan for something, He speaks it forth. And when He speaks it forth, power is released for it to be created.

God had a plan for Joseph's life, so surely He had already spoken over Joseph's life before Joseph had the dreams. Before Joseph ever endured a test, God had already spoken regarding the final outcome He had planned. Long before Joseph stepped into his destiny, the power of God's words had already been released to carry him toward that destiny.

God has a plan for every one of us, just as He did for Joseph. And as we have just seen, when God has a plan for something, He *speaks*. That means God has *already spoken* His plan over each one of us. He has *already spoken* a specific word over your life, and He has *already spoken* a specific word over mine. And when He spoke, the power was released to carry us toward the destiny He has planned for us.

The Prophetic Test: God's Word for Your Life

One night in 1993, God gave me a vision for ministry. He said, "I want you to build a church of thirty thousand people, which reaches three hundred thousand in the Dallas-Fort Worth Metroplex. I also want this church to reach three million in Texas, thirty million in America, and three hundred million around the world." The next morning, I was reading the Bible during my quiet time, and I came across 1 Samuel 11:8: "When he numbered them . . . the children of Israel were three hundred thousand, and the men of Judah thirty thousand." Immediately the Lord confirmed in my heart that the dream I had the night before was from Him!

Seven years later, we planted Gateway Church. A few months into our fledgling ministry, I was having my quiet time, and I read that verse again. The Lord said to me, "I'm going to remind you what I've called you to do, and I'm going to confirm these numbers to you again."

Instantly, I remembered that when we first planted the church, another church gave us $30,000.

Later, that same day, I had lunch with a man who had visited our church twice, and at the end of the lunch he said, "My family and I are going to join the church, and we're excited about it! Every now and then, we have some resources we can sow into the kingdom. The Lord put an amount on my heart I want to give the church." As he handed me the check, he said, "God told me to tell you this amount is going to confirm something to you."

I thanked him and told him how grateful we were. We said goodbye, and after I got in my car, I reached into my pocket and pulled out the check. It was for $300,000! The Lord had confirmed both numbers He had given me in a dream seven years before!

There's no doubt in my mind these numbers and this dream were from God. He wanted to do something, and at the time, I had no idea what the full destiny would look like. But my part was, and is, to continue passionately serving Him with all my heart. It's up to God to accomplish His word, and it's up to me to obey.

As I continued to pray about the vision God had given me for ministry, I read Matthew 16:18, where Jesus says, "I will build My church." Another way of looking at it is, "I [Jesus] will [meaning there's no doubt] build [He's the One doing the building, not me] My [it belongs to Him] church [it's a body; it's all of us; it takes all of us to do it]." I knew God was telling me if I would take care of the depth of my relationship with Him by having a personal, daily, intimate, and thriving relationship with Jesus Christ, He would take care of the width of my ministry. He would take care of the numbers.

This is part of my story, but God has called each one of us for a specific purpose. There is no one else who can do what God has called you to do; there is no one else who can do what God has called me to do. But it's up to us to discover the specific words God has spoken over our lives. And it's up to us to believe the prophetic words God has spoken and then obey Him.

That's what the Prophetic Test—the test of God's word—is all about. Will we believe God's words and stand on them, come what may?

To "prophesy" means to speak as if divinely inspired. It means God, who is divine, has spoken to someone. He can speak through a dream (as He did with Joseph), during a worshipful moment, through the Bible, or through a friend, mentor, or pastor.

God had spoken a prophetic word over Joseph's life, but Joseph went through some tough times when it seemed as though God's words and plans would never come to pass. In those times, Joseph was tested *by the words God had spoken over him*. Would he believe God's words or the words of despair and hopelessness that his circumstances seemed to confirm?

The Bible describes how Joseph experienced this test: "He sent a man before them—Joseph—who was sold as a slave. They hurt his feet with fetters, he was laid in irons. Until the time that his word came to pass, the word of the LORD tested him" (Psalm 105:17–19).

It says in this passage that they hurt Joseph's feet with fetters, which are chains, and that he was laid in irons, so we know that Joseph experienced some real physical suffering during this trial. But it also talks about something else that tested Joseph's character. It says, "The word of the LORD" (Psalm 105:19) also tested Joseph.

When I saw this verse, it jumped off the page at me. I love looking at the original languages the Bible was written in, so I did some research. In the English translation of this verse, "word" occurs twice, but in the original Hebrew, there are actually two completely different Hebrew words with two very different meanings. They are the Hebrew words *dabar* and *imrah*. This verse actually says, "Until the time that his [*dabar*] came to pass, the [*imrah*] of the LORD tested him" (Psalm 105:19).

Now let me explain something to you about these Hebrew words. The first word, *dabar*, is used 1,441 times in the Old Testament and is the Hebrew term most frequently translated as "word." The word *dabar* means "a matter" that is spoken of.[1]

With this in mind, we can see that the first part of this verse is actually saying, "Until the time that [the *word that was spoken* over Joseph's life] came to pass, the word of the LORD tested him."

Now, the second "word" in this verse is the Hebrew word *imrah*. The word *imrah* appears only thirty-seven times in the Old Testament. It means "commandment," "speech," or "word" and refers to the very Word of God—the literal Word of God.[2] This word is not used very often in the Bible. Let me give you a few passages in which the word *imrah* is used.

> The words of the LORD are pure words,
> Like silver tried in a furnace of earth,
> Purified seven times. (Psalm 12:6)

> As for God, His way is perfect;
> The word of the LORD is proven;
> He is a shield to all who trust in Him. (Psalm 18:30)

> Your word I have hidden in my heart,
> That I might not sin against You. (Psalm 119:11)

In each of these verses, *imrah* refers to the literal Word of God. Let's also note that the word "tried" in Psalm 12:6 and the word "proven" in Psalm 18:30 can also be translated as "refined, tested, or purified."

So what Psalm 105:19 is actually saying about Joseph is this: until the time that Joseph's *prophetic* word (or *spoken* word) came to pass, the *literal Word* of God tested and refined him. The New Living Translation of this verse says, "Until the time came to fulfill his dreams, the LORD tested Joseph's character" (Psalm 105:19). This verse is the synopsis of this entire book! But here's an important insight: prophetic words tend to test our *faith*, but the literal Word of God, the Bible, tests our *character*.

I have two questions for you to consider: Do you test the Bible, or does the Bible test you? Do you judge the Bible, or does the Bible judge you?

I love to study Bible commentaries, but there's a right way and a wrong way to study them. Some people read the Bible, and then they go to a commentary to see if what the Bible said is true. When I read something in a commentary, I go to the Bible to see if what the commentator said is true because the literal Word of God, the Bible alone, is my standard.

How do we know murder is wrong? The Bible tells us so. How do we know the difference between murder and manslaughter? The Bible tells us so. How do we know lying is wrong? The Bible tells us so. How do we know stealing is wrong? The Bible tells us so. How do we know adultery is wrong? The Bible tells us so. Paul confirmed this when he wrote in the New Testament that he wouldn't have known coveting was wrong if the Law, God's Word, had not told him so (see Romans 7:7).

Some people say truth is ever-changing. No, it's not! Our understanding of truth may change, but truth itself never changes. Contrary to popular belief, absolute truth is not subject to personal opinion or current scientific, political, or popular beliefs. We can all have differing opinions, but if something is true, it's true regardless of personal opinion. Absolute truth is absolutely true for everyone—no exceptions. No matter what we think we know, the Bible will always be the source of absolute truth.

Other people say the laws of the land set the standard. That's not true either. Laws can be wrong. At one time, slavery was legal in our country. Segregation was legal. Killing unborn babies was (and in some places still is) legal. Yet we know the truth—*every life* is precious to God. Legality is not the standard for truth or morality. The Bible is!

The Bible is the Word by which all truth must be measured. The Bible is also the Word by which all other words from God must be measured. That's why it's absolutely essential we know the Bible.

Right now, whether you know it or not, you are being tested by the Word of God. It is testing your character. Whether you reach your destiny or fail to reach your destiny is directly related to how well you know God's Word. I can't emphasize this enough: *you need to know the Word of God!*

Whether you reach your destiny or fail to reach your destiny is directly related to how well you know God's Word.

I see believers all the time who are trying hard to make progress, but they seem stuck. And the reason is really quite simple: they are violating Scripture! I'm going to make a strong statement: there are some people who will never fulfill their destiny unless they change some things, because their lives don't line up with the Word of God.

For example, some people won't submit to authority, even though the Bible says they should (see Romans 13:1-7; Hebrews 13:7; Titus 3:1). Some people won't tithe, even though the Bible says not tithing is robbing God (see Malachi 3:8). Some people won't honor the Sabbath or take a day off, even though it's one of the Ten Commandments (see Exodus 20:8-11). The sad part is that most of these people probably don't even know they're violating Scripture.

If you never read the Bible, how will you know what it says? And if you don't know what it says, how will you know how to live?

Know What the Bible Says

Some of you picked up this book because you have a dream from God, and you want me to tell you how to fulfill your destiny. Well, here's what I'm telling you: know what the Bible says. And the only way to know what the Bible says—what God says—is to read and study it. So read it, listen to it, meditate on it, memorize it, and obey it. As a friend of mine says, "If you're a Christian, you might as well face it: sooner or later, you're going to have to read the Bible!"

When I got saved, I wanted to know as much as possible about the Bible. And I still do! When I study the Bible, I'm studying God's words, and who wouldn't want to do that? Something in me just craves God's Word. I don't read many other books. I wish I did sometimes, because people ask me all the time whether I have read this or that book. But there's something about *God's Book* I just can't get away from. I can't seem to get enough of it.

When I prepare a message, I never have a problem coming up with Scripture passages to use. My problem is I always have too many Bible verses, and I have to leave some out. I study and study, and sometimes I end up with hundreds of verses, too many to share in a single message. As I'm preparing, I'm always thinking, *I guess I can take this verse out or maybe that one. I suppose I can make this point with just four verses instead of forty-seven!*

That may seem excessive to some, but not to me—I simply love God's Word! Ever since I met Jesus Christ and He changed my life, I have wanted to know Him as intimately as I can.

The good news is you and I can get to know Him through His Word because He reveals Himself to us in the Bible. The Bible is not only the book of His words—it's also the book of His life. I want to know as much as I can about the Bible, not because I'm a minister but because I'm a Christian—because I have met Jesus Christ, and I want to know more about Him.

When I first got saved, I spent hours and hours reading the Bible. I wanted to know how the book of Mark related to Lamentations and how Hosea related to Acts. I wanted to put the whole thing together as one book.

For years, I read ten chapters a day, which took me about an hour. But there were times I would read fifty chapters a day, and that would take me about five hours. There were a few times I was able to read a hundred chapters a day. Now I realize not every person is able to do this—I'm in vocational ministry, so my job allows me to spend a great deal of time in the Word. But anyone—including you—can read through the whole Bible in a single year by reading a little more than three chapters a day. And if you read ten chapters a day, you can go through the whole Bible in four months, or three times in a single year. But the most important thing is to get started and spend time in the Word of God every day.

Let me just say that I know there are some people who struggle to read the Bible daily or don't know where to start. If that's you, I encourage you to ask the Holy Spirit to renew in you a passion for His Word. As you read or listen to the Bible, ask God questions about things you don't understand or ask Him to give you His perspective on a Scripture. He is faithful to answer!

The Bible is the greatest book there is. Its words are "life to those who find them and health to one's whole body" (Proverbs 4:22 NIV). The words in the Bible are "gold" (Proverbs 25:11). God Himself has said, "I am watching to see that my word is fulfilled" (Jeremiah 1:12 NIV).

Not only is the Bible important, it can be fun, too! Before we had apps on our phones, I used to buy Bible trivia books. Every time a new one came out, I would get it. When I was in traveling ministry and Debbie and I were on the road, I would have her quiz me. The books had a beginner section, an intermediate section, and an expert section. So we'd be driving down the road, and she would ask me questions, such as, "Who were Uz and Buz?" Now you might think it's not very important to know the answer to this question, but it was interesting to me because I wanted to know *everything* I possibly could about the Bible. (And in case you're wondering who Uz and Buz are, check out Genesis 22:20–24.)

I would also say to Debbie, "Name a chapter in the Bible. Any chapter." She would randomly pick a chapter like "Ezekiel 45." Then I would try my best to tell her all about that specific chapter. I wanted to memorize as much as I could, so if she asked me about a chapter and I couldn't tell her what it talked about, I would have her read it to me, and then I would focus on memorizing it.

Then I would say to Debbie, "Name a Scripture. I'll see if I can tell you what the chapter says, what the context is, and if I can tell you some other cross-references relating to it." If she said, "Mark chapter 7," I would try to tell her what happened in that chapter. I would try to tell her where that same story is found in Matthew and Luke, and whether it's in all four of the Gospels or just in the Synoptic Gospels.

This may sound a bit extreme to some (okay, to most!). But my love for the Bible comes straight out of the hunger in my heart to know God's Word. It isn't because I'm a pastor; it's because I'm a believer. And it isn't because I want to win trivia contests or pass theology tests; it's because Jesus Christ radically changed my life. He gave me His written Word so I could know Him and become more like Him. I treasure His every word!

If you want to know God, get to know His Word. It's that simple.

If you know a man or woman who is being used greatly by God—whether they're a schoolteacher, stay-at-home parent, plumber, construction worker, doctor, or pastor—I guarantee they spend time in God's Word. That's what sets them apart.

If you want to know God, get to know His Word.

I personally believe any person who reaches his or her destiny in God will be a person who knows His Word.

How well do you know the Bible? If you don't read it, meditate on it, memorize it, or study it, your thoughts about God and your destiny will become all jumbled and confused. The Word is what keeps you aligned with God even through the toughest seasons. If you want to reach your destiny, you must come to the place where you know and love the Bible.

The Bible is God's Word. And until the time your dream comes to pass, God's Word is testing you. It's testing your character. Remember, testing means "to refine, prove, or purify." God is not testing you so you'll fail. He's testing you to help you become stronger in your conviction and in your character. Are you a man or woman of God? Can you be trusted with the destiny He has planned for you? God's Word will build your faith and bring you to your destiny.

There's a reason why I positioned this chapter in the middle of the book. It's because the Prophetic Test is often in the middle of the journey toward your destiny.

As you go through trials to reach your destiny, will you hold fast to God's Word? No matter what you hear, see, or experience, will you be faithful to the word God has spoken? Will you hold fast to God's Word, no matter what your circumstances might be saying?

God Still Speaks Today

We are very blessed to have the Bible. Joseph didn't have the written Word of God. All he had was the word God put in his heart—the prophetic word of God. And since that was all he had, I believe he held on to it tightly. But we are doubly blessed today. We are blessed to have God's written Word in the Bible, which is our standard, and we must hold on to it. And we are also blessed to have God's prophetic word, and we must hold on to that as well.

Let me repeat that. God continues to give us His prophetic word, and we need to cling to it—because God still speaks today!

If you are or have been part of a theological or doctrinal system that says God doesn't speak today, I want you to know something very important: that idea simply does not agree with Scripture! God did not lose His voice two thousand years ago. Why in the world would you pray if you couldn't get an answer to your prayers? While He never says anything contrary to what He has already said in the Bible, He does still speak. He hasn't lost His voice.

It saddens me to hear that many seminaries today are teaching that God stopped speaking two thousand years ago. Sadly, that's also what I was taught in Bible college. I was taught that God said everything He's ever going to say through the Bible, and He doesn't speak anymore. But it's not true. He does speak! And one way He speaks to us is by speaking to our hearts.

I remember a particular incident that happened when I was at Shady Grove Church. The Spirit of God began to move, so Pastor Olen was called in front of the church's denomination credentials committee to be questioned.

For three hours, Pastor Olen was grilled by this committee about the nature of the Holy Spirit, the gifts of the Spirit (specifically speaking in tongues), and whether God still moves today. At the end of three hours, the committee asked him, "Do you believe when a tongue is interpreted or when someone prophesies that God could be speaking through that person?"

"Yes, I do," Pastor Olen replied. "I don't believe it's always God who is speaking when that happens. But, yes, I do believe God sometimes speaks in that way today."

"That's where we've got you!" they said. "Because the Bible contains everything God has said, and He does not speak to us anymore. If you say God told you something and you can't give us the 'chapter and verse,' then you're adding to the Bible—and you know what happens when you add to the Bible!"

Pastor Olen replied, "You men have been questioning me for three hours now, and I've been answering your questions. Now, may I ask each of you a question?"

After they agreed, he said, "You're telling me that God doesn't speak today. So I have just one question for you: if God doesn't speak today, then who called you to preach?"

At that, all five committee members began looking at their shoes. They had nothing to say.

So Pastor Olen addressed the chairman of the committee. "Doctor, I asked you a question. Who called you to preach?"

Dr. So-and-So cleared his throat and then reluctantly answered, "God did."

"Good," Pastor Olen said. "Would you mind giving me the 'chapter and verse' in the Bible for that?"

But Dr. So-and-So had no reply.

So Pastor Olen said, "It's obvious that God must speak today because He spoke to you in your heart when He called you to preach. We know God never says anything contrary to the Bible, but He does speak today."

That was a word of wisdom the Holy Spirit gave Pastor Olen for that moment. But in spite of that word of wisdom, they still kicked him and Shady Grove Church out of the denomination! Pastor Olen didn't mind, though. He understood the truth that God still speaks today, and if God is speaking, we shouldn't let anyone or anything talk us out of it!

The apostle Paul must have encountered a problem similar to Pastor Olen's because he wrote to the church at Thessalonica, "Do not quench the Spirit. Do not despise prophecies. Test all things; hold fast what is good" (1 Thessalonians 5:19-21).

According to the Bible, God has some things to say to us today through prophecies, and we are not to "despise" those prophecies. If we do, Paul says we run the risk of "quenching" the Holy Spirit Himself.

God speaks to us through His written Word, and we must always hold on to what He has said in the Bible. But according to this passage, God also speaks to us through prophetic words, and we are commanded to "hold fast" to those as well.

If we are to hold on to the prophetic word of God, there are some things about prophecies we must understand.

Prophetic Words Are Only Part of the Puzzle

It's important for us to know that prophetic words are only part of what God is saying. There are many verses about prophecy in 1 Corinthians chapters 12 through 14. First Corinthians 13:9 has this to say: "For we know in part and we prophesy in part." "We know in part" means we don't know everything. Only God knows everything. What we know is miniscule by comparison. Since we don't know everything, our prophecy is only part of a bigger picture. That's why "we prophesy in part."

The bigger picture is like a huge puzzle. God knows every piece of the puzzle and how each piece fits together. After all, He designed it! We must realize that the few pieces we discover and fit together—the prophecies we receive—do not finish the puzzle. Our prophecy is not the whole picture; it's just part of the puzzle.

If you were perfect, you could prophesy perfectly, but no one is perfect. Only God is perfect. There is always a human element to prophecy. The Bible tells us, "The spirits of the prophets are subject to the prophets" (1 Corinthians 14:32). So we have to take every prophetic word and consider it in light of the bigger picture.

God has given us prophetic words to encourage us and cause us to seek Him. But again, prophetic words do not give us the whole picture. We must take every prophetic word God has spoken to us and submit it to the bigger Word that God has spoken in the Bible, which is the perfect Word of God. When we put the prophetic word God has spoken to us together with His perfect written Word, we come up with a more complete picture of what God is saying.

Here's a good illustration of how this works.

On the last day of December, it's not uncommon for me to have a prophetic dream regarding the coming year. This doesn't happen every year, but there are certain years when this has occurred. (I think it depends on what I eat that night—just kidding!)

Years ago, I had one of these dreams on New Year's Eve. In the dream, I was riding in a car with my friend Mark Jobe, who is an evangelist. A pastor friend of mine was in the driver's seat, I was in the middle, and Mark was sitting to my right, by the passenger door. All three of us were together in the front seat.

The three of us began to discuss what God was saying about the coming year. Mark told us he had just preached a prophetic message God had spoken to him, and in Mark's message, God was saying that the coming year was going to be a year of darkness.

The pastor said, "You know, Mark, I don't want to argue with you at all. I'm really just trying to understand what God is saying. But I really believe God spoke to me also. And when God spoke to me, He said this was going to be a year of light."

Mark said quite pleasantly, "Well, I understand that, and I wouldn't want to disagree. But I really believe God spoke to me. And He said it's going to be a year of darkness."

"I certainly appreciate that," the pastor replied. "But I believe it's going to be a year of light."

Mark responded, "Well, I understand what you are trying to say, but . . ."

The conversation went on and on. It wasn't an argument by any means; it was a discussion. But they kept going back and forth, and I was sitting in the middle watching them, as if I were watching a tennis match.

Then suddenly I broke in. "Guys, don't you understand? Don't you remember the story in the Bible about the ninth plague in Egypt? Darkness covered the whole land, but the children of Israel had light in their dwelling places. So both of you are right! God is saying it's going to be a year of darkness for those who are not following Him and a year of light for those who are following Him."

When I woke up from that dream, I knew the Lord had just spoken to me about the coming year. I didn't come up with that on my own—I'm not that smart!

Here's my point: in the dream, each man had a part of what God was saying, and it was only when I put the parts together that the full message of God could be understood.

It's important we understand this. All too often we choose the prophecies we like and only listen to those. Or we choose the pastors or ministers we like and only listen to them. But *all* the ministry gifts have a part in God's puzzle, and if we leave some out, we won't see the full picture.

When we're listening to various pastors and speakers on television or YouTube, for example, we shouldn't tune in to watch only those who strike the "right chord" for us at that moment. Instead, we ought to be asking, "God, what are You saying through this preacher? What are You saying through this one? What are You saying through that one?" We need to take heed of all the ministry gifts because they are all pieces of the puzzle.

If we had heard those two prophecies from my dream, we might be tempted to see which one suits our fancy. "Let's see, now. A year of darkness, and a year of light. Hmm. I think I like that one about a year of light. Yes, I think that one about a year of light is from the Lord! That is God's word for me!" If we do that, we are embracing one prophecy and ignoring the other. Yet God is speaking through both.

As humans, we know only "in part"; therefore, we prophesy only "in part" (1 Corinthians 13:9). So if you receive a prophetic word, you must understand it's not the whole picture. It's only a part. And because God wants us to follow Him by faith, oftentimes He doesn't tell us everything or show us the whole picture.

Because God wants us to follow Him by faith, oftentimes He doesn't tell us everything or show us the whole picture.

Similarly, Joseph's prophetic dreams displayed only a portion of his destiny—his brothers bowing to him. It wasn't until much later in his life that he learned the full extent of his destiny.

Prophetic Words Are to Be Judged

One time, a guy shared with me a word he felt was from God. The only problem was I had about ten Scriptures that proved it couldn't be a word from God.

He said, "But Pastor, I have a word!"

So I picked up my Bible and said, "I have one, too. And if your word doesn't line up with this Word, it can't be from God."

I judge *all* words against *the* Word. That might offend you, but judging a prophecy is completely biblical. In 1 Corinthians chapter 14, Paul is talking about prophecies when he says, "Let two or three prophets speak, and let the others judge" (1 Corinthians 14:29).

This verse makes it clear that we are to allow prophecies to be spoken. But it also says when those prophecies have been spoken, we are to *judge*, or test, them. Why? Because when we speak prophetically, there is *always* a human element involved. None of us is omniscient. None of us is infallible. So it's up to us to discern, or judge, what is truly from the Lord and what is human influence. That's why the Bible tells us to judge prophecy.

Prophecy is like pure water from a hose sprayed through a window screen. This illustration was given to me by a pastor after I had ministered prophetically at his church. After the meeting was over, he said to me, "Thank you for coming to my church with a clean screen."

"A clean screen?" I asked. "I've never heard that expression. What do you mean by a clean screen?"

So he explained exactly what he meant.

God's words are the pure water, and our human spirits are the window screens. Prophecy is like pure water coming out of a hose. It comes from God and goes through us. But sometimes our screens are dirty. So even though the water is clean and pure, if there is dirt on our screens, the water will have some dirt in it when it comes out on the other side.

There are prophets who have ministered at our church whose screens were dirty. It was like they were hearing from God, but everything they were saying was tinted with harshness or judgment.

So when that pastor said, "Thank you for coming with a clean screen," he was just thanking me for allowing God's prophetic words to flow to his congregation without mixing in "dirt" from my own personality or my own issues.

This pastor had learned to do what the Bible says to do in 1 Corinthians 14:29: judge prophecies. That's what we must learn to do as well. We must learn to discern what is dirt from the screen and what is the pure word that comes from God.

How We Judge Prophecy

We Judge Prophecy by the Word of God

So how do we judge prophecy? The first way is by testing, or comparing, it against the Word of God. The written Word of God is always our authority, and God's true prophetic words are always confirmed by God's written Word. You can't test a prophecy against itself—you have to prove it with the Word of God. (Remember, the word for "test" can also mean "prove.")

One time, Debbie and I bought a home and soon found out it had a longstanding water leak. The previous owner hadn't known about the leak, which had caused mold in the walls behind the drywall. He was a believer, and when he found out about it, he wanted to pay for the mold remediation.

So I asked a friend in the home building business if there was anything we needed to be concerned about with the mold remediation process, and he told me something interesting. In the state of Texas, there's a law that one company cannot both test for mold *and* remediate it. If one company tests for the mold, a different company has to remove it. Then the testing company comes back again to inspect and confirm that the remediation company got rid of the mold completely. He said it used to be a different process years ago, but it changed because mold removal companies weren't held accountable. They were testing against themselves, and fraud ran rampant. They would charge a lot of money for testing and to get rid of mold, but they wouldn't really fix anything. But now, legally, all mold remediation work needs to be inspected by another company to prove the mold is gone.

Similarly, we must have an outside standard by which we prove and confirm our prophetic words. We have to test all prophetic words by God's Word.

This is why it's so important to know the Bible. How can we test a word with the Word if we don't know the Word? God never contradicts Himself, so a true prophecy will never contradict the Word of God.

God makes this very plain in Deuteronomy chapter 13. He warns us that there will be prophecies that contradict His Word and that these false prophecies will sometimes even be accompanied by signs and miracles.

> If there arises among you a prophet or a dreamer of dreams, and he gives you a sign or a wonder, and the sign or the wonder comes to pass, of which he spoke to you, saying, "Let us go after other gods"—which you have not known—"and let us serve them," you shall not listen to the words of that prophet or that dreamer of dreams, for the LORD your God is testing you to know whether you love the LORD your God with all your heart and with all your soul. (vv. 1–3)

God is letting us know that we should never listen to a prophecy that contradicts His Word—even if that prophecy is accompanied by the prediction of a sign or miracle that comes to pass. If a prophecy contradicts God's Word, it's not a prophecy from God, because God never contradicts Himself! He never says one thing in His Word and something else through prophecy. That's why God's Word must always be our standard.

And in this passage, God says He is *testing* us in these situations. Will we love the Lord our God with all our heart and with all our soul? If we do, we will hold fast to His Word, no matter what. We will cling to His Word, not to signs or miracles or false prophecies. We must judge every prophecy by the Word of God, allowing His Word to be the final answer.

I never cease to be amazed when people tell me, "God told me to do this" or "God told me to do that," yet it's all too obvious that God never told them anything of the kind because what they had been "told" to do was a clear violation of His Word! God will never contradict what He has said in the Bible.

For instance, the Bible says to honor the Lord with the first 10 percent of your income. That's a fact. I've studied tithing and stewardship for more than forty years. So, if you receive a word or have a dream that contradicts this, it's not from God. And if you don't honor the Lord with your finances, you won't reach your destiny.

God's Word is the standard by which we measure everything. It has nothing to do with whether someone gives you a prophetic word and you think or feel that word is right. If your word doesn't line up with God's written Word, it's not right! If you read something in the Bible that's different than your beliefs, do you change your beliefs or do you try to change the Word? Please hear me on this: God's Word doesn't adjust to us. Don't tell me God told you to do something that contradicts what the Bible says. He didn't. He won't. If it's contrary to Scripture, then you have not heard the voice of God.

We Judge Prophecy by Our Inward Witness

The second way we judge prophecy is by our inward witness—by holding it up to what God is saying to us in our own hearts. After all, the Bible says, "The Spirit Himself bears witness with our spirit" (Romans 8:16). This means our own human spirit can recognize the

Spirit of God when He is talking. When our spirit recognizes the Holy Spirit, the Holy Spirit is bearing witness with our spirit. And the more we know God, the more readily we will recognize His voice.

There may be times when you receive a prophetic word, but it doesn't seem to agree with what God has been speaking to you personally. It doesn't contradict God's written Word, yet it doesn't seem to line up with what the Holy Spirit has been speaking to you in your own spirit. If this should happen, don't be concerned about it. Just put that prophecy on the shelf. If the word is from God, He will eventually confirm it in your own spirit. And if it is not from God, it can just stay on the shelf!

Someone once asked me, "Aren't I supposed to be faithful to the prophecy?"

"No," I replied. "You're supposed to be faithful to God! Just stay faithful to Him. If you don't understand a prophecy, tell God about it and give it to Him. Say, 'God I don't understand this right now. If this is Your word for me, I will embrace it. But for now, God, I choose to embrace *You*. I choose to trust *You*. I trust that every word *You* have spoken will come to pass in my life.'"

Judge every prophecy by the Word of God and the faith of God.

In Jeremiah chapter 35, there's a great example of a situation in which prophecy had to be judged by the inward witness. The Rechabites had received a word from their father, Jonadab, not to drink wine, and then they received another word that contradicted the first one (vv. 5-6). Were they to listen to the "prophet" Jeremiah? Or were they to hold fast to the word their father had commanded them?

God had told Jeremiah to go set wine before the Rechabites and tell them to drink it (see Jeremiah 35:1-2). So Jeremiah obeyed God. He called the Rechabites, put wine in front of them, and said, "Drink wine" (Jeremiah 35:5). What were the Rechabites to do? Their father had commanded them not to drink wine, but now a true prophet of the Lord was telling them to drink wine! Do you know what the Rechabites said to Jeremiah? They said, "You are telling us to drink wine, but that can't possibly be right, because God already gave a word to our father, Jonadab, that we were not supposed to drink wine. God has already spoken to us about this" (Jeremiah 35:6-8 paraphrase).

Jeremiah was a true prophet of the Lord, and he was obeying God by telling them to drink wine. But *this was a test*, and the word Jeremiah spoke to the Rechabites did not bear witness with them. It didn't contradict God's written Word, but it did contradict what God had *already told them to do* through their father, Jonadab. The prophetic word of their father still witnessed with them as being the true word of God, so they judged the prophecy from Jeremiah, and they did not obey it. They obeyed the prophetic word that had first been given to them—the word that seemed right.

Then God said to Jeremiah, "Now you go and tell Israel about this. Tell them, 'The Rechabites are obeying the word that was given to them by their father—but you Israelites are not obeying the words that I gave to your fathers'" (Jeremiah 35:12-14 paraphrase).

God told Jeremiah to do this so He could show us something. When God has spoken to us, we must hold fast to His Word and obey it. We must hold fast to His written Word, and we must also hold fast to His prophetic word. And we must judge every prophetic word by the Word of God and the witness of our spirit.

Every Word from God Is Submitted to the God of the Word

There is a human element to prophecy because prophets are human beings speaking God's words to other human beings. And all words from God must be submitted to the God of the Word. That means that every word of prophecy must be submitted to God who has spoken it. Now, can I blow up your theology for a minute?

The Bible tells us of another true prophet who had a word from God, *but that word did not come to pass*! That prophet was Jonah. I would say Jonah was definitely a true prophet, wouldn't you? After all, he did get his very own book of the Bible! But Jonah spoke a prophecy from God, and that prophecy did not come to pass. We tend to think that if someone is a true prophet, then all of his or her prophecies will come to pass. But that's not always the case.

Jonah disobeyed God's command at first, but then later he obeyed. He went to Nineveh and said what God told him to say—that Nineveh would be destroyed in forty days. Notice Jonah didn't say, "Repent, or you will be destroyed." No, he simply said, "Yet forty days, and Nineveh *shall* be overthrown!" (Jonah 3:4, emphasis added).

But forty days went by, and guess what happened? Nineveh was not destroyed! Why? The word Jonah had spoken was a true word from God, but *all words from God are submitted to the God of the Word*. When the people of Nineveh heard God's word, they decided they didn't want to be destroyed, and they repented. The Bible says when they repented, "God relented from the disaster that He had said He would bring upon them, and He did not do it" (Jonah 3:10).

In other words, their repentance caused God to change what He said He was going to do. When the people of Nineveh turned to God, God turned the prophecy.

You would expect Jonah to have been happy to see an entire city saved from destruction through his prophetic ministry. Jonah had obeyed God and spoken God's prophetic word to Nineveh; as a result, the city had repented and was not destroyed. But Jonah was *not* happy about it. Instead, he was very angry because now it looked as though he was a false prophet. Because of God's mercy on Nineveh, Jonah's prophecy had not come to pass!

Jonah even admitted to God that this was why he had refused to obey Him in the first place and had fled to Tarshish.

> Therefore I fled previously to Tarshish; for I know that You are a gracious and merciful God, slow to anger and abundant in lovingkindness, One who relents from doing harm. Therefore now, O LORD, please take my life from me, for it is better for me to die than to live! (Jonah 4:2–3)

Because now it looked to the people of Nineveh as though Jonah was a false prophet, he decided it would be better to die rather than face the fact that the prophecy he had spoken did not come to pass. He was more concerned with the word God had spoken through him than with pleasing the God who had spoken it.

I'm sorry to say that I have personally seen this occur sometimes with those who move in the prophetic—they would rather be right about their prophecies than have a whole nation turn to God! (That's a pretty strong statement, isn't it?)

Jonah's situation was not unusual, though. Isaiah was a true prophet of God as well, and he also spoke a word from God that did not come to pass. God sent Isaiah to King Hezekiah and told him to say, "Thus says the LORD: 'Set your house in order, for you shall die and not live'" (Isaiah 38:1).

That was a true word of prophecy from the Lord. But when Hezekiah heard the prophecy, he prayed and asked God to change His mind. Then the word of the Lord came a second time to Isaiah: "Go and tell Hezekiah, 'Thus says the LORD, the God of David your father: "I have heard your prayer, I have seen your tears; surely I will add to your days fifteen years"'" (Isaiah 38:5).

Because Hezekiah humbled himself and prayed, God had mercy on him. God changed His mind and spoke another word about Hezekiah's future—a word that was radically different from the first one. So Isaiah's first word from the Lord was true, but it did not come to pass.

You see, there are some prophetic words from God that are unconditional. That means they don't depend on man to come to pass. We don't have to respond in a certain way for it to happen. For instance, Jesus is coming back. This is an unconditional prophetic word because it's happening no matter what we do! It's not dependent on you.

Then there are conditional prophetic words that rely on our response. Their success depends on whether we make it through these character tests. There's a lot of "If . . . then" phrasing. These are the prophecies that test us as we wait for them. And it's these conditional prophecies that are submitted back to the God of the Word.

Remember, you are the only one who can delay or derail your destiny. God may set a path for you, but if you turn from it or walk another way, you will not arrive at the destination He has planned for you. It's conditional on your response. In other words, some of God's words are dependent upon you.

Whether or not you end up at your destination depends on how well you go through these tests. Again, God is so gracious that if you fail one, He'll just let you keep taking it over and over until you pass it because He wants you to step into your destiny. Think of it like a GPS—if you make a wrong turn, God simply says, "Recalculating," and lets you take the test over again.

We must hold on to prophetic words, but we also have to judge and test them to see if they're truly from God. We judge them by the Word of God and our inward witness. And then we must stay submitted to the God who has spoken those words.

The God of the Word is full of mercy. The God of the Word is Love. His heart will always be made manifest through the words He speaks, and it's important to remember that.

Hold On to Prophetic Words

Throughout our lives, we will encounter circumstances that seem to contradict the words God has spoken over us. One of the most important things we can do if we want to pass the Prophetic Test is to simply hold on—hold on to the words God has spoken to us. Because there will be many opportunities to let go of those words or stop believing that what God said is going to come to pass.

As I've said, God tests our faith with the prophetic word, and He tests our character with the written Word. We absolutely must continue to believe those things God has spoken over our lives. And the way we hold on is by faith.

In April 2020, we celebrated Gateway Church's twentieth year of ministry. Around that time, I was talking with someone about the word God had given me so many years earlier to reach thirty thousand, three hundred thousand, three million, thirty million, and three hundred million people. I said, "I actually don't know if those numbers are literal or figurative." I just didn't see a way it could happen.

Not long after that conversation, I was on an elders' retreat, and as soon as I woke up one morning, I felt like the Lord put His finger in my face and said, "Who gave you permission to say those numbers were figurative? Did Moses stand on the banks of the Red Sea and talk about walking across on figurative land? Who are you to say those numbers I gave you are not literal just because you don't see a way?"

God had confirmed those numbers to me again and again. In that moment, I was convicted and realized that I needed to hold on tightly to the words the Lord had spoken to me about my destiny.

In times of doubt, I've had to declare, "God, I'm going to stand in faith that You're going to use me to help and to minister to multitudes. I'm going to have faith in the words You've spoken and keep a clear conscience so You can use me."

If God has spoken something to you, hold on to it! If God has said you are going to do a certain thing for Him, hold on to it! Don't let go of the word God gave you, no matter what happens. And don't stop believing in the words He has spoken.

If God has spoken something to you, hold on to it!

Joseph could have given up and let go of the things God had spoken about his destiny. But if Joseph had let go of those dreams, he never would have made it to the destiny to which God had called him. All through Joseph's trials, he had to hold on to the word of God. He had to keep on believing that the things God had spoken over his life would be fulfilled.

The apostle Paul understood the importance of holding on to the prophetic word of God. Remember what he wrote to the church at Thessalonica: "Do not despise prophecies. Test all things; hold fast what is good" (1 Thessalonians 5:20-21). Paul is telling them to test all prophecies and to hold fast to those prophecies that are good. Good prophecies are those that are from God.

If we are going to hold on to God and those prophecies, it's going to require some effort on our part. Paul described that effort as "pressing on." In Philippians 3:12, Paul says, "Not that I have already attained, or am already perfected; but I press on, that I may lay hold of that for which Christ Jesus has also laid hold of me."

Paul is talking about his destiny. He is saying that Jesus Christ has laid hold of him for a specific purpose, and Paul wants more than anything to lay hold of that purpose. He wants more than anything to hold on to the things Jesus Christ has called him to do. He wants to keep believing the words God has spoken about his destiny. But in order to do that, Paul says he must "press on." In other words, he has to push forward, resist the enemy, and exert some effort if he is going to keep a tight grip on the words God spoke over his life.

Timothy was Paul's son in the faith, and Paul wrote to let Timothy know about this test and the struggle all of us must go through.

This charge I commit to you, son Timothy, according to the prophecies previously made concerning you, that by them you may wage the good warfare, having faith and a good conscience, which some having rejected, concerning the faith have suffered shipwreck, of whom are Hymenaeus and Alexander, whom I delivered to Satan that they may learn not to blaspheme. (1 Timothy 1:18-20)

Paul is reminding Timothy of the prophecies that had been spoken over his life, and he is exhorting Timothy to hold on to those prophecies. Paul says it is *by those prophecies* that Timothy will "wage the good warfare, having faith and a good conscience." This is pretty amazing! According to Paul, not letting go of that prophetic word is absolutely critical to Timothy fulfilling God's call on his life. It's the same for us. We also need to take the prophecies spoken over us, receive them fully with faith and a clear conscience, and then use those prophecies as weapons against disappointment, disillusionment, and temptation to go astray.

Immediately after encouraging Timothy to do this, Paul tells a cautionary story of two young men who did not hold on to the prophetic words of God—Hymenaeus and Alexander. Paul says that these young men rejected the prophecies made over their lives; they didn't receive them in faith or with clean consciences. And because of that they suffered shipwreck, meaning they didn't reach their destination—their destiny—in God (see 1 Timothy 1:19-20). Then Paul even says that because Hymenaeus and Alexander rejected God's word for their lives, he had turned them over "to Satan that they may learn not to blaspheme" (v. 20). It sounds to me like Paul is saying that rejecting a true word from God is blasphemous. These are pretty strong consequences for rejecting the prophetic word of God—"delivered to Satan" and "suffered shipwreck" (vv. 19-20)—but that's what the Bible says!

So if God has given you a word about your life, *hold on to it.* As I said before, there is only one person who can prevent you from walking into your destiny, and that person is *you.* Don't block your destiny. Hold on to the things God has spoken over your life.

Forty-something years ago, God spoke to me about leaving an employer. When I left, that employer said to me, "You will never amount to anything if you leave me." But, even as a young man, that didn't affect me at all. Do you know why it didn't affect me? Because God had spoken to me about my destiny. So I just held on to what God said.

This reminds me of the time I found a little surprise as I was looking through some of my old computer files and came upon one titled "Elaine's First Prophecy." Elaine is my daughter, and when she was a young girl, she received her first prophecy. So she typed it up and saved it on my computer. She wanted to be sure to save it because, apparently, she was planning on getting more!

I was somewhat blown away by this, I have to admit, and a bit humbled as well. Here was a young girl holding on to the prophetic word she had received, and yet so many adults do not. So many adults have let go of the things God has spoken over their lives. They have forgotten what God has said about their destiny, or they have simply stopped believing in it. They have allowed the circumstances of their lives to cloud their vision and convince them that the things God said they will do for Him are never going to happen. Don't let that be you. Hold on in faith to the words God has spoken over your life and believe Him!

One of Elaine's prophetic words in the document I found was that an anointing of ministry would come to her. It said, "You're going to speak to multitudes one day." She's now in her thirties, and in the last few years, I've seen this word come to pass. The first time she shared a short, three-minute message during worship at our women's conference, she walked away with thirty speaking engagements. Elaine and her husband, Ethan, now pastor a church together in Houston, Texas. Over the years, I've seen her speak at major conferences, at events, and on TV. Millions have heard her share God's Word. She's an incredible communicator, but it's the anointing of God on her that makes all the difference. Elaine has gone through her own journey of testing—her life hasn't been all roses. It's her story to tell, but she has held on to her prophetic word. And as she steps into new levels of her destiny, she continues to pursue God's Word. She *knows* the Bible.

That's what Joseph had to do. And that's what you and I must also do if we want to pass the Prophetic Test.

Until the time the prophetic word of God comes to pass in your life, the written Word of God will test you. So get to know His Word. Study the Bible. Meditate on it. Memorize it. Remember that knowing what God has said in His written Word is the key to seeing His prophetic words fulfilled in your life.

As you wait for the fulfillment of your destiny, keep in mind that there is only one Person you need to please, and that Person is God! As long as you serve Him, no one else can stop what He has planned for you.

God has a destiny for your life. He has someone He wants you to engage. He has someone He wants you to reach. He has a ministry for you, even if it is not a vocational ministry. So press on to that destiny God has promised. Hold on to the prophetic word of God, no matter what happens. When you do that, you will pass the Prophetic Test. And one day you will step into your destiny. One day you will see every word God has spoken over your life come to pass.

CHAPTER SEVEN

The Power Test

When our daughter, Elaine, was a little girl, it was not uncommon for me to walk into a room and find all her dolls neatly lined up, while she dictated orders to them. She would say, "Now you go over there, and you go here; you do this, and you do that." What struck me the most about this scene was the way that even a small child could express the inward desire to rule over the world around her—even if her authority extended only to her dolls!

Has it ever occurred to you that the desire for power is built into human nature? That it's part of who God made us to be? It seems to me that human beings are hardwired to want to rule and have dominion over the world around them. If you don't believe me, just get your children a dog. Dogs can really take a licking in the pecking order of family life, but especially from the youngest member of the household, who is usually in the position of being ruled over by everyone else. That was Elaine in our family. She would say, "That's *my* dog" and boss it around because she got told what to do by her mom, dad, and two older brothers. It's amazing how even the smallest child will jump at the chance to finally have something to dominate or rule over. No matter how young, they don't seem to need any lessons in how to boss the dog around!

If we watch children, we quickly see that every person arrives on this earth with a desire to rule. To put it another way, we all have a desire for power. But where do we get that desire for power? We get it from God! I know you may have never heard this before, but you actually have a legitimate and righteous desire for power in you.

All too often we think of the desire for power only in negative terms. Of course, there's a wrong desire for power—a desire the enemy has twisted that's rooted in selfishness. But there's also a right desire for power.

Jesus told His disciples that if they desired to be great in the kingdom, they had to be a servant (see Matthew 20:26). Note that He didn't tell them they were wrong or had bad motives for wanting to be leaders—He actually gave them instructions on *how* to get there! And 1 Timothy 3:1 says, "Whoever aspires to be an overseer desires a noble task" (NIV).

It's not wrong to want power. God put this desire into each one of us when we were created. God is all-powerful, and the Bible says He created us in His own image. So when we were created, we were created in the image of an all-powerful Ruler.

Genesis 1:27–28 tells the story.

So God created [humankind] in His own image; in the image of God He created [humankind]; male and female He created them. Then God blessed them, and God said to them, "Be fruitful and multiply; fill the earth and subdue it; have dominion over the fish of the sea, over the birds of the air, and over every living thing that moves on the earth."

God created humankind "in His own image," and the very first thing He told Adam and Eve to do was to "have dominion" over the earth and to "subdue" it. From the very beginning, God not only created us to have power but also commissioned us to use it. He planned for us to have power and use it the way He does—to do good and make life on Earth better. We are made in the image of an all-powerful God who uses His power to bless people, minister to people, and help people.

The Power Test: Learning to Steward Your God-Given Authority

God created us to have power, and He wants to give His power to us, but He is looking for those who can be trusted with it. What will we do with the power He gives us? Will we use it wisely as His stewards on this earth?

This is the Power Test.

So far, most of the tests we've studied have involved the way we respond when bad things happen in our lives. But the Power Test is different. This test has to do with how we respond when something *good* happens. The Pride Test is how we respond to the dream, but the Power Test is how we respond to the destiny itself. In other words, it's the test of success, and it's the hardest test I've ever taken!

This may come as a surprise to some, but God's blessings can be just as much a test as tribulations can. Why? Because blessings involve responsibility, and responsibility requires character. Success may have a better view than a prison or a pit, but it's still a test. In some ways, this test was more difficult for me than the ones I went through when we couldn't pay the bills. Let me explain.

It's a lot of responsibility to be a leader with vast resources and the power to make decisions that affect people's livelihoods. There's immense pressure to ensure you're making wise, godly choices. People often only see the perks of power—wealth or influence. They see decisions that are made (and often gripe and complain about them). But they don't see the nights the leader is wide awake, thinking and praying at three in the morning. They don't see the weight the leader carries into his or her everyday life.

I've had conversations with employees who were not happy, and they made it known to me in very harsh ways. I had the power to end their employment right then and there, but I had to keep myself in check. I knew they were frustrated or going through a tough season, and God was asking me to extend grace.

Other times, I've sat in rooms where we've been presented with several different ways to use budget and influence, and they all seem like wonderful options. The question in those scenarios is not *if* we have the resources, but what does God *want* us to do with our resources? That's also difficult to navigate and requires attentiveness to the Holy Spirit.

When you have power, you have to choose *when* and *how* to use it, because your decisions can greatly affect multitudes of people. Power requires a different kind of restraint, discipline, and responsibility than the other tests.

So how do you respond to success? How do you respond to power? How do you respond to authority? How do you respond to influence? How do you respond to God's blessings? It's what you do with the power and blessings of God that is the true test of your character. This is the essence of the Power Test.

If God blesses believers but they don't have the character necessary to handle that blessing, they will fall or misuse that blessing for selfish reasons. That's why God spent so many years building Joseph's character before giving him the responsibility to rule over Egypt.

Now, you might be thinking, *I've never been able to take this test. I would love to have some power!* Let me assure you, every person will go through the Power Test at different times in their life because every person has some degree of authority and responsibility. You might not believe you have much authority, but if you think carefully, you'll realize there is something God has given you responsibility over. It might be something as small as a puppy or as seemingly insignificant as a room full of dolls, but you have dominion over *something* in your life! And in that area of authority, you will be tested.

Since I'm a pastor, an example that easily comes to my mind is a man who starts out serving in the church parking lot. Every week he is faithful in that responsibility, following orders and parking cars "for Jesus." After a while his faithfulness becomes apparent to everyone, and eventually he is made the parking lot captain. So the next week he shows up with a uniform, a bullhorn, and a huge flashlight that looks like a prop from a *Star Wars* movie. That parking lot is now his place of dominion!

The point I am trying to make is this: we all have responsibility over something, and we will all be tested by that responsibility, especially as we begin to step into our destiny.

Genesis tells the story of how Joseph was called from the dungeon to interpret Pharaoh's dreams. At that time Joseph had been in Egypt for thirteen years, and it had been two full years since he interpreted the dreams for the butler and the baker. He was thirty years old, and he probably didn't think he was anywhere close to his destiny. But things were about to change.

Then it came to pass, at the end of two full years, that Pharaoh had a dream; and behold, he stood by the river. Now it came to pass in the morning that his spirit was troubled, and he sent and called for all the magicians of Egypt and all its wise men. And Pharaoh told them his dreams, but there was no one who could interpret them for Pharaoh. Then the chief butler spoke to Pharaoh, saying: "I remember my faults this day." Then Pharaoh sent and called Joseph, and they brought him quickly out of the dungeon; and he shaved, changed his clothing, and came to Pharaoh. (Genesis 41:1, 8-9, 14)

Pharaoh then asked Joseph about these dreams. Not only did Joseph give Pharaoh the interpretation of his dreams, but he also gave Pharaoh some free advice about how to prepare for the coming years of famine (see Genesis 41:25-36). Joseph's advice was so full of wisdom that Pharaoh concluded he must be filled with the Spirit of God. (I find it interesting that three unbelievers—Potiphar, Pharaoh, and the keeper of the prison—all recognized that the Spirit of God was with Joseph.) Here's what happened next:

So the advice was good in the eyes of Pharaoh and in the eyes of all his servants. And Pharaoh said to his servants, "Can we find such a one as this, a man in whom is the Spirit of God?"

Then Pharaoh said to Joseph, "Inasmuch as God has shown you all this, there is no one as discerning and wise as you. You shall be over my house, and all my people shall be ruled according to your word; only in regard to the throne will I be greater than you." And Pharaoh said to Joseph, "See, I have set you over all the land of Egypt."

Then Pharaoh took his signet ring off his hand and put it on Joseph's hand; and he clothed him in garments of fine linen and put a gold chain around his neck. And he had him ride in the second chariot which he had; and they cried out before him, "Bow the knee!" So he set him over all the land of Egypt. Pharaoh also said to Joseph, "I am Pharaoh, and without your consent no man may lift his hand or foot in all the land of Egypt." (Genesis 41:37–44)

When Joseph stepped out of the dungeon, he stepped into the Power Test. He was quickly given a position of great power and authority. Pharaoh gave Joseph his signet ring, which represented his rights and authority as the ruler of Egypt. He clothed Joseph in fine linen and put a gold chain around his neck, representing the riches Joseph would now enjoy. Pharoah also had Joseph ride in his chariot, with people crying out, "Bow the knee!" as he went by, which represented the royal position in which Joseph now stood. He had the three Rs—rights, riches, and royalty. Now, that's *power!*

In what must have seemed like the blink of an eye, Joseph found himself stepping into the first phase of his destiny, but the tests didn't stop there. And if Joseph had handled the power given to him in the wrong way, he never would have been able to fulfill his destiny in the way God intended. Similarly, just because you are starting to walk in the destiny God has for you doesn't mean you stop taking tests. I believe the Power Test is the first one we encounter as we take our initial steps into our destiny.

The Power Test Comes Suddenly

The Power Test often comes suddenly. Just like Joseph, you may work hard for ten, fifteen, or twenty years, and then in a single day, God can suddenly change everything about your circumstances! God can bless you and put you into your destiny. You could be called into your boss's office today and walk out with a promotion. It could all happen in the snap of a finger.

That's what happened to Joseph. God saw that he had been faithful, and He made his dream a reality. Notice that Genesis 41:14 says, "They brought him quickly out of the dungeon." Joseph shaved, changed his clothes, and was given a place of great power and authority—it was fast! One morning Joseph woke up in a dungeon, filthy and hungry, and the next day he woke up clean-shaven in the palace. One morning Joseph woke up as a prisoner, and the next day he arose as the second most powerful man in the world! The Power Test comes very, very suddenly.

In a single day, God can suddenly change everything about your circumstances!

Power Comes from God

Psalm 62:11 tells us power comes from God: "God has spoken once, twice I have heard this: That power belongs to God." This verse is saying that if we have power, it came from God. He is the only One who can give us power.

One of my favorite Scripture passages about power is in John chapter 19. Pilate is talking to Jesus, and he doesn't seem to realize his power comes from God.

Then Pilate said to Him, "Are You not speaking to me? Do You not know that I have power to crucify You, and power to release You?"

Jesus answered, "You could have no power at all against Me unless it had been given you from above. Therefore the one who delivered Me to you has the greater sin." (John 19:10–11)

I think this is one of the most humorous passages in the Bible because Pilate is actually talking to the Creator of the universe and saying, "Don't You realize that I have power over You?" Pilate just didn't understand, did he?

Jesus straightened him out when He said, "You could have no power at all against Me unless it had been given you from above." Jesus let Pilate know that all power and all authority come from God Himself.

God has given every person power in some area of his or her life, and every person is a leader to some degree. What kind of a leader are you? Are you a humble leader? Are you a servant-leader? What are you doing with the power God has given you?

Like so many of the other tests, this test is also about stewardship. God is looking for people He can trust to steward His power. Power isn't ours to own, and it can be taken away just as quickly as it is given. God wants us to recognize that all power comes from Him, and He wants us to walk in humility.

How Do We Receive Power?

So how do we receive power? It's very simple. As with everything else in the Bible, if you want to have power, you just do the opposite of what you think you're supposed to do! I don't know if you've noticed this yet, but in the kingdom of God, everything is opposite. This has been called the spiritual law of paradox.

If you want to have authority, you must be under authority (see Mark 9:35). If you want to truly live, you must first die (see Matthew 16:25). If you want to receive, you must give (see Luke 6:38).

With God, it is all opposite of the world's ways. So to get power, you must *give up the right to power*. You must become a servant.

James 4:10 says, "Humble yourselves in the sight of the Lord, and He will lift you up." We already know power comes from God, and it's God who lifts us up and gives us power. This verse is telling us that if we want God to lift us up and give us power, we must *humble ourselves* in His sight.

First Peter 5:5–6 tells us how:

> Likewise you younger people, submit yourselves to your elders. Yes, all of you be submissive to one another, and be clothed with humility, for
> > "God resists the proud,
> > But gives grace to the humble."
> Therefore humble yourselves under the mighty hand of God, that He may exalt you in due time.

Again, the Bible tells us the way to promotion is to humble ourselves. God's Word tells us to "be submissive . . . and be clothed with humility" (v. 5). To our natural minds that may sound like the least likely way to get power, but remember, everything is opposite in the kingdom of God. God says if we do these things, then He will "exalt [us] in due time" (v. 6). In other words, God will give us authority, responsibility, and influence when we pass the test.

Notice 1 Peter 5:5 also says, "God resists the proud." I want to tell you something very important: having the Creator of the universe resist you is *not* a good thing! To help illustrate this truth, I'm going to compare the Christian life to a game of American football.

I think football is a fun game. In much the same way, I think the Christian life is a fun way of life. In fact, I think the Christian life is the most fun way of life there is, and one reason it's so much fun is that God lets us "run with the ball." God doesn't make all the touchdowns. He wants *us* to make the touchdowns! God hands us the ball, and then He says, "Here, you can teach. Here, you can pray for the sick. Here, you can lead someone to Jesus. Here, you can be a group leader at church. You can do this!" Then He adds, "The only thing I ask you to do is to just stay behind Me. If you *stay behind Me*, I'll take care of all the obstacles."

In the beginning, it's easy for us to stay behind God. The first time we're asked to lead in some kind of ministry situation, we know we can't do it on our own. For instance, one day your small group leader says to you, "I'm going to be out of town next week. Will you teach?"

And you say, "I don't think I can do this. I'm not a leader. I've never taught a small group. I can't do it. It's not my gift. You have to get someone else."

Then the leader responds, "Well, I prayed about it, and I really believe God told me you're supposed to lead next week while I'm out."

That's when God says, "You don't have to be a leader. You just have to follow. Follow Me."

So you reluctantly agree, even though you're scared to death all week. You prepare thoroughly and work really hard. You follow very closely behind God because you know that without Him, you can't do anything.

Then, when the night comes, everything goes amazingly well. God's hand is on it. And after you finish leading, everyone cheers like you made a touchdown. People come up to you afterward and say, "That was a great lesson! You're a really good leader!"

It feels pretty good, so the next time God says, "Here, take the ball again," you're a little more confident. When God hands you the ball, you say, "Okay! Okay! I've got it, Lord."

This time you might even step out and dodge a little bit, showing off a few moves. Pretty soon, everything is going great, and before you know it, you've become used to the fact that God is out in front of you.

But then a time comes when God hands you the ball, and you say, "You know, God, I don't think I need to stay behind You anymore. I think I've got this figured out now. I can do it myself, Lord. You can go and sit down. I've got it covered."

Let me tell you something: *God does not sit down!* Remember, "God resists the proud" (1 Peter 5:5). And when we walk in pride, this is what happens:

God hands you the ball and says, "Just stay behind Me."

You say, "That's not necessary anymore. I don't need You, God. I think I can do this by myself."

Then you step out from behind God, and you try to move forward on your own.

"Okay," God says, but then He steps in front of you, turns and faces you, and assumes a tackling position—and God is one *big* linebacker, if you know what I mean!

Then He says, "C'mon, let's see how far you can get now."

This is what happens when we walk in pride. The Bible makes it very clear that God opposes us, resists us, and blocks our moves when we walk in pride.

To further illustrate this important point, let me share a story about a good friend of mine. He is an elder at another church and has a prophetic gift. He's a wonderful, godly man, and we laugh about this story now.

Years ago, I was invited to a church in Arkansas to pray and prophesy over their leaders and congregation during three different presbytery services over the course of three days. I asked my friend to come with me, and he said, "I can't do that!"

His response wasn't all that surprising to me—not many of us would readily volunteer to publicly prophesy over people we'd never met! But I told him I thought he'd be great, and since we had a long drive to get there, we could talk about it on the way.

I picked up my friend, and the whole drive he asked me questions about prophecy and how to hear God for someone else's edification. He said, "I just want you to know that I'm not prophesying over anyone the first night. I will sit and learn. The second night, maybe. The third night, I'll see."

The first service started, and when the first couple came to the front of the congregation to be prayed over, my friend immediately jumped out of his seat! He approached the couple and prophesied a beautiful word from God over their lives. It was spot on. The next couple came up, and he did the same thing. He prophesied over every person who came up that first night! We even had a time at the end where we could speak prophetic words over people in the congregation, and my friend shared many encouraging words from the Lord. God's anointing was all over him!

Following the service, we went to the host pastor's home for dinner, and then we retired to the living room to continue talking. During our conversation, the pastor looked right at me and asked, "When you get a word from God, do you sense an impression, or do you actually hear words and sentences in your mind?"

Before I could answer, my friend stretched his arms along the back of the couch and said, "Well, I'll tell you . . ." and started answering the pastor's question for me. It was kind of amusing—he went from novice to expert in one night!

The next day we had another prophetic service, and when the first couple came up to the platform, I looked at my friend. He shook his head and whispered with a hint of panic, "I don't have anything,

Robert. You have to go. I don't hear anything." I encouraged him throughout the service, but he continued to shake his head.

Afterward, he said, "Why was it so easy last night and so difficult tonight?"

I shared with him that I thought there was a reason for it. The first night he was humble. He knew he couldn't do it without God. In other words, he was scared to death! And that's a good place to be. That's why God used him to bless others. But the second night he got prideful. And the Lord does not entertain pride. Power and success come to the humble.

Joseph was a prime candidate for pride. He struggled with it when he was younger, and we know from what we've read so far that he was handsome, intelligent, and very capable. He was the favorite son, even though he had ten older brothers. He even had the affirmation and endorsement of God on his life, and yet when given an opportunity to take credit for something, Joseph walked in humility.

> And Pharaoh said to Joseph, "I have had a dream, and there is no one who can interpret it. But I have heard it said of you that you can understand a dream, to interpret it."
>
> So Joseph answered Pharaoh, saying, "It is not in me; God will give Pharaoh an answer of peace." (Genesis 41:15–16)

Pharaoh had heard that Joseph could interpret dreams. But Joseph refused to take the credit for his gift. Joseph said, "No, it is not in me to interpret dreams. It's only God who can do it." Joseph understood he needed to stay behind God. That's the humility Joseph walked in. And because of Joseph's humility, God was able to trust him with His power.

Humility is always attractive, and pride is always ugly. Have you ever noticed that? Think about it for a moment. Have you ever met someone who was very successful but also arrogant, conceited, and prideful? Are you drawn to that person? Do you want to spend more time with them? Probably not, right? Because pride is repulsive! No matter how successful someone might be, pride has a way of making people very unattractive. On the flip side, have you ever met a successful, accomplished person who was humble? That's very attractive, and you typically really like them and want to be around them more. What a difference humility makes!

I must admit there is one thing I really don't understand: someone who has never been successful at all yet still manages to be prideful. It's just downright silly! Pride always looks foolish, and to illustrate my point, I'm going to tell on myself.

Growing up, my father was very successful. Naturally, I wanted to be successful too (or at least appear to be). So, when I was in my twenties, a friend gave me a really nice pair of shoes because they were too small for him. (And truth be told, they were too small for me too, but I wore them anyway.) I didn't have any nice clothes at that time. We didn't have much back then in the way of material things, and these were really expensive, lizard skin shoes. It was the style at the time, and important, successful people wore shoes like these. Whenever I walked around in them, I felt like the king of the jungle. I thought, *Everyone probably thinks I'm rich when they see me in these shoes. When I walk into a room with these shoes on, people just can't help but notice me.*

I wore those shoes everywhere—to the grocery store, my kids' soccer games, *everywhere*. I thought those shoes said wonderful things about who I was!

Then one Saturday I went to a car wash, and the place was packed with people. I went inside to wait and saw they had a place where you could get your shoes shined. I thought to myself, *I'm going to get my shoes shined so everyone here can see how important I am. Hopefully, they didn't see me get out of that Ford Fairlane. I'm sure when they see these shoes, they'll think that Mercedes out there is mine.*

So I got my shoes shined, stepped down, and began to walk down the long glass walkway where people watched their cars being washed. Everyone was standing at the glass, so I walked very slowly, taking my time in my nice and shiny lizard skin shoes. As I passed, everyone turned slightly, and when they turned, I noticed their eyes would get really big. Everyone was glancing down at my feet. *Wow,* I thought, *This is great! These shoes are real attention-getters!*

I was just loving it. I got to the end of the walkway and thought to myself, *I'm just going to glance down and see how nice these shoes look.* When I looked down, I could see that the guy who shined my shoes had rolled up my pant legs and forgot to put them back down after he finished. People were staring all right—at my skinny legs and knee-high socks!

Pride always looks foolish, doesn't it? But humility is appealing and attractive. And when we are humble, God will show up and lift us up for His purposes. When we walk in humility, God will give us power. All power comes from God, and we get it by being humble. We get it by giving up the right to power and becoming servants instead.

We must also remember that we have a part to play. There's a balance between "It's all God," and "I worked very hard, and God blessed me." I'm sure you've heard someone say the phrase, "It's all God!" This expression has made its way through Christian circles for a long time, and although I appreciate the heart behind wanting to give the Lord credit, I think it sometimes swings the pendulum too far into false humility.

Years ago, I was having lunch with my good friend who is an award-winning music artist, and he told me a story I will never forget.

He said, "Robert, God convicted me of false humility."

At the time, I had never heard of false humility, so I asked him to explain.

He proceeded to tell me the story about one of his recent concerts. Afterward, he walked off the platform and saw a guy standing there. The guy said to him, "Brother, that was good!"

My friend responded with something he'd been saying a lot: "Well, it's all God!"

And the guy replied, "Well, it wasn't *that* good."

The truth is if it had been "all God," it would have been *incredible*!

My friend realized that whenever someone complimented him, he had gotten into the habit of saying "It's all God" in an attempt to be humble, but it was actually an attempt to puff up his performance and his pride. He should have responded with "Thank you," because he showed up and worked hard, and God blessed his effort. That's the way to walk in true humility.

What Is the Purpose of Power?

The Bible tells us God gave power to Jesus when Jesus walked this earth. Acts 10:38 says, "God anointed Jesus of Nazareth with the Holy Spirit and with power, [He] went about doing good and healing all who were oppressed by the devil, for God was with Him."

What did Jesus do with that power? He went about doing good deeds. God gave Jesus power so He could do good—so He could heal people and set them free from the oppression of the devil. Please understand this: God gives power so we can help other people.

God did not give power to Joseph for Joseph's sake. God gave Joseph power so he could feed the world during a severe famine! God looked down and said, "There are seven years of famine coming. I need someone I can trust to take care of these people for Me during the famine. Otherwise, a lot of people are going to die." In Joseph, God found a man who would be humble, faithful, and a good steward—a man He could trust to feed the nations.

God's heart is always for people, so God's power is always given to help people. That's what power is for, and God wants us to remember that.

God's heart is always for people, so God's power is always given to help people.

In Deuteronomy 8, the Lord lets the Israelites know He is going to help them enter the Promised Land, and they will possess many good things through His power. He tells them not to forget about that after they have entered the land, and He reminds them that power comes from Him.

Finally, He warns them against saying in their hearts, "'My power and the might of my hand have gained me this wealth.' And you shall remember the LORD your God, for it is He who gives you power to get wealth, that He may establish His covenant which He swore to your fathers, as it is this day" (Deuteronomy 8:17–18). God wants His people to remember that power comes from Him, not from their own efforts. God says the purpose of power is so He may "establish His covenant." The purpose of wealth is so He may "establish His covenant." The purpose of influence is so God may "establish His covenant." God wants to establish His covenant in this earth, and His covenant is one of blessing, healing, and deliverance from sin and darkness!

You see, God owns all the resources in the world—actually, the *universe*. He even owns Mars! One day when Elon Musk gets there, it will say "Property of God." In one hand, God has all the resources. And in the other, He has all the hurting people—all the hungry, broken people who need the Good News, food, money, medicine, and hope. A businessperson would say that God has all the supply in one hand and the demand in the other. And what's in the middle? *We are*. We are the connecting piece between all the resources and those in need. God works through His people. We are the distributors. He is simply looking for humble stewards through whom He can channel all His resources and power. He wants to get all those resources to all those people who need them. And every time God promotes us or gives us a position of influence, it's because He has *people* in mind. He has someone specific He wants us to minister to and bless. The world says power is for self, but the Bible says power is for others.

Years ago, God gave our church a great piece of land and a beautiful building in a highly visible location on a major highway. Did He do this so we can say how big and nice our building is? No, He did this so we can help more people. God gave us that land because He wanted to *establish His covenant* with the people in that area. God looked down and saw forty thousand cars driving by that property every day—most of them driven by people destined for hell unless someone tells them about Jesus Christ.

Since then, God has given us influence all over the world. Is it so we can say we're famous? No, it's so we can share the gospel of Jesus Christ and minister to broken and hurting people. And whatever our level of influence might be in years to come, we have determined to keep serving people. We are going to keep doing the same things we started out doing when our church was smaller: loving people, helping people, seeing marriages restored, supporting missionaries around the world, and so much more! The more God increases our influence, the more people we can reach for His kingdom!

It's truly wonderful when people who have been given power use it to help people. I see this modeled all the time at our church. I'm somewhat biased, but I honestly believe that some of the world's greatest servants are in our church. Members are willing to stay late, come in at odd times, and lay down their lives to serve others. They truly care for one another as Paul exhorted us to do: "Let each of you look out not only for his own interests, but also for the interests of others" (Philippians 2:4).

I see this illustrated beautifully when God uses one of our pastors to speak a prophetic word of encouragement to someone in the congregation. I look out over the congregation and see the Spirit of God ministering to that person, and it blesses me. Then I notice that the people nearby are just as happy and excited as the person who is being ministered to. And that blesses me even more! People are happy God is blessing their brother or sister in the Lord, and that is the right attitude!

One day, a lady in our church was driving her daughter to school, and her heart was breaking for her little girl. Her husband had recently abandoned the family, leaving her and the children to fend for themselves. And now it was "Father-Daughter Day" at school.

When this mother pulled up to the school, she was thrilled to see one of our pastors standing at the curb. The little girl ran up to him and hugged him, her day obviously brightened by this surprise. Then she asked, "Pastor, what are you doing here?"

"Would it be okay if I joined you at school today?" he replied. The biggest smile you have ever seen appeared on that little girl's face, and off they walked, hand in hand. She would have a "daddy" at school with her that day, just like the other little girls!

As a pastor, I love to see such love demonstrated, and I believe God loves it, too. Why? Because God's heart is for people. He loves people, and He likes to see His children serving and ministering to one another. It's why He gives us power, blessings, and ministry gifts.

Some years ago, some friends introduced me to a lady one Saturday evening after church. She and her husband had been missionaries to Mexico for forty years. We talked for a few moments, and then I asked, "Is there anything I can pray with you about tonight?"

She said, "Yes. Two months ago something happened with our visas, and I was ordered to leave Mexico after forty years, but my husband had to stay. They won't let him out, and they won't let me back in. We've been apart for two months. Could you pray about that?"

I immediately thought about a man in our church named Juan Hernandez who was a political strategist and very influential presidential campaign manager in Mexico. At that time, the current president of Mexico had been elected largely because of Juan's brilliant work. Then, Juan led the president and thirteen out of twenty-four cabinet members to Christ. I thought perhaps Juan could do something to help. I asked the missionary to give me her name and contact information, and I told her there was someone in our church who might be able to help.

Later that evening, after the next service, another couple came up to me and introduced themselves. The husband said, "My name is Jose, and I'm Juan Hernandez's cousin."

I said, "Oh! I'm trying to get in touch with Juan. I don't know if he's out of town this weekend, but I need to speak with him."

I began to tell Jose the story about the missionaries, and he immediately replied, "I will take care of it."

"Really? Do you have some contacts?" I asked.

"I'm the minister of immigration of Mexico."

It was the first time I had met him, and I didn't want to impose, so I said, "Well, listen if you run into any problems . . . " I was trying to let him off the hook if he didn't want to help. But I will never forget how he stopped me mid-sentence, looked me right in the eyes, and said, "I will not run into any problems. I will take care of it."

That conversation happened on a Saturday. On Monday, the missionary had his visa. On Tuesday, he boarded a flight and came home to his wife. Their missionary organization gave the couple a full year furlough in the States, and at the end of that year, the man passed away. But he got to spend the last year of his life with his wife. You know why? Because a man had power, and he knew how to use that power. He knew his power was to help people.

That is what influence is for. *That* is what power is for. God gives us power and influence because *He loves people passionately.* He wants us to use His power to reach them with His love.

Power is not a bad thing. It's a good thing, and it comes from God. Power is given for the purpose of helping others. You may not be second in command of all of Egypt like Joseph or even know how much influence you have, but you do have influence. The Power Test is all about recognizing that any power, influence, or success we experience is not for our own purposes. We may work hard and respond well to God's voice, but it all belongs to Him. He is watching to see if you will steward that power wisely and use it to do His work. He is watching to see if you will use your influence and authority to share His love with a lost and dying world. That is the Power Test. Will you pass it?

CHAPTER EIGHT

The Prosperity Test

It was a 1973 Ford station wagon with 130,000 miles. It was the first car Debbie and I ever paid cash for, but when the Lord provided for us to purchase another vehicle, we knew He wanted us to give this one away.

When we met a single mother in our church, we knew immediately we were supposed to give the car to her. She had been getting rides to work from someone, but the person was suddenly moving away. If she couldn't get a car within two weeks, she was going to lose her job. When she shared her prayer need at church, we knew our station wagon was for her.

It was an older car, but it was reliable and in good condition, and we had recently put new tires on it. We were thrilled to give her that car, and she drove it for many years. It helped her keep her job and provide for her family. God blessed us when we purchased it, and we, in turn, were used by God to bless her and help meet her needs.

As we discovered in the previous chapter, power will test your character. But so will money. In fact, money is really just another form of power. Money can give us the power to do certain things or meet certain needs, and in the same way, the lack of money can hinder us from doing certain things. Therefore, money empowers us to some extent. It also tests our character.

The Prosperity Test: Using Money Wisely

So we must ask ourselves, *What do we do with the power that money brings us?* Do we use it as God would have us use it—to further His purposes for our lives and the lives of others? Or do we squander it in foolish ways, or worse yet, in ways that are actually harmful?

This is the Prosperity Test. (I could have named it "The Money Test" or "The Resources Test," but I'm sure by now you've noticed that all the tests start with the letter P.) Every one of us has taken this test, and we will continue to take it as long as we're living, because we need material things to survive. We need food, we need shelter, and we need clothing. Money is just something we use to exchange for the things we need.

If you think you're too spiritual to bother with material things, try going without food and clothing for a while. You'll quickly discover that while money cannot provide happiness or contentment, the lack of it can certainly create problems!

This is why God is so interested in the way we handle our money. Our money is a medium God uses to further His purposes on this earth. God wants people to have food and clothing and to be provided for, and He uses *people* to distribute His resources. He uses *people* to distribute money and take care of needs on this earth. God used Debbie and me to help provide for that single mom. It blessed her, *and* it blessed us. God looks for good stewards—those who know how to manage money wisely, according to His principles.

He found such a person in Joseph.

In Genesis 41:2-7, we find the account of Pharaoh's perplexing dreams. First Pharaoh dreamed he saw seven fat cows and seven thin cows, and the seven thin cows ate the seven fat cows. Then Pharaoh dreamed he saw seven plump stalks of grain and seven thin and blighted stalks of grain, and the seven thin stalks ate the seven plump stalks. The Bible tells us Pharaoh's spirit was troubled about these dreams (see Genesis 41:8). Somehow, he knew these dreams were significant. So he desperately searched to find someone who could tell him their meaning. This is why Joseph was called out of the prison to stand before Pharaoh. Let's pick up the story in verse 25.

> Then Joseph said to Pharaoh, "The dreams of Pharaoh are one; God has shown Pharaoh what He is about to do: The seven good cows are seven years, and the seven good heads are seven years; the dreams are one. And the seven thin and ugly cows which came up after them are seven years, and the seven empty heads blighted by the east wind are seven years of famine. This is the thing which I have spoken to Pharaoh. God has shown Pharaoh what He is about to do. Indeed seven years of great plenty will come throughout all the land of Egypt; but after them seven years of famine will arise, and all the plenty will be forgotten in the land of Egypt; and the famine will deplete the land. So the plenty will not be known in the land because of the famine following, for it will be very severe. And the dream was repeated to Pharaoh twice because

the thing is established by God, and God will shortly bring it to pass."
(Genesis 41:25–32)

Two times Joseph said, "God has shown Pharaoh what He is about
to do" (vv. 25, 28). God had a purpose in showing Pharaoh those
dreams—a purpose of blessing, provision, and deliverance from starvation! God knew seven years of famine were coming, and He wanted
to make sure people didn't starve. So He showed Pharaoh what was
about to happen.

But there was more God was trying to do. God had a plan to provide
food for *everyone* during the famine, but He needed someone whom He
could trust to carry out His plan. God needed someone who was a good
steward and who would obey Him in the area of money. Joseph was
that person. He understood God's principles about managing finances.
And as God's faithful servant, Joseph offered wisdom to Pharaoh.

> Now therefore, let Pharaoh select a discerning and wise man, and set
> him over the land of Egypt. Let Pharaoh do this, and let him appoint
> officers over the land, to collect one-fifth of the produce of the land
> of Egypt in the seven plentiful years. And let them gather all the food
> of those good years that are coming, and store up grain under the
> authority of Pharaoh, and let them keep food in the cities. Then that
> food shall be as a reserve for the land for the seven years of famine
> which shall be in the land of Egypt, that the land may not perish during
> the famine. (Genesis 41:33–36)

God had a plan to provide food for everyone when the years of
famine came. But His plan would have failed in the hands of someone
who didn't know how to manage money wisely. God couldn't choose
someone who wouldn't let Him be first in their decisions and whose
bank account was in disarray. He couldn't choose someone with a

pattern of unrestrained spending, who didn't know how to save for the future. If He had chosen someone like that, the grain would have been depleted before the famine arrived! God looked for someone who was a good steward, someone who knew how to manage material things according to His principles. The Prosperity Test was a huge part of Joseph's destiny. Would he manage the wealth of those years of plenty as God wanted?

The Prosperity Test is a huge part of your destiny as well. Until you are found faithful with money, you will not be able to step into your destiny to the full extent God desires. Why? Because God's plans for you will always involve bringing His blessings and provision to others.

Like it or not, it takes money to do that! It takes money to meet the needs of hurting people and carry the gospel around the world, and it takes money to support your family while you're doing that. God will give you everything you need to carry out His plans for your life. Can He trust you to handle it wisely? Or will you squander what He gives you by foolish spending? That is the Prosperity Test.

You might be saying to yourself, *I never have any money. I always seem to be broke. How could I be taking the Prosperity Test?* The truth is everyone has financial resources to manage. Every time you get your paycheck, you're taking the Prosperity Test. Every time you get extra money, you're taking the Prosperity Test. Even if you're living on welfare, you take the Prosperity Test each time you get a check from the government. (Remember, Jesus took note of how people gave offerings in the Temple, including the widow with only two mites to her name [see Mark 12:41–44].)

It's unavoidable. We will all be tested in how we handle our money, and it seems that here in the United States we have a lot more money to test us!

You Take the Prosperity Test Every Day

I know you've probably heard this before, but it's worth repeating: The United States is one of the most prosperous nations in the world. According to *Forbes Magazine*, "The poor in the US are richer than around 70% of all the people extant."[1] So if you live in the United States, you likely take the Prosperity Test every day.

Let me give you some statistics to help you see what I mean. According to the World Bank, the average annual household income of someone living in the United States in the year 2021 was $65,900.[2] Now let's compare this figure with the average annual household income for people living in other countries that same year:

Finland	$49,600		France	$42,300
Japan	$41,600		Germany	$47,000
Saudi Arabia	$21,900		Israel	$43,100
Chile	$13,500		Poland	$15,300
Argentina	$8,900		Mexico	$8,500
Turkey	$9,100		Ukraine	$3,500
Russia	$10,700		Cambodia	$1,500
China	$10,600		Sudan	$650
Nigeria	$2,000		Afghanistan	$500
India	$1,900			

These figures show the difference between the income the rest of the world lives on and the average income we live on here in the United States. Now, this doesn't account for cost-of-living rates, which we know vary around the world and are rather high in the United States. But when we look at these numbers, they help us understand that most people in the United States still enjoy a greater degree of material prosperity than nearly everyone else on this planet.

Here in America, we are so prosperous that we often pray for things the rest of the world would only imagine. We pray for things like new clothes or a bigger home. While the rest of the world is praying for a bicycle for transportation or food to put on the table, we pray for a better car than the one we're already driving.

A friend of mine is involved in full-time mission work, and when he first began traveling as a missionary, he didn't have much experience with the economic differences between our country and most others. This became painfully obvious on one occasion when he was preaching a message on suffering. He made the mistake of using an illustration he had developed here in America—his family "getting by" with "only" one car for a year. That was his example of suffering! Yet he was preaching this message in a country in which 96 percent of the people did not even own *one* car and whose average citizen earned about $2,000 a year!

Sadly, many of us have absolutely no comprehension of how the rest of the world lives. Here in America, many people live in a prosperity bubble, and most of us have no idea how richly blessed and prosperous we really are. We are living the Prosperity Test every day. Whether we realize it or not, we have been entrusted with great material wealth.

The critical question is, *What are we going to do with this wealth?* In the same way power tests the true character of every person, money tests it too. Every time you get your paycheck, you have a test handed to you.

Unexpected income is a particularly revealing test. Have you ever had a windfall, such as a raise or a surprise bonus at the end of the year? When you did, you took the Prosperity Test. It doesn't matter whether it was a $10,000 raise, a $1 per hour raise, a $1,000 bonus, or a $50 bill. Every time you receive extra money, you have a chance to show God how well you're going to manage the income He gives you.

What did you do with that extra money? Did you save it, spend it, blow it, pay down your debt, or something else?

It's amazing how we pray and ask God for extra money, but then when it comes into our hands, we're not always faithful to do what God would want us to do with it. Why would God continue to give us extra funds if we're not faithful with the funds He has already given us?

Every person will be tested by money, whether he or she has only a little or a lot. That's why Jesus said, "Where your treasure is, there your heart will be also" (Matthew 6:21). In other words, Jesus says your *money* will always be tied to your *heart*.

God is very interested in our hearts. The Bible says, "For the LORD does not see as man sees; for man looks at the outward appearance, but the LORD looks at the heart" (1 Samuel 16:7). God is looking at our *hearts* to see if they truly belong to Him. The way we handle money is a primary indicator of where our hearts really belong.

So it's very important to settle these questions: What has first place in your heart—God or money? Does money control you, or do you control money?

Does money control you, or do you control money?

Let God Be First

The most important principle I can tell you about money can be summed up in four simple words: *Let God be first!*

I always feel burdened to share this principle with people because it's so important. I feel so passionate that I even wrote a whole book about it called *The Blessed Life*. When God is number one in your life, everything else adds up! And the way you put God first in your life is by *honoring* Him above all else. The Bible tells us, "Honor the LORD with your possessions, and with the firstfruits of all your increase" (Proverbs 3:9).

This is really what tithing is all about: giving God the honor and thanks for everything we have. We do this by giving Him the first 10 percent of our income—the *firstfruits* of what we earn. I don't know why God decided on 10 percent, but I think He decided on a percentage because it's fair to everyone. Regardless of whether you make $40,000 or $400,000 a year, it's always 10 percent. You may have heard a lot about tithing throughout your life, or this may be the first time, but tithing is really very simple. It's about *putting God first*.

Finances are just one way we can show honor to God and let Him know He is first in our lives. Joseph honored God and let Him be first in everything he had. Joseph even honored God in the naming of his children. In the midst of the seven years of plenty, Joseph had two sons. Genesis 41 tells the story.

And to Joseph were born two sons before the years of famine came, whom Asenath, the daughter of Poti-Pherah priest of On, bore to him. Joseph called the name of the firstborn Manasseh: "For God has made me forget all my toil and all my father's house." And the name of the second he called Ephraim: "For God has caused me to be fruitful in the land of my affliction." (vv. 50–52)

The name Manasseh means "to forget," and the name Ephraim means "to be fruitful." But the first thing Joseph had to say about the names of his children was "for God"! *"For God* has made me forget. . . . *For God* has caused me to be fruitful" (emphasis added). Joseph recognized it was God who made him forget his troubles, and it was God who made him fruitful. Joseph had stepped into a place of incredible power and wealth, but in that place of privilege and comfort, he did not forget God. As the ruler of Egypt, Joseph was still thanking God and honoring Him. His two sons were the firstfruits of his body, and Joseph chose to *honor God* with those firstfruits! He used their names as a way to give honor to God for all He had done for him. It was an outward reflection of the gratitude in his heart.

God has always been interested in knowing what is *first* place in our hearts.

Why did God accept Abel's offering but not Cain's? Because Abel's offering was the *firstborn* of his flock! Cain's offering was *not* the firstfruits of his crops, so his offering was not blessed (see Genesis 4:3–5). Because of His preeminence, God cannot accept second place. He must always be first.

When the Israelites first entered the Promised Land, God commanded them to give all the silver and gold from Jericho to Him (see Joshua 6:19). Why? Jericho was the *first* city they conquered, so it was the *firstfruits* of the Promised Land. Notice God didn't tell them to first take ten cities and then give one of those cities to Him when it was all over. No, God commanded them to give everything from that *first* city to Him, and after they did, He said they could have the goods from all the other cities.

This is how the principle of the firstfruits works in our lives: giving the *first* to God causes the rest to be blessed. God told the Israelites if they would *honor Him* with that first city, then He would help them conquer all the other cities. Further, He would allow them to keep everything from all the other cities. But when Achan kept part of the silver from Jericho for himself, the Israelites saw that God was no longer helping them. Instead of having God's help, they were on their own—and the battle did not go well for them! Until they made that "dishonoring" situation right with God, they were not able to go on and capture any more cities (see Joshua 7). The tithe is blessed and consecrated to God. But if you take it (or keep it), it's cursed!

The tithe is always the *first* part, not the last. God said that when the Israelites' sheep had lambs, they were to give the *first* lamb to Him. God did not say to let the sheep have ten lambs, and then give one of the ten to Him. He said to give Him the *first* one. Why? *Because it takes faith to give the first one!* It takes faith to give the *first* 10 percent, not the last 10 percent. Tithing means a tenth part, but it's about giving the *first* tenth to God!

Giving the last 10 percent instead of the first 10 percent is saying, "Once I'm sure all my needs are taken care of, I will give to You, God. If I have enough room in my life for You, I will honor and obey You." That is not really very honoring to God, is it? But when we give God the *first* 10 percent, we are taking a step of faith and trust. We are saying, "God, I want to obey and honor You by giving to You first. You are first place in every area of my life. I trust You to provide for me and meet all my needs."

Tithing is a test of your heart. You can *claim* God is first place in your life, but let me see your bank account! By observing where your money goes, I can tell you who or what is *really* first place in your life. It could be the mortgage company, the electric company, or your local pizza place. Amazon, Bass Pro Shops, Walmart, or Nordstrom might be first in your life. I'll tell you what is first place in a lot of people's lives. Can you guess? It's Visa!

But let me tell you who ought to be first—God! He doesn't care about how much stuff you have. *He cares about how much stuff has you.* He cares about your heart.

God doesn't command us to tithe for His sake—He has all the resources in the world. He tells us to do it for our benefit! Malachi 3:10 says, "'Bring all the tithes into the storehouse, that there may be food in My house, and try Me now in this,' says the LORD of hosts, 'If I will not open for you the windows of heaven and pour out for you such blessing that there will not be room enough to receive it.'" In verse 11, God tells us that if we put Him first in our finances by tithing, He will "rebuke the devourer for our sake." But if you keep the tithe, the Bible says you are robbing God and are cursed with a curse (see Malachi 3:8-9). Scripture is so clear on this principle. I don't know about you, but I'd rather 90 percent of my income be blessed than 100 percent of it be cursed!

I've been in ministry for more than forty years, and I often hear testimonies from tithers and non-tithers. They all say the same thing. The tithers say, "Pastor, we're so blessed." And the non-tithers say, "We can't afford to tithe." What does this tell you? When God says He will "pour out for you such blessing that there will not be room enough to receive it" (Malachi 3:10), He means it! This shouldn't be *why* we tithe, but it's a resulting benefit. And for those who are not tithing, *all* their finances are under a curse.

I have to pause here and mention that God Himself doesn't curse us. We live in a fallen world—a cursed world. But God wants to redeem you and your finances. Please hear my heart on this. The reason I'm so passionate about people understanding the principle of tithing is because I'm tired of seeing people lose their jobs, income, health, family, kids, and marriages because the enemy is devouring them. It's better to tithe than it is to stand in a room and yell at the devil. We can stand firm on the promise that God rebukes the enemy for us when we tithe.

The Lord also says, "Try Me now in this" (Malachi 3:10). So if you're still not convinced, try tithing for a year and see what happens. I've told our congregation that if they're not fully satisfied, we'll give them their money back. It's a money-back guarantee! I can say this with complete confidence because I know God's promises are true. But I am also sure to explain that we don't need the funds. We have never passed an offering plate at Gateway, yet we are one of the highest-giving churches in America. We don't need the money; it's not why I want people to tithe. It's because, as a pastor, it breaks my heart to see people living outside the blessing of God. It's because I know that when God is first in your life, everything else lines up and is blessed. This is a principle we see throughout the Bible, and yet many Christians refuse to acknowledge it.

When God is first in your life, everything else lines up and is blessed.

In June 2013, Barna Research Group released the results of a five-year study about American Donor Trends. The study showed that the proportion of households in the United States that tithe their income dropped from 7 percent in 2009 (before the financial crisis) to just 4 percent in 2010 and 2011 and then 5 percent in 2012. These numbers have been in this range consistently for the past fifteen years. So according to this respected research organization, only 5 percent of households in the United States tithed in 2012.[3] Also, since the Barna report considers giving to non-church charitable organizations as part of someone's tithe, the percentage going to the Church is even smaller.

I believe God has blessed this nation because we have sent missionaries all around the world to spread His gospel message. America has been living in years of prosperity and blessings from God. But I also believe that years of famine are right around the corner if we do not start honoring Him with the firstfruits of those blessings.

We have been blessed because of God. If we turn our backs on Him, we are going to be in trouble! So let's make a commitment to make God first.

How can you do your part? After you receive your paycheck, give your tithe first. I get paid the fifteenth and thirtieth of every month. On those days, the first thing I do during my quiet time is go online and give 10 percent of my income to the church. I want to give God the first part of all my increase, not the last part! But I'm not legalistic about it. If I have an early morning meeting, I might have my quiet time and give our tithe later in the day. If Debbie happens to go to the grocery store before I tithe, I don't say, "Oh, that's great, honey. Now we're cursed! You gave our tithe to the grocery store!" It's about my heart. God knows my heart to have Him first in our finances.

Any time you receive some unexpected money, you have a great opportunity to let God be first. When you get a bonus, do you tithe on it? Do you honor God first? Imagine the message it sends when someone prays, "God, please help me! I need extra money!" But when God answers that prayer by sending extra money, they don't tithe on it!

Isn't it amazing how quickly we forget it was God who met our need and sent us the money? Tithing is simply a way of expressing our gratitude to God and acknowledging that it came from Him. But if we immediately forget God and don't honor Him with the tithe on that money, we are not putting Him first.

Please understand me. This is not law—this is *love*. This is expressing love and gratitude and honor to God, the One who has given us everything!

God is so gracious and compassionate. When we are in a tight spot, God will say, "I want to bless you. I want to help you. Even though you have some things out of line in your life, I know you need this money right now. You are My child, and I love you. So I'm going to help you. I'm going to put it on your boss's heart to give you a raise, even though no one else in the company is getting a raise right now." God loves you so much that in some cases He will move upon the heart of an unbeliever just to provide for you. So be sure to thank Him for it! Be sure to honor Him for all He does for you.

Just a few months after I got saved, I heard a sermon about tithing and decided to try it. At the time, I was making $600 a month, so I gave $60 in the church offering. The very next day, I went to work, and the owner called me into his office. He said, "I'm going to give you a $200 a month raise." Then he added, "And I have no idea why I'm doing this." In other words, it wasn't because I deserved it. I put God first, and I was blessed, but more importantly, my heart changed. Tithing works on your heart, not just your wallet.

One morning when Josh was young, I was sitting at my desk paying bills. Back then, we paid all our bills with checks, and I always wrote our tithe check first. That day, after I wrote the check for our tithe, I set it aside and continued writing checks for our other bills. Josh was old enough to read and understand numbers, so when he saw the amount I wrote on the check, he said, "Wow! That's a huge amount of money, Dad. Why do we give so much to the church?"

I sat him on my lap and said, "Son, I'm going to tell you something I've never told you. Your daddy was not always a Christian. As a matter of fact, before I met Jesus at nineteen years old, my life was a total wreck. But God saved me and delivered me and blessed me. So I will gladly give God the first of all my income—not out of duty or compulsion but out of gratitude."

Tithing isn't only about making sure you're not under a curse or about moving forward in your destiny. It's also about gratitude and showing God that He has the first place in your heart.

So let God be first—this is the first principle of the Prosperity Test. Joseph understood this principle and put God first in every area of his life.

There are also other important financial principles that were essential to his success in his destiny as ruler of the world's food supply during the years of famine. Of course, Joseph understood the most important principle—he allowed God to be first in every area of his life. But Joseph also understood the importance of something else we would all do well to comprehend: *learning to wait.*

Good Things Come

For those seven years of abundance, Joseph made the Egyptians store up, store up, and store up some more. After a while, I'm sure some of the people probably said, "We've got enough grain stored up by now! Why can't we just use some of this grain instead of storing it?" Joseph most likely replied, "No, you don't understand. If you don't store it up now, you're not going to have it later when you need it."

Joseph understood the importance of waiting. The Egyptians could have used all that extra grain right away, or they could have sold it and made themselves rich overnight. But they would have starved during the famine.

Did you know the Bible says it's not a good thing to try to get rich quickly? Proverbs 28:20 says, "A faithful man will abound with blessings, but he who hastens to be rich will not go unpunished." According to the Bible, get-rich-quick schemes are bad for you, and if you get involved in them, you'll be punished! In other words, if you try to get rich quickly, you can expect to encounter problems. Please understand this simple fact: if it sounds too good to be true, it probably is.

It's amazing to me how many people get involved in get-rich-quick gimmicks. This isn't meant to make you feel bad if you've been lured into a scheme or you've been scammed. I know how tempting some of these deals look, especially if you're struggling financially. Over the years, I've had people want me to get involved in these enterprises, but I've learned the reason they want me involved is because they see the gift of God on my life. They think they can somehow make themselves rich by using that gift—a gift God has given to me so I can help people and bring them to Him.

I made a firm decision long ago that I am not going to get involved in any quick money-making enterprises. Many of these ventures appear legitimate, and some actually are. But most are never as lucrative as they say, and some are downright scams.

I'm saddened to note that nearly everyone goes after the church as a business target. Many do this because the tightly knit community that exists within the church makes it a great place to network. Church folks are a favorite target, so watch out for shortcuts to wealth. Your best safeguard—and this should be no surprise—is God's Word. In fact, when it comes to wealth, the Bible teaches us to *wait*. The Bible teaches us to *be faithful* and *be good stewards*.

The reason most people try to get rich quickly is they are not willing to live as they ought to financially. They don't want to wait or be patient. They want to have what they want and have it now! They should be learning to save money and live below their means, but they don't like that idea, so they turn to some shortcut.

We must learn to wait. We need to be patient when it comes to purchases. I know so well how tempting it is to click "Buy Now" and have it show up at your house two days later. But it's wise to walk away from a possible purchase and think it over for a while. We should look at our budget and ask God if this is His will right now. We live in a society of instant gratification, and it's all too easy to fall into the pattern of buying whatever we want at the moment, without being patient or seeking God's counsel about it. (Remember my story from chapter 2 about the Suburban!)

This is something I believe is really important for married couples to understand if they are going to pass the Prosperity Test. Husbands and wives must realize they sometimes put pressure on each other to buy things they really cannot afford. Wives put pressure on their husbands, and husbands put pressure on their wives to purchase things that are simply unwise at that point in their lives. Sometimes the reason is greed or selfishness, and often the reason is pride. They want to have expensive things like other couples have, and they feel a need to "keep up with the Joneses." But this is really just pride. And it can lead to financial problems if it's not recognized and dealt with accordingly.

Can You Afford It?

Thankfully, there's a very simple way to defuse this type of conflict. You can prevent pressure from dominating your financial decisions by having a budget.

Because Joseph understood God's principles of financial management, he had a budget. Joseph said,

> Let Pharaoh . . . appoint officers over the land, to collect one-fifth of the
> produce of the land of Egypt in the seven plentiful years. And let them
> gather all the food of those good years that are coming, and store up
> grain under the authority of Pharaoh. (Genesis 41:34–35)

Joseph didn't vaguely say, "Well, I think it would be a good idea for us to save some of the grain during the years of plenty. Maybe we should think about doing that." No, he had a *plan* in advance, and that plan involved very *specific* amounts—one-fifth (20 percent) to be exact. He knew that to make it through seven years of famine, they had to be prepared. Joseph's plan also involved *accountability* using Pharaoh's officers.

Joseph's plan was so good that he not only fed Egypt and his family, he also fed the whole world during the seven years of famine. Other nations came to Egypt to buy food, and Joseph extended Egypt's empire by trading land in exchange for life-saving grain.

Now, your planned-out budget may not help you feed the world, but it will help you define *specific limits* for your spending and keep you and your spouse *accountable* to those limits. It's hard to say no to your spouse when he or she wants something. I understand that. But you can both keep emotions out of your financial discussions if you simply make a budget and stick to it. Your spouse may come to you and say, "Can we buy a bigger house? Can I buy a new car? Can I have this or have that?" And there is a correct and peaceful answer that goes like this: "I would love to see you have that, but let's see what the budget says."

Then you look at the budget and say, "Oh, I'm sorry. I guess Mr. Budget says, 'No.' I would gladly buy it for you if it fit into the budget. But Mr. Budget says 'No.'" When you let the budget (or Mr. Budget, as I like to call him) make the decision, you will have a much more peaceful discussion—and a much less stressful financial life!

Shortly after I shared this principle one weekend at church, a woman told me she and her husband decided to get serious about their budget. They had a lot of school debt and wanted to pay it off. So they made a strict budget and started using the "Mr. Budget" phrasing with their kids. They decided they would go to McDonald's once a week for a treat, and one day their four-year-old daughter asked, "Mom, can we go to McDonald's twice this week?"

The mom responded, "Honey, I would love to take you to McDonald's twice this week, but Mr. Budget says 'no.'"

A little while later, the mom heard the four-year-old mumble, "I hate Mr. Budget!"

We all hate Mr. Budget at times! But I guarantee you will eliminate 90 percent of the stress in your life if you bring this area under control. Without a budget, it's difficult to know where your money is going or even how much money is coming in and going out. So if you don't have a budget, you're not going to be able to succeed financially. You're not going to be able to plan for your financial future either.

I've had people ask me, "Do you think we should buy this new house?" Before they ask me, they need to understand the decision to buy a house is not a matter of thinking. It's not a matter of feeling. It's a matter of numbers! Usually, it's not really my advice they want but rather my blessing or my endorsement of their decision. But I don't know what their income is. I don't know what their expenses are. I will not even offer an opinion until I have asked at least one very important question: *"Can you afford it?"* And all too often the answer I receive goes something like this: "Well, we *feel* like we can."

You can't make your mortgage payment with feelings. It takes money! Financial management isn't about opinion. It's about math. It's also about being in alignment with the Lord and stewarding your resources well. You might get to a place where you can buy just about anything you want. You could be blessed financially, but that doesn't mean you *should* buy anything you want. The question, "God, is this Your will?" is always important.

Having a budget is a practical step in the right direction. It helps to make seemingly difficult decisions quite simple. First, you calculate all your expenses and compare them to your income. You set aside your tithe and determine how much you want to give in offerings. Then you subtract your taxes, insurance, bills, food, clothing, and so on. Finally, you come down to a number that is left for the mortgage, and that number will tell you whether you can buy the house or not. It's that simple! (And if that doesn't sound simple, there are many apps and online resources available to help you.)

Change Your Life—Make a Budget!

There are certainly more reasons to make a budget than I can list here, but I want to mention seven reasons why it's important and valuable to have a budget. If you implement the principle of budgeting, it will change your life in the following ways:

1. *It helps you see things more clearly and objectively.* A budget puts a number on everything, which helps you see financial issues more clearly and objectively. Questions about finances are reduced to the simple comparison of income versus expenses. This helps you keep emotions out of the picture and differentiate between reality and feelings. Without a budget, many people have no

idea what their actual monthly income and expenses are. But if you put all the numbers down, you will see your financial situation very clearly. A budget shows you in black and white what exactly you can and cannot afford. Years ago, we had to do this all on paper, but now there are great computer programs and budgeting apps available that can filter and organize your finances. You might have to figure out which one you like best, but many are very user friendly and helpful in visualizing where your money is going.

2. *It makes you examine and clarify your values and priorities.* When you need to make decisions about how to spend your income, you're forced to examine what's most important to you. How much do you value expensive clothing versus saving or giving? How much do you value owning a certain kind of car versus sending your children to college? Which one is a higher priority? How much do you value letting your children have braces as you drive a five-year-old car versus getting a new one? A budget helps you clarify the answers to those questions. A budget helps you see needs versus wants, now versus later, and important versus unimportant.

3. *It provides a basis of discussion and agreement.* The most powerful tool you have in marriage is unity, yet few married couples are in unity where their finances are concerned. A budget can help you find a place of unity because it provides an opportunity for listening, talking, praying, and hearing each other's hearts. When you talk and pray about your budget, you have a foundation for finding a place of agreement about your finances. Agreement is the most powerful tool in marriage, while strife and division are deadly.

4. *It provides accountability.* Mr. Budget helps keep you from overspending because he has already decided how the money is going to be spent. Mr. Budget can say "no" to an impulse purchase and provide accountability, which helps keep your finances on track. When you have already determined not to spend outside of your budget, Mr. Budget will tell you whether or not you can buy something.

5. *It helps you live within your means.* A budget provides clear and impartial numbers, letting you know what your actual income is and what you must do to not spend more than you make. In this way, a budget helps you to live in a land called "Reality" rather than the lands of "Fantasy" or "Denial." In other words, a budget helps you to live within your means. Many people live with unnecessary stress because they have foolishly taken on financial obligations that are bigger than their actual income. A budget helps by revealing the lifestyle your income can realistically support. Many people could greatly reduce the stress in their lives if they would simply downsize their lifestyle to fit their income.

6. *It helps you live without debt.* God wired you to benefit from patience. He wired you to enjoy looking forward to things. He wired you for something called hope. Do you know what debt does? It robs you of the opportunity to hope. When you borrow every time you want something, you don't have to hope for it anymore; instead, you just put it on the credit card. This is why people who are in debt are the most discouraged people in the world. They have no opportunity for delayed gratification, and that robs them of the joy and happiness that come when a hope is fulfilled. If you just pull out the credit card every time something

strikes your fancy, you'll live in continual discouragement. That discouragement can start a cycle of debt in which you want to buy something every time you feel discouraged. Then the debt increases, which creates more discouragement, and the cycle goes on. Perhaps you know exactly what I'm talking about. When you get a little low, you just want to buy something in order to create that short-lived surge of excitement. It's seductively easy to get in the habit of buying things without hope.

7. *It builds character and discipline in your life.* A budget holds up a set of numbers and asks you to live within them. Will you stick to the commitment you made to God and your spouse when you prayed and set up that budget? Or will you go back on your word when the pressure is on and the temptation to spend is tugging at you? Sticking to a budget is like sticking to any other commitment. It takes character. It takes discipline. And these are vital qualities to have if you're going to fulfill God's destiny for your life.

I want to emphasize this statement because it's so important: *you will never fulfill the spiritual destiny God has on your life if you cannot pass the Prosperity Test.* If you can't handle money correctly and according to biblical principles, how will you be able to handle the other issues that are important to your destiny?

As with everything else God has given you stewardship over, He is watching to see if you will handle money wisely. Having a budget is a first step toward taking responsibility for your money and showing God that you will be faithful with the things He has placed in your care.

Joseph had a budget. And Joseph developed his budget so well that after seven years of savings, he fed the entire world during seven years of famine. Now *that* is God's style of budgeting! And one way Joseph did it was by living on less than the amount that was actually coming in—this is called "living below your means."

Live Below Your Means

Most people think they understand how to live below their means, but they really don't. Spending 90 to 95 percent of your income is not living below your means.

Truly living below your means actually requires living on about 70 percent of your income. Just add it up and you'll see what I mean. For instance, if you tithe 10 percent, put 10 percent in savings, put 10 percent in retirement or other investments, and give something in offerings above your tithes, you're going to be living on 60 to 70 percent of your income at the highest level. Yet, rather than living below their means, many people are living above them.

Many people do not have the income to support the lifestyle they're leading, and oftentimes the reason they're living that way is pride. They want to drive the same type of cars their friends are driving, and they want to live in the same type of homes or apartments as their friends. But they do not make enough income right now to do that, so they get themselves into all kinds of financial difficulties.

When Debbie and I first got married more than forty years ago, I bought a used manufactured home. Well, to be honest, it was a trailer. And only five hundred square feet. In the summertime, we had to put aluminum foil on all the windows so the temperature inside could cool to eighty-five degrees.

We had some friends who lived in nice, new apartments. They were beautiful and air conditioned, and they didn't need to put foil on their windows to stay cool. One night after visiting with one of the couples at their apartment, Debbie said to me, "I really don't care where we live, but I wouldn't mind living in one of those apartments."

And I said, "Sugar, if you'll stay with me, we will live in some very nice homes. But we cannot do that right now. It doesn't make sense. And, quite honestly, our friends may not have anything left after they finish their one-year lease!"

I bought that trailer for $6,000, and a year later, I sold it for $7,000. Then we lived with a widow for six months while we saved up for our first home. We have since lived comfortably, but that might not have been the case if we had tried to live like our friends. Instead, we consistently lived below our means—as frustrating or unpleasant as it was at times—and reaped the benefits.

God never intended our financial decisions to be dictated by what other people are driving or wearing—or where they are living! In fact, God tells us quite clearly the approach He wants us to have toward our money and our lifestyle.

> Now godliness with contentment is great gain. For we brought nothing into this world, and it is certain we can carry nothing out. And having food and clothing, with these we shall be content. But those who desire to be rich fall into temptation and a snare, and into many foolish and harmful lusts which drown men in destruction and perdition. For the love of money is a root of all kinds of evil, for which some have strayed from the faith in their greediness, and pierced themselves through with many sorrows. (1 Timothy 6:6–10)

God says if we have food and clothing, we should be content. He does not say to be content with these things if you live in India or Africa or Haiti. The Bible doesn't put forth a different standard for those of us who live in the United States. No, He simply says believers are to be *content* with those things. This is not a cultural issue—this is the Bible! As long as we have food and clothing, we are to be content.

The love of money and the desire to be rich will tell you that you should not be content with mere food and clothing. Greed will tell you that in order to be content, you must have more. It will tell you that you can never be happy unless you buy "this" or have "that." Greed is *never* satisfied. That's why this Scripture passage says those who are greedy "fall into temptation and a snare," and "pierced themselves through with many sorrows." Ecclesiastes 5:10 says, "He who loves silver will not be satisfied with silver; Nor he who loves abundance, with increase."

Greed will push you to buy things you don't really need. Because of this, many Americans put themselves under a burden of debt, and they end up with ulcers and other health problems brought on by financial stress. But God never intended us to live that way! God does not want us to live in debt, continually stressed out about our finances. God wants us to be content. As believers, we should walk in more contentment than anyone else. We should be content with God's provision. True godliness brings with it contentment, while greed will rob you of contentment and push you to live beyond your financial reality.

True godliness brings with it contentment.

When you live above your means, you are making a declaration to God. You are saying, "God, I'm not content with Your provision, and

I'm not content with You. I know You have said there are certain ways You have of doing things, but I'm not willing to wait for You to work in my life. I'm not willing to wait for the things I want. I must have them now! So I'm going to figure out a way I can get more without You." Do you think God is going to bless a person like that? When God looks down and sees a selfish, greedy person who is violating His scriptural principles, do you think He says, "I'm going to give him more"? No. A person like that may end up getting more, but he is getting more by working more, not by the blessings of God.

Make no mistake about it: God *wants* to give us more. He wants to bless us and give us the desires of our hearts. But it's so we can bless others! And as with everything else, in order to have God's blessings, we must be willing to do things His way and abide by His principles.

I wrote my book *Beyond Blessed* for just this reason. In *The Blessed Life*, I primarily focused on living out the biblical truth of generosity and how to begin giving extravagantly. But over the years, I encountered so many believers who weren't stewarding their finances well. Some people truly didn't know any better, and I understand that. But how can you be generous if you have nothing left? The truth is the blessed life walks on two legs: generosity and stewardship. So I wrote *Beyond Blessed* to give people practical and biblical principles for budgeting, saving, and stewarding.

I have a tremendous burden for people to understand that living the blessed life is not only about being generous; it's also about stewardship and the importance of managing their finances according to biblical principles. I believe once people become better stewards and get their finances in order, they're more likely to break free from bad financial habits and debt patterns. Understanding these biblical principles changes *everything*!

It really bothers me when I see believers struggling financially and then blaming God for their situation. Some people even reach a place of such discouragement that they don't believe God wants to bless them. They blame God, as if He is letting them down, yet the reason they are struggling financially is because they have violated scriptural principles with their unbridled spending.

They are not content as God commanded us to be, so they live gluttonous, materialistic lives. Then they end up borrowing money they should not be borrowing, just to support a lifestyle they shouldn't be living. Because of their own poor financial management, they end up in trouble, and then they wonder why God doesn't seem to be blessing them the way they think He should. They blame God for not coming through, but their financial problems are their own fault, not God's. They have fallen prey to the *deceitfulness* of riches.

Don't Be Deceived

Yes, riches can be deceitful. In 1 Timothy 6:9–10, the apostle Paul tells us that riches can cause people to fall into a snare and stray from the faith. Jesus put it this way:

> Now these are the ones sown among thorns; they are the ones who hear the word, and the cares of this world, the deceitfulness of riches, and the desires for other things entering in choke the word, and it becomes unfruitful. (Mark 4:18–19)

You can go to church and hear the Word. You can read your Bible, listen to podcasts, and watch preachers on television, but if you're not careful, the deceitfulness of riches can *choke the Word of God* that has been planted in your heart and make that Word unfruitful. In other words, the deceitfulness of riches can stop the Word of God from producing good fruit in your life as God intended.

The deceitfulness of riches has even caused some people to stray from their faith! Paul says, "Some have strayed from the faith in their greediness, and pierced themselves through with many sorrows" (1 Timothy 6:10). People have abandoned their families because of money. Some have actually abandoned the Church because of money.

I have known people who have tried attending church and giving because they think doing so will automatically bring them financial blessing. When that doesn't work for them, they just abandon the church and go somewhere else. They heard someone preaching about the blessings that come from giving and decided to try it, but the motive for their giving had nothing to do with a pursuit of the heart of God. Their motive was to get rich! Do you think God's blessing is going to be poured out on that sort of giving?

Do you know why riches are deceptive? It's because the enemy has created a tempting lie that money equals happiness. Wealth promises joy, security, identity, and popularity. Yes, money is useful and needed, but God is the only One who can give you what you really crave. And God says that if we have food and clothing—if our basic physical needs are met—we are to be content (see 1 Timothy 6:8). But if we're not careful, riches can deceive us.

I'm sad to say that as a pastor, I witness this on a regular basis. For more than thirty years now, I have been counseling people about their finances, and I'm still shocked to hear about the trouble that some believers get themselves into. They come to church every week, and they (supposedly) read the Bible every day. Yet they are not applying the most basic precepts of God's Word to their financial decisions. They're not even applying common sense!

If you think that sounds a bit harsh, let me give you just one example. When we receive requests for financial assistance, quite often it's to help someone make a car payment. One time our staff was ministering to a couple who wanted us to make their car payments. So we asked them, "Well, how much are your car payments?"

"One is $600, and the other one is $500," they replied.

"Hmm. That amounts to $1,100 per month just for your car payments then, doesn't it?" we asked. "And how much is your income each month?"

"$3,300 a month."

"So $1,100 of your $3,300 monthly income is going to car payments?!"

Please understand—you simply can't do that! I don't know how they came to believe they could afford that amount in car payments with their monthly income. The numbers simply did not add up. This is not rocket science or even a deep spiritual revelation—this is common sense.

I am shocked at how deeply in debt many people are today! Some people don't know any better because they weren't taught how to budget or be good financial stewards. But I believe the reason why most people are under a crushing load of debt has to do with the expensive cars they drive, the trendy clothes they wear, the latest technology they buy, and the pricey apartments (not even the houses!) they rent. They don't have the income to live that way. But pride, greed, ignorance, and the need for instant gratification don't allow them to choose a car or apartment that fits their financial reality.

I know my words are strong, but it's important for me to share the truth, even though some may not like it.

Whatever happened to driving an affordable, reliable car? Whatever happened to buying a two- or three-year-old car that has already taken the biggest drop in depreciation, really taking care of it, and driving it until it no longer works?

These are wisdom principles we can follow to help us live below our means. Joseph understood these principles, and he utilized them as he saved during the years of plenty!

If you make enough money to drive expensive cars and live in an expensive home, that's fine. But if you don't make that kind of income, don't buy expensive vehicles and live in an expensive home. Don't live above your means!

As long as I am giving examples of living above your means, let me share something I see all too often, and I admit that it concerns me. I see people spending five dollars for a cup of coffee—and they have two cups of that pricey coffee every day! Five dollars may not seem like a lot once, but people don't realize how much the little things add up. Now if you are living on 60 to 70 percent of your income and still have enough extra money to do that, then go ahead and spend ten dollars a day on coffee. But if you're living on credit card debt, it's absolutely foolish to spend five dollars on a cup of coffee. I don't care how many of your friends are at that trendy coffee shop! If your budget does not make room for it on a regular basis, then order water or stop going.

People have been a bit shocked and appalled that I would suggest such a sacrifice, but sometimes it's the smaller things that can really make a difference. That's how you live below your means and save to invest in your future.

Joseph understood the principles of budgeting and saving for the future. And because Joseph was such a wise manager of material things, God placed him in charge of the food supply for millions of people. Being faithful in the area of money was essential for Joseph to step into his destiny, and it's equally essential for you.

Jesus said if we are faithful in that which is least, He will set us over much (see Luke 16:10). If we cannot faithfully manage the finances God has blessed us with, how can we expect to manage the destiny He has promised us?

Luke 16:11 is very clear: "Therefore if you have not been faithful in the unrighteous mammon, who will commit to your trust the true riches?" This really sums up the Prosperity Test. Our destinies are all about handling the true riches of the kingdom. It seems like Jesus is saying, "If you can't handle money, how will you be able to handle your spiritual destiny?"

It's possible you may be feeling convicted after reading this. I know many people have been living above their means for years, and it has become a lifestyle. If so, I want to ask you to allow the Holy Spirit to work in your heart. Allow the principles you have just read to change your thinking about finances and change the way you're living.

This message can change your life if you take it to heart and decide to do something about it. If you make the decision today to live below your means, even if you have to downsize for a season, you will be so grateful ten years from now.

I love people, and my heart is burdened when I see the financial difficulties many of God's people are living with, especially the younger generation. It breaks my heart when I see the places they're living, the vehicles they're driving, and the clothes they're wearing because I know most of them are doing it entirely on debt. They are digging a hole for themselves that may take years to escape.

I'm not trying to condemn anyone with this teaching, but I do pray that the conviction of the Holy Spirit will help those in that situation to repent. I pray they will change their way of living and change their minds about the way they're managing their money because it's so important to their destinies in God.

Each of us has a spiritual destiny God has planned for our lives. But there are those who will not reach their destinies if they do not get their finances under control. Again, this may seem like a harsh statement, but it's true. Debt and financial pressure can keep believers in bondage and hold them back from doing the things God has called them to do. Some people have already missed opportunities to do great things for the kingdom of God because of poor financial decisions. Some have even missed opportunities to have the desires of their heart answered because poor financial management has hindered their path.

But God never intended for us to miss out on realizing our God-given dreams, and God will give us everything we need to fulfill the destiny to which He has called us. The question is, *What will we do with the things He has given us?*

Let God be first in your finances. Honor Him with the firstfruits of all your increase. Make a budget, live below your means, and learn to wait for the good things God has promised. When you have been found faithful in handling money, you will pass the Prosperity Test. Then God will be able to promote you, just as He did Joseph, and use you as a channel to distribute His wealth and resources to a hurting and destitute world.

And reaching a hurting world is the first thing on God's mind when He is dreaming about your destiny. So walk in it!

CHAPTER NINE

The Pardon Test

What would it be like to narrowly escape being murdered by
your own brothers—only to have them sell you as a slave into
a lifetime of bondage and degradation? As Joseph trudged through
the desert to Egypt, hot sand probably stung his eyes, ropes cut into
his tender skin, and the cruelty of the traders who had bought him
must have seemed small compared to the cruelty and betrayal he had
experienced at the hands of his own brothers.

What was going through Joseph's mind as he made that long
and painful journey to Egypt? As he stood on an auction block
and was sold to the highest bidder? As he served in the house of
Potiphar as a slave? As he became a husband and a father but could
not share his joy with his father, all because of his brothers' sin and
hatred?

Did Joseph have valid reasons to feel betrayed and abused? Most certainly, yes! What had been done to him was not an accident or some sort of misunderstanding. It was treachery.

The Pardon Test: Forgiving Wrongs

The suffering Joseph endured came about because of the deliberate cruelty and malice of others, so Joseph most certainly had reason to be hurt, angry, and hungry for justice. He could have spent all those years consumed by bitterness. He could have spent endless nights going over and over in his mind the horror of what had been done to him. Yet he didn't do that. Instead, *Joseph made the decision to forgive.*

How do we know? The answer is quite simple. We know he chose to forgive his brothers because we're told "the LORD was with Joseph," and he prospered in everything he did (Genesis 39:2-3). If Joseph had been walking in unforgiveness, the blessing and presence of God would not have been with him, and that would have kept him from stepping into the destiny God had prepared for him all along.

This is the Pardon Test, and every one of us will have to face this test and pass it. Just like Joseph, every one of us will have to deal with hurtful relationships and wrong or even malicious behavior. It can be easy to forgive when the offense is something minor, but what about when it's major? Like being sold into slavery by your brothers? Yet Joseph passed the Pardon Test with flying colors.

We're going to jump ahead in the story to after Joseph's family joins him in Egypt and after his father passes away because I want you to see the moment when Joseph shares his decision to forgive his brothers. Let's read about it.

When Joseph's brothers saw that their father was dead, they said, "Perhaps Joseph will hate us, and may actually repay us for all the evil which we did to him." So they sent messengers to Joseph, saying, "Before your father died he commanded, saying, 'Thus you shall say to Joseph: "I beg you, please forgive the trespass of your brothers and their sin; for they did evil to you."'" Now, please, forgive the trespass of the servants of the God of your father." And Joseph wept when they spoke to him.

Then his brothers also went and fell down before his face, and they said, "Behold, we are your servants."

Joseph said to them, "Do not be afraid, for am I in the place of God? But as for you, you meant evil against me; but God meant it for good, in order to bring it about as it is this day, to save many people alive. Now therefore, do not be afraid; I will provide for you and your little ones." And he comforted them and spoke kindly to them. (Genesis 50:15–21)

This passage is the very first time the word "forgive" is used in the Bible. This word in Hebrew means to "absolve fully" or "release from punishment." Most of the time it's not translated "forgive" but rather "bear up" or "lift up.¹"

I find this so interesting because it's exactly what the Lord Jesus Christ did with all our sins. He *bore* them. He *lifted them off* us. When He forgave us of our sins, He took the burden of sin from us and put it on Himself (see Isaiah 53:6–12). That's what the word "forgive" really means. It means to take a burden off someone completely and totally and *release* that person. It does not mean to take only part of it off or just help them carry it. It means to lift it off entirely.

The message Joseph's brothers claimed to be bringing from their father asked Joseph to do just that. Their message begged Joseph to *lift off* the sin they had done against him. Their message asked Joseph to forgive them completely—in other words, to absolve them of guilt and pardon them.

I really like the word "pardon" because when you pardon someone, you're not holding anything they have done against them anymore. And that's the way God forgives us. He has fully forgiven us, and He is not holding our sins against us anymore!

Now think about this: *Is that the way you're forgiving other people?* Are you releasing them, absolving them, and pardoning them fully and freely, as God does? That is true forgiveness. In order to step into your destiny, you must forgive *the same way God has forgiven you.* I know I've said this about every test, but until you do this, you will never fulfill your destiny!

A popular analogy compares holding unforgiveness in your heart to drinking poison and hoping it will hurt the other person. But the reality is that *you* are the only one who will get hurt! Unforgiveness causes you to live in torment.

Jesus describes this for us in Matthew chapter 18, where He tells the story of the servant who refused to forgive his fellow servant. This is one of the most profound teachings on forgiveness in the Bible, and I encourage you to read the entire passage. Jesus says the master of the unforgiving servant "delivered him to the torturers until he should pay all that was due" (Matthew 18:34). What Jesus is sharing through this parable is that when you refuse to forgive, you will be tortured and tormented. Until you release that person, *you* will be in bondage, not them.

When we hold unforgiveness in our hearts, it hurts us. But it also hinders us from moving forward into our destiny. Now, I realize we live in a fallen world, and we may have a million reasons not to forgive others. But if we are going to step into the things God has planned for our lives, we must deal with unforgiveness and leave it behind. We must learn to forgive as God has forgiven us.

Keys to Forgiveness: Release, Receive, and Believe

I believe the Holy Spirit has shown me some keys about walking in God's forgiveness. In order to forgive as God has forgiven us, we must learn to release, receive, and believe.

Release

To forgive others completely is to release them in your heart from all charges against them. Even though what they have done is wrong, they are acquitted. They are no longer held guilty for the things they have done. True forgiveness does not continue to look for justice or vindication. True forgiveness releases the wrongdoers from the punishment they deserve.

Remember, this is the way God forgives us! Every one of us has sinned against God and deserved eternal separation from Him as a result. But God placed our sins on Jesus, and Jesus took the punishment for our sins. God, in turn, *released us* from the punishment we deserved. He is no longer holding our sins against us. That is how He expects us to forgive one another. When we forgive as God forgives, we *release* the person fully.

Joseph made the choice to *release* his brothers and forgive them completely for everything they had done to him. He had to choose to go on with God or be consumed with bitterness for the rest of his life. Joseph chose to move forward with the blessing of God, and

I believe he did this long before he had this conversation with his brothers.

Let's stop for a moment and do some math. Joseph was seventeen when his brothers betrayed him. He was thirty when he stepped into his destiny. Then, there were seven years of prosperity and seven years of famine. He met his brothers again about two years into the famine, so he was thirty-nine years old. His father, Jacob, died twenty years later, so Joseph was fifty-nine years old at the time of this conversation with his brothers in Genesis 50. Joseph had almost a whole lifetime of years to forgive and move on. I believe he truly did forgive them, because he had already accomplished much of his destiny by fifty-nine years old, and it was the only way he could have had such a great attitude during this encounter. The Bible even says that "he comforted them and spoke kindly to them" (Genesis 50:21)!

Now, let me point out something interesting about this story. After their father, Jacob, died, Joseph's brothers sent messengers to Joseph, saying,

> "Before your father died he commanded, saying, 'Thus you shall say to Joseph: "I beg you, please forgive the trespass of your brothers and their sin; for they did evil to you."' Now, please, forgive the trespass of the servants of the God of your father." And Joseph wept when they spoke to him. (Genesis 50:16–17)

I don't know if you've ever noticed this before, but the message Joseph's brothers sent to him was steeped in manipulation! As far as we know, Jacob never sent such a message to Joseph. The Bible does not say anything of the sort. In fact, it does not even state whether Jacob was ever told the full truth about what had happened to Joseph. What it does state quite clearly is that Joseph's brothers were afraid

Joseph would finally take vengeance on them after their father died. They said to each other, "Father is dead. Maybe Joseph is going to repay us now" (see Genesis 50:15).

I believe his brothers came together and made up this message. I imagine their conversation going something like this:

"Here's what we'll do: we'll try to get Joseph to believe that Father knew all about it, and that he still wanted Joseph to forgive us for what we did."

"That's good. But let's throw in the word 'commanded.' Don't say 'ask.' That's not strong enough."

"Oh, and don't say, 'Jacob commanded.' Say, '*Your father* commanded'—that will carry more weight."

"Great idea! And don't just say, 'Your brothers.' Let's say, 'The servants of the God of your father.' Let's get God in on this thing— you know how much Joseph wants to honor God in everything."

I'm sure they tried to get the wording exactly right. So for final emphasis, they said, "Before your father died he commanded" (Genesis 50:16). In other words, they wanted Joseph to believe this was the dying wish of his beloved father. Talk about manipulation!

Then their message said, "For they did evil to you" (Genesis 50:17). I think this was perhaps the most hurtful part of the entire message because there was never a "*we* did evil against you." There was never an apology! They had twenty years to repent, but as far as we know, Joseph's brothers never asked for his forgiveness. They never went to him and said, "*We* did wrong." They phrased it very indirectly, as though it was a message from their father, saying, "*They* did wrong." And instead of going to Joseph themselves, they sent messengers (see Genesis 50:16).

This is what I am trying to show you: Sometimes those who have wronged us will realize it and apologize. Sometimes they will repent and change. But what if they don't? What if they continue to lie and manipulate? What if they never admit they have been wrong? What if they never change their ways?

You see, it's one thing to forgive someone who has wronged you when that person admits it. It's easier when he or she comes to you in brokenness and humility and says, "I'm so sorry. I don't know why I said that. I was tired today, and I said something I didn't mean. Please forgive me."

When someone is truly repentant, it's easy to say, "Yes, I'll forgive you."

But what about the people who refuse to repent? What about the people who continue to sin against you—who lie and manipulate? Who walk in pride and won't admit they have done anything wrong? Will you forgive them? Can you forgive people even when they don't repent? That is the true test of forgiveness and the essence of the Pardon Test. We must forgive, even if those who have wronged us never realize what they've done or repent of it. We must *release* them and leave the situation in God's hands.

It's very important to understand this because if we refuse to forgive, we are putting ourselves in the place of God. But God is the only One who has the right to hold something against someone and the only One who has never wronged anyone. You and I are not the judge— God is the Judge!

Joseph understood this truth. It's why he told his brothers, "Do not be afraid, for am I in the place of God?" (Genesis 50:19). Joseph understood that only God had the right to judge his brothers' actions because *only God is truly just*. God has justified us by the blood of His Son, and He is the only One who is just enough to forgive sin.

The Bible says, "If we confess our sins, He is faithful and just to forgive us our sins and to cleanse us from all unrighteousness" (1 John 1:9). God is a just Judge. He has forgiven us of our sins, and when He cleansed us of our sins, we became sons and daughters of the Judge. As children of the Judge, we are commanded to forgive and to release.

Any time you hold unforgiveness against someone, you have set yourself up as judge and jury. You have made yourself the one who determines that person's guilt or punishment. When you do this, you are taking the place of God and leaving Him out of it.

But when you forgive someone, you release God to act in the situation, in your life, and in that other person's life. You let Him be the Judge He rightfully is. You release God to enact justice and healing on the scene—because He is the only One who can! As hard as you might try to bring justice to a situation, you will never be able to because you are not just! Not one of us is.

Vengeance may seem necessary and even epic or adventurous, but there's a reason why vigilantes in pop culture are typically portrayed as tortured and lonely souls. The truth is, until you forgive someone and release him or her, you cannot free yourself from torment. Forgiveness releases you from the bondage of trying to make a situation right.

There was a season in my life when I was having a hard time forgiving someone. Thoughts about it seemed to flood my mind, no matter where I was. As I was driving down the road, I would be going through an argument in my mind about why he was wrong and I was right. This didn't just happen once. I would go through this argument in my mind day after day.

Like many Christians, I knew how to play the game. I convinced myself I had forgiven this man. I would justify my thought patterns in this way: "Of course, I've forgiven him. But one day I will have to talk to him about this. I will need to help him understand the darkness he walks in." And I actually believed I had forgiven him!

One night I couldn't sleep. It was about two o'clock in the morning, and I had been replaying this obsession over and over in my mind. Have you ever been there? If you have, you know what I'm talking about. You just keep replaying that offense until you can't even go to sleep.

As I was lying in bed, replaying it over and over in my mind, suddenly the Lord broke in on my thoughts. (It's so wonderful when He does that!) He spoke very clearly in my heart and said, "Forgive him!" His tone almost sounded like He was tired of me obsessing over it.

"But I have forgiven him," I replied.

"No, you have not," the Lord said. "You are holding this against him. You continue to think about it, and you even talk to other people about it. You have not released him. You have not forgiven him the same way I have forgiven you because I am not still thinking about your sin. I am not going around talking to other people about it, either. Now, forgive him!"

"But, God," I said with absolute sincerity, "He was wrong."

"Of course he was wrong," the Lord said to me. "There's no need to forgive people when they are right!"

You don't need to forgive people for being right! I had never thought about it that way. When you have to forgive people, it's usually not because they have been baking cookies for you, is it? It's because they have been wrong!

God said to me again, "Yes, he was wrong. Now forgive him!"

"But, Lord," I said, "I wasn't wrong in this situation."

I wasn't quite prepared for the Lord's reply. "No, you weren't wrong," He said to me. "But how would you like for Me bring up some of the situations in which you *were* wrong? *How much time do you have?*"

Ouch! Then the Lord reminded me of a situation from my past. It was a situation in which I had been the one who was wrong, and it was not a pleasant remembrance. Then He said to me, "Was what he did to you worse than what you did in that situation?"

"No, Lord," I replied. "What I did was much worse than what he did to me."

"That's right," the Lord said. "And I forgave you, didn't I? *Now forgive him.*"

When God said that last "forgive him," I knew He wasn't just *encouraging* me to forgive. He was *telling* me to forgive! After all, He *is* Lord and Master. That means He can *command* us to do something, and we had better obey!

God told me, "Forgive him and release him."

So I forgave him and *released* him completely, and I prayed for him.

But I had to be careful not to pick up that offense again! The enemy is crafty, and he will tempt you to pick up what you released. Just because you have forgiven someone doesn't mean the enemy won't subtly try to remind you of that person or wrongful situation. He will try to get you to entertain the offense and play it out in your mind. Pretty soon you'll find yourself back in a place of unforgiveness, and you'll have to choose to forgive them again. It doesn't mean you didn't really forgive them the first time. It just means you have to do it again!

I realize with major injustices and offenses it may take time to forgive. There are times when we try to forgive to the best of our ability, but there is a healing process that needs to occur to fully and completely release someone. That process is worth it. Keep chipping away at your unforgiveness. Forgive again and again and again until it's gone.

Years ago, when I first met James Robison, he gave me a Bible, and inside it, he wrote two sentences that changed my life: "I have nothing to prove. I have Someone to please." I've never forgotten those words. The One I want to please is the Lord Jesus Christ, and I am not pleasing Him if I do not forgive! If you do not forgive, you will live your life searching for vindication. You will live your life always trying to *prove something* rather than trying to *please Someone*. That's a lonely and miserable way to live.

You will live your life always trying to *prove something* rather than trying to *please Someone*.

Joseph could have done that. He could have lived the rest of his life trying to vindicate himself and get justice for the terrible things that happened to him. When his brothers asked, Joseph could have withheld his forgiveness. He could have lashed out and made them grovel. He could have watched them squirm and said to himself, *Well, my brothers will have to honor me now.* But after a lifetime of testing, Joseph knew that pleasing God was the only answer. He forgave them and *released* the situation to God. He went on with his life and allowed God to vindicate him.

Let me show you some Scriptures that talk about releasing those who have wronged you.

> You shall not take vengeance, nor bear any grudge against the children of your people, but you shall love your neighbor as yourself: I am the LORD. (Leviticus 19:18)

Dear friends, never take revenge. Leave that to the righteous anger of God. For the Scriptures say,

"I will take revenge;
I will pay them back,"
says the LORD.

Instead,

"If your enemies are hungry, feed them.
If they are thirsty, give them something to drink.
In doing this, you will heap
burning coals of shame on their heads."
Don't let evil conquer you, but conquer evil by doing good.
(Romans 12:19–21 NLT)

Perhaps you are more familiar with this translation of Romans 12:19: "'Vengeance is Mine, I will repay,' says the Lord" (NKJV).

God says vengeance belongs strictly to Him, and He forbids us to take vengeance for wrongs done to us. We are supposed to leave that up to Him because He is the only One who can bring righteous judgment to any situation. That's why vengeance belongs to the Lord.

Receive

The Bible makes it very clear that there is a connection between our forgiveness of others and God's forgiveness of us. I'm sure most of you have prayed the Lord's Prayer at one time or another. Jesus taught us to pray this way: "And forgive us our debts, as we forgive our debtors. And do not lead us into temptation, but deliver us from the evil one. For Yours is the kingdom and the power and the glory forever. Amen" (Matthew 6:12–13).

Before we go further, I want to break down a few things from these verses you may not have noticed. Not only is Jesus saying something about forgiveness here, He is also highlighting a correlation between forgiveness and temptation. If you don't forgive, you will be led into temptation. Then Jesus prays for deliverance from the evil one. There's a connection here as well. If you don't forgive, you're in bondage.

When you pray this prayer, do you realize you're asking God to forgive you *in the same way you forgive other people?* (I'm sure you're thinking, *This would have been helpful information to have before I prayed this prayer!*)

In the verses immediately following the Lord's Prayer, Jesus explains, "For if you forgive men their trespasses, your heavenly Father will also forgive you. But if you do not forgive men their trespasses, neither will your Father forgive your trespasses" (Matthew 6:14–15). That is an amazing Scripture passage, but I have to admit I sometimes wish it were not in the Bible! Jesus Himself said if we do not forgive others, then He is not going to forgive us.

Now, I want to reiterate that God forgave all humanity of all sin with Jesus' death on the cross. The whole world has already been forgiven, and our salvation is not in the balance with this verse. I believe this passage is about walking in the freedom Jesus intends for us. As I've said, the word forgive means "release." And if we don't forgive, we are held in bondage in our minds, emotions, and attitudes. No one is holding us there except ourselves! This verse essentially says that Jesus will not release us from the bondage that comes with our unforgiveness unless we release others. Only *you* can make this choice. *You* have to choose to forgive and walk in the freedom Jesus bought for you. So we better forgive! And the way we forgive is in the same way we have been forgiven.

I believe the Lord showed me that one reason many people have a hard time *giving* forgiveness is because *they have never received it.* You can't *give* something to others that you don't *have* yourself. There's something inside us that just seems to have a hard time believing God has totally and completely forgiven us. And because we haven't *received* His forgiveness, it's difficult for us to *give* it to others.

Jesus said: "Freely you have received, freely give" (Matthew 10:8).

Do you realize the word "forgive" contains the word "give"? The only way you can *freely give* something is if you have *freely received* it. And until you *receive* His forgiveness fully and freely, you won't be able to *give* it fully and freely. We have to come to a place where we forgive the way God does.

If you believe you must somehow *earn* your forgiveness, you will make other people earn their forgiveness, too. If you believe that somehow you are *paying* for your forgiveness, you will make others pay for forgiveness also.

We fall into this trap all too often. Sometimes we live as though God Himself is keeping score, even though He gave us the best gift He had—His beloved Son—to set us free from the penalty of our sins! We pray as if God is getting back at us for all the stuff we've done wrong. We look at misfortunes in life as God's way of getting even.

If we're a little short in our bank account at the end of the month, we might think God is getting back at us for being late with our tithe. We might even say, "Oh, yes, thank You for getting back at me, Lord. Now we're square. That's good."

Or if we get a flat tire on the way to work, we might think God is getting back at us for neglecting our morning prayers. We might say, "Yes, thank You, God. I knew You were going to do this because I didn't have my quiet time this morning. I was supposed to have it, but

I got up late. Oh, and now it's starting to rain! That's really a good touch, God. I will really remember this lesson now! Thank You, Lord, for getting back at me. *Now we're even.*"

Can I tell you something very important? *God will never get back at you.* He is never going to get even with you or punish you or make you pay for the wrongs you have done. Why? Because Jesus already paid your penalty in full! Isaiah 53:10 says, "It pleased the LORD to bruise Him." How could it have pleased God to bruise His own Son? It pleased Him because all our sin was atoned for, and He could once again have a relationship with us. That is the goodness of God. That is the forgiveness of God. But for some of us, it seems too good to be true. We have to learn to *receive* it.

This reminds me of an incident that happened about thirty-five years ago when Debbie and I lived in a very small house. (We had a tiny house before tiny houses were popular!) Our tiny house had a tiny bathroom. It was so small that you could wash your hands while sitting on the toilet! Any time we were getting ready to go somewhere, we had to do a bit of strategic maneuvering around each other. We were getting ready for church one morning, and Debbie was standing at the bathroom sink putting some moisturizer on her face. She was still barefoot and wearing her bathrobe, but I was already dressed for church, complete with hard-soled dress shoes. I went into the bathroom to brush my teeth, and as I reached for something, the full weight of my body came down on her little toe!

She screamed! But at first her screams had no sound to them. She was in too much pain to make any real noise!

"I'm sorry, I'm sorry, I'm sorry!" I exclaimed over and over.

"It's okay. It's okay," Debbie said, as she hobbled toward the bed to sit down.

"I'm sorry, I'm sorry, I'm sorry!" I frantically repeated.

"I know," she said. "I know. It's okay—it was an accident."

I continued to apologize, "No, no! I'm sorry, I'm sorry, I'm sorry!"

I kept saying it over and over again, and I think it was making her agony worse. She was probably thinking, *Just leave me alone and go away!* But she said to me, "Really, it's okay! I forgive you."

I kept saying, "No, no. I feel so bad! I feel so bad!"

And she kept saying to me, "It's okay."

Finally, I said to her, "No, it is not okay. I want you to hit me!"

"What?!" she said. "I don't want to hit you!"

"You don't understand," I said. "I feel bad, and I will feel better if you just hit me!"

The problem was not that Debbie was not *giving* forgiveness. The problem was that I wasn't *receiving* forgiveness. I wanted somehow to even the score between us!

Sadly, there are a lot of Christians who have a "hit me" mentality. They have not received the forgiveness God has freely provided for them, so they want God to "hit" them. They think if God punishes them, it will make them feel better about the wrong they have done! This is the essence and origin of doing penance.

John 1:12 sets us straight on this point: "But as many as *received* Him, to them He gave the right to become children of God, to those who believe in His name" (emphasis added). The book of Hebrews says God *disciplines* His children, but that word is not *punish*. He corrects behavior because He loves us, but He does not punish us.

I want to just say it again: God will never punish you. Jesus already took your punishment when He bore your sins—completely and totally. His blood paid the price for every sin you have ever committed or will ever commit so you would not have to pay the price of forgiveness. *But you have to receive His forgiveness.*

If you have a problem *giving* forgiveness, it's probably because you have a problem *receiving* forgiveness. But you must forgive others in the same way God has forgiven you. Until you receive the forgiveness God has freely given, you won't be able to give it to others.

Until you receive the forgiveness God has freely given, you won't be able to give it to others.

And if you have a problem *receiving* God's forgiveness, it could be because you have a problem *believing* it.

Believe

Perhaps you have a hard time believing God could forgive you completely and totally release you from the penalty of sin. After all, the Bible tells us God is holy and pure. It says He is so pure that He cannot even look upon evil. Habakkuk 1:13 says, "You are of purer eyes than to behold evil, and cannot look on wickedness." God cannot even look at wickedness and sin! That is how pure His eyes are. Yet every one of us has messed up and missed the mark.

Isaiah 53:6 says, "All we like sheep have gone astray; we have turned, every one, to his own way." All of us have gone astray. All of us have transgressed God's commands. All of us have sinned and done things God could not even put His eyes upon.

But Job 36:7 says, "He does not withdraw His eyes from the righteous." And 1 Peter 3:12 says, "For the eyes of the LORD are on the righteous, and His ears are open to their prayers; but the face of the LORD is against those who do evil." According to Scripture, God cannot even look on our sin, but His eyes are on the righteous every day. How does that work? You might be thinking, *I'm definitely not righteous, but I sure wish God's eyes were upon me every day!*

How can a God who is pure, just, and holy accept us when we have fallen so far short of His perfection? The truth is, God wanted to be in relationship with us, so He had to do something about our sin. And He did! All the sins of the world—past, present, and future—were placed on Christ on the cross. Second Corinthians 5:21 tells us: "For He made Him who knew no sin to be sin for us, that we might become the righteousness of God in Him." Listen to me: we were all born sinful. But Jesus, who was perfect, became sin for us. He lifted it off us and bore it Himself. Romans 6:14 says, "For sin shall not have dominion over you." When Jesus died on the cross, sin was destroyed! Jesus destroyed it!

I want to clear up a common misunderstanding about sin. Did you know that no one goes to hell because of sin? People don't go to hell for their sin—they go to hell for *unbelief.* They're separated from God because they won't believe. Everyone's sin has already been absolved. It's *belief* that makes the difference. Jesus said in John 6:47, "Most assuredly, I say to you, he who believes in Me has everlasting life." And John the Baptist said, "He who believes in the Son has everlasting life; and he who does not believe the Son shall not see life" (John 3:36). Please settle this in your heart today: if you believe in Jesus, your sins are forgiven!

Jesus made that exchange so we could be *made righteous*, just like He is; so *we* could be made the *righteousness of God Himself!* And all of this is done "in Him"—in Christ Jesus! When we receive the forgiveness Jesus paid for on the cross, we are *made righteous*.

And something miraculous happens. Psalm 103:12 tells us, "As far as the east is from the west, so far has He removed our transgressions from us." God cannot look at our transgressions, *so He removed them*! He scattered them so far away that He cannot see them anymore! All my sin has been laid on Jesus and removed from me. Now God can look at me. Now He can talk with me. Now He can walk with me all day long.

I can have a relationship with God, and it's not because I did something good or somehow earned it. The only reason I can have a relationship with God and stand before Him without guilt, sin, or shame is because God laid all my iniquity on His Son, Jesus Christ. When God looks at me now, He sees me washed in the blood of Jesus, and that blood makes me pure and holy in His sight. His eyes are upon me every day because He has made me righteous through the blood atonement of Jesus Christ. In God's eyes, I am perfect.

This is what you must believe: You *are* righteous! His eyes *are* upon you! God has *removed your sin*. You can have a relationship with Him now. He wants to walk with you, speak to you, and show you great things every day.

Why am I telling you this over and over again? Because I want you to understand that you are forgiven. You have been completely pardoned by the sacrifice of Jesus Christ! *And because you have been pardoned, you can now pardon others.* Because you've been forgiven, you can now forgive!

It doesn't matter what anyone else has done to you. Is it worse than all the bad things you've ever done in your whole life? And even if it is, we can't compare our bad deeds with other people's. We can only compare our deeds to Jesus' perfection, and compared to His perfection, our bad deeds are all despicable.

Think of all the wrong you have ever done—God has forgiven all of it! You have been forgiven. Now you need to share that forgiveness!

I want to tell you a wonderful story of forgiveness. This is the true story of a young Jewish man named Yakov and a young Jewish girl named Rachel. They lived in Europe during the time of the Holocaust. Yakov was in his early twenties, and Rachel was a teenager, but Rachel had already caught Yakov's eye. He was falling in love with her.

But times were terrible for the Jews and getting worse by the day. One night, Rachel's parents gathered a group of young people around them and said, "We believe the Nazis are planning to kill us, and no one is going to make it out of here alive. We want you to try to escape." Then they took all the money they had and sewed it into Rachel's coat. "Maybe this will help to keep you alive," they told her. "It will be of no use here."

So that night Rachel and her sister, along with Yakov and about twenty other young people, tried to escape from the Nazis. In the escape attempt, Rachel's sister was shot, and Rachel ran back to help her. But it was too late—Rachel's sister died in her arms. Then Rachel was shot in both legs, and it seemed she too was going to die. But two boys grabbed her by the arms and dragged her into the woods to safety.

What were they to do with Rachel? She needed medical care, or she would die. They were desperate, so they took her to the house of a German family. "Please help her," they said. "Look, she has money, and you can have all of it if you will take care of her." So the German family took Rachel into their home. They treated her wounds and told everyone that she was one of their own children. Rachel lived with that family and survived the war.

Things were more difficult for Yakov. He and about fifteen other young men lived in the forest for over a year. They dug a large pit in the ground and covered it up to conceal themselves. They would sneak into town at night and forage for food, then go back to the forest and hide during the day.

After about a year, someone found out about their hiding place. Nazi soldiers soon came to the pit where they were hiding, apprehended the young men, and sent them to a prison camp.

When they arrived at the prison camp, the German commandant came out of his office and looked at his young prisoners.

"Are any of you boys a tailor?" he asked.

"I am a tailor, sir," said Yakov.

"You step over here, then," the commandant ordered. And then he had the other young men stand in a line.

Immediately Yakov realized they were going to shoot all of his friends. So he shouted out, "I must have an assistant! I can't sew clothes without an assistant!"

"All right," the commandant said. "Then I will let you pick one— only one though. You choose."

Yakov had lived with all those young men for over a year as they struggled to survive in the forest. Among them were two brothers who were Yakov's best friends. In a split second, Yakov had to choose which one lived and which one died. He chose one of the two brothers, and the boy came over to where Yakov was standing. Then the two watched as Nazis shot the brother and the rest of their friends.

Yakov's ability to sew saved his life, and he made it through the rest of the war by sewing uniforms for the German soldiers at the camp.

Toward the end of the war, the Russian army was getting closer and closer to the camp, and the Nazi guards were afraid of being captured by the Russians. The Nazis made plans to escape on horses, so they gave orders to Yakov and his friend to go and get their horses saddled for them. But Yakov said, "They're going to kill us before the Russians get here, so we have to leave." As soon as those horses were saddled, the boys jumped on the horses and rode as fast as they could toward the Russian lines. Sure enough, the Nazis killed all the Jews in the camp and left before the Russians arrived. But Yakov and his friend safely escaped and ended up surviving the war.

Soon, the years of unspeakable horror had passed, but Yakov had not forgotten about Rachel. He went looking for her after the war. When he found her, they got married and became Mr. and Mrs. Yakov Waldman. They had a son and named him Marty. Years later, Marty became a rabbi, and now he leads a large congregation of Messianic Jews. It's my privilege to call him my friend.

When Marty was growing up, it used to bother him that he didn't have any relatives. People would ask, "Are you related to these Waldmans or those Waldmans?" Marty dreaded that question because he always had to say, "No, I'm not related to anyone." All his grandparents, uncles, and aunts had been killed in the Holocaust. Only one of his parents' sisters had survived.

Several years ago, Marty went to the death camp at Auschwitz to see where his family had died. The man who accompanied him on the trip was also a believer and the grandson of a Nazi prison guard. These two men stood in Auschwitz—the grandson of a Jewish Holocaust victim and the grandson of a Nazi prison guard—and they hugged and prayed for the German and Jewish people.

How could that happen? How could those two men do that? I asked Marty those questions, and he just smiled at me and said, "Jesus forgave me." The only way these two men were able to stand together on ground so tainted with wickedness is because they had first received God's forgiveness. It's the only way they could give His forgiveness freely to others.

Like Marty and his friend, God has sorrow because of our sins, but He does not hold them against us. Through Jesus, He has provided forgiveness for every sin we have ever committed or will ever commit. And when we receive His forgiveness, we are able to give it to others, no matter how traumatic and awful the situation may be. We can forgive others as He has forgiven us.

Perhaps you are hurting because unjust things happened to you or your family. Joseph knew what that felt like. Why allow that hurt to live on? God has made a way through Jesus for *every* wrong to be forgiven. He has already paid the price for every sin. And now, in His grace, He is asking, "Will you forgive the same way I have forgiven you? Will you release that person fully and freely? Will you let it go?"

When you hold on to unforgiveness, you are only hurting yourself. But when you forgive, you will be gloriously free! You will be free of torment, free of judgment, and free to move forward into the destiny God has planned for your life.

CHAPTER TEN

The Purpose Test

Twenty-two years had passed since Joseph was sold into Egypt. He had spent thirteen years working as a slave, and part of that time included being imprisoned in a dungeon as punishment for a crime he did not commit. Now, at thirty-nine years of age, Joseph had been the administrator of Egypt for nine years. He had seen the country through seven years of plenty, and now he was helping Egypt thrive during the early years of the famine. And Joseph was about to receive a surprise.

Suddenly, after more than two decades, his brothers—the very ones who had betrayed him and caused him so much suffering—were right in front of him. They were bowing down before him, "with their faces to the earth" (Genesis 42:6), just as his dreams had symbolically depicted so many years before! The Bible tells us what Joseph was thinking at that moment: "Then Joseph remembered the dreams which he had dreamed about them" (Genesis 42:9).

In other words, Joseph had a sudden realization. He realized what God had shown him in those dreams so many years before had been part of His plan all along. Joseph finally understood the *purpose* behind his dreams. What could have been a moment of supreme triumph, grief, or even revenge, instead became a moment of revelation.

> Then Joseph said to his brothers, "I am Joseph; does my father still live?" But his brothers could not answer him, for they were dismayed in his presence. And Joseph said to his brothers, "Please come near to me." So they came near. Then he said: "I am Joseph your brother, whom you sold into Egypt. But now, do not therefore be grieved or angry with yourselves because you sold me here; for God sent me before you to preserve life. For these two years the famine has been in the land, and there are still five years in which there will be neither plowing nor harvesting. And God sent me before you to preserve a posterity for you in the earth, and to save your lives by a great deliverance. So now it was not you who sent me here, but God; and He has made me a father to Pharaoh, and lord of all his house, and a ruler throughout all the land of Egypt." (Genesis 45:3–8)

The Purpose Test: Understanding Your Destiny

When you read these verses, you see that Joseph finally understood his purpose. He not only understood the dreams God had given him but also the *purpose* those dreams had foreshadowed. Joseph realized he had finally stepped into the destiny for which God had created him.

In essence, Joseph was telling his brothers, "You don't seem to understand. It was God who sent me here. So I don't want you to be angry with yourselves. I don't want you to be upset or grieved or sad. I want you to forgive yourselves just as I have forgiven you. God had a *purpose* for my life, and it was to fulfill *His purpose* that He sent me here to Egypt!"

Joseph had been through many difficult experiences during those years, but at last he was able to clearly see the vision, the purpose, and the destiny God had planned for his life.

Joseph had passed the Purpose Test.

Every one of us will take this test because every one of us has a God-ordained purpose. Is it possible to understand your purpose and live it to the fullest? Absolutely—Joseph did!

So how do you find your purpose? That's the number one question deep down in every person's heart. And there are keys that can help you discover and fulfill God's purpose for your life.

Believe You Have a Purpose

In 1952, Campus Crusade for Christ founder Dr. Bill Bright created an evangelistic booklet called "Have You Heard of the Four Spiritual Laws?" This booklet has been used for decades to introduce the plan of salvation to unbelievers by explaining the four spiritual laws that govern our relationship with God. The first spiritual law is this: "God loves you and has a wonderful plan for your life." This law is essential for believers to know and understand.

In order to discover the purpose God has for your life, you must first *believe* you have one! We know God has an eternal purpose for everything, and the body of Christ has an overall purpose in God's eternal plan. But it's important to know that you, as an individual, have a *specific purpose* as well, and you simply must *accept* it by faith. As I've said throughout this book, God has a unique destiny for you, and you are the only one who can fulfill it.

God has a unique destiny for you, and you are the only one who can fulfill it.

God is a *"purpose-full"* God. He is not a "purpose-less" God! Everything He created has a purpose. Ecclesiastes 3:1 says, "To everything there is a season, a time for every purpose under heaven." Every animal, every plant, every tree, and every person—including you!—has been created for a time and a purpose. (I'm not sure what purpose mosquitoes have, but everything else has one, so they must have one too!)

The Bible says God formed you in your mother's womb, and when He formed you, He had a purpose in mind. The psalmist says of God,

For You formed my inward parts;
You covered me in my mother's womb. . . .
My frame was not hidden from You,
When I was made in secret,
And skillfully wrought in the lowest parts of the earth.
Your eyes saw my substance, being yet unformed.
And in Your book they all were written,
The days fashioned for me,
When as yet there were none of them. (Psalm 139:13, 15–16)

This passage tells us that God's purpose for you was written in His book before you were even born! Yes, before God created you, He had a plan and purpose for your life to help other people. He wants you to discover what that purpose is and fulfill it to its wonderful fullest.

Do you realize you have the intellect, ability, talent, and gifting to do something special for God? He designed you for a specific role, and you will never be truly happy until you discover what it is. And once you discover your purpose and begin fulfilling it, your life will take on new energy and excitement.

An example that comes to mind from my own life involves the gift of preaching. I have a purpose for my life, and part of that purpose involves sharing God's Word with others. So preaching is a gift I have, and I enjoy it! I get pumped up when I speak. I am more energized when I preach than when I do anything else!

Years ago, I discovered what a difference a sense of purpose can make. Our children were small at the time, and at the church we were attending, parents with children were required to work in the nursery once a month. Now I might be gifted to preach, but I am definitely not gifted to work in the nursery! Every time I worked in the nursery, I had to have a nap when I got home. It didn't energize me at all! On the contrary, I was totally and completely worn out by it. I remember dreading it every time my week came around.

Oh, no, I would think to myself. *In two more weeks, it will be my week to work in the nursery again.* Then I prayed, "Oh, God, would You please help me to get through this?"

After a lot of grumbling—I mean, praying—the Lord finally said to me, "What are you gifted to do?"

"I'm gifted to preach!" I said.

"Then preach!" the Lord replied.

So I decided to take the Lord's advice. The next week I went into the nursery ready to preach! I said to those little babies, "Open your

Bibles to Isaiah. I'm going to share with you some truths from God's Word." Then I preached to those little babies. They just took it all in, as babies do, but when I left the nursery that day, I was jazzed! Instead of being worn out, I was energized.

Here's my point: When God created you, He had a specific purpose in mind, and He has given you a specific gifting related to your purpose. You need to find out what your gifting is because when you discover the gifting God created in you, it will bring energy and excitement to your life. More importantly, it will help other people. And as you begin to move in your gifting, you will begin to understand your purpose.

If you're not sure what your purpose is, just look at the way you have been created. If you look at the way something is made, it helps you to understand the purpose of it. Even examining the design of inanimate objects will give you clues to their purpose.

Let me use an extremely mundane example—a toilet plunger. If you had never seen a toilet plunger before, then you could initially imagine all sorts of purposes for it. You might speculate that it could be used as a ring-toss game, a birdbath for hummingbirds, a cookie cutter (not sure who would want those cookies!), or maybe even a bizarre hat for bald people. But none of these ideas really makes much sense. When you look carefully at the way a toilet plunger is made, it soon becomes obvious that it was created with a very specific purpose in mind. (I won't elaborate further.)

In the same way, God, the great Designer, created you for a specific purpose. I was the class clown and the kid who wouldn't stop talking in school. And look what I do now! God designed me with a gift of speaking and humor and He has me using it to help other people. You, too, have a unique design. If you could see what you look like "in the spirit," it would help you to better understand your purpose.

For example, if you were designed to help with freedom ministry (or as some call it, deliverance ministry), then "in the spirit" you probably look a lot like the plunger I was just describing. (That gives you an idea of what I think of demons, doesn't it?)

In all seriousness, God has a unique purpose for your life, and it's vitally important for you to believe it—to *believe* He created you with a specific purpose in mind. I encourage you to make every effort to discover what your purpose is. As you move toward discovering His purpose for your life, you will also be moving toward your destiny.

Understand God Is in Control

Have you ever heard the story about the pessimistic parachutist? The sergeant was giving him instructions as the plane was climbing to ten thousand feet. "After you jump out of the plane," the sergeant said, "You're going to take your right hand and put it on your left shoulder, pull the rip cord, and your parachute will open. If for some reason it doesn't open, pull the emergency cord on your right shoulder and your emergency chute will open. You will land in a field about ten miles north of town, and there will be some trucks waiting there to pick you up."

When it was time for the pessimistic parachutist to jump out of the plane, he went for it! He pulled the rip cord on his left shoulder, but it didn't open.

"I knew it!" he said.

So he pulled the emergency chute on his right shoulder, but that wouldn't open either.

"I knew it!" he said again.

The last thing everyone heard him scream as he fell without an open chute was, "I bet the trucks will be late too!"

Obviously, this is a joke. But the truth is, many of you are living your lives expecting the worst out of every situation.

We've already established that on the journey toward your destiny, you're going to experience difficulties. You're going to have setbacks, people are going to say or do things against you, and the chaos of life is going to happen.

But here's what I want you to know: God is in control.

If you don't believe God is in control, you will live in a sad, anxious, and bewildering world—a world with little purpose. When you can't see the hand of God working, you will eventually reach a point where you only see the bad in everything and always expect the worst to happen. The world is rampant with pessimists. (If you don't know whether you're an optimist or a pessimist, just ask your spouse or your best friend. He or she will know!) The problem is that pessimists often lose sight of their purpose. Don't let this happen to you.

If you truly believe God is in control, it will serve as an anchor for understanding your purpose. You will begin to see the good in everything because God is good! And you can rest in the knowledge that He is working for good in every situation, no matter what the circumstances are. There is peace in knowing God is in control.

God is good! And you can rest in the knowledge that He is working for good in every situation, no matter what the circumstances are.

Joseph had this attitude about the things that happened in his life. His brothers were dismayed in his presence because of all the evil they had done to him (Genesis 45:3). But Joseph was not dismayed. He explained it to his brothers this way:

> But now, do not therefore be grieved or angry with yourselves because you sold me here; for *God sent me* before you to preserve life.... And *God sent me* before you to preserve a posterity for you in the earth, and to save your lives by a great deliverance. So now *it was not you who sent me here, but God*; and He has made me a father to Pharaoh, and lord of all his house, and a ruler throughout all the land of Egypt. (Genesis 45:5, 7–8, emphasis added)

Joseph told his brothers *three times* that God sent him to Egypt, not them. Joseph understood God was ultimately in charge of his destiny. That's why he was able to believe God was working, even in circumstances that were terribly wrong and unjust. Although his brothers' actions were wrong and caused him to suffer, Joseph could see the hand of God in his situation. He was able to see that God had a purpose for sending him to Egypt and that He had been working out His purpose all along.

We, too, must come to trust God as Joseph did. We need to stop thinking we're not going to fulfill our destiny because of something someone else did. I'm telling you—whether it was your parents or an abusive pastor or a boss who wronged you—no one can stop God's destiny for you! We must understand that God can take even the wrongs done to us and use them for our good.

And He can do much more than that! God can also take our own mistakes and failures and turn them for our good. (As you know, we're often our own worst enemy.) I want you to know something very important: God is bigger than your mistakes and failures! And He's much bigger than your own thinking and reasoning.

God says, "For as the heavens are higher than the earth, so are My ways higher than your ways, and My thoughts than your thoughts" (Isaiah 55:9). Our thoughts will never be as expansive or great as God's thoughts. Because we are human, we sometimes overlook this truth. But we don't need to grieve over mistakes we have made. Our failures and shortcomings do not have the power to short-circuit the purposes of God.

Years ago, my son Josh had an opportunity to embrace God's providence in what he viewed as a failure on his part. When he moved to Amarillo, Texas, we went with him to help him find an apartment and get settled. We didn't know the area, so we just did the best we could to find an apartment for him to rent. After he'd lived there for a while and had gotten to know the area, he found some better places to live for less money. We were talking about his move when he came home for a visit.

"I wish I hadn't signed a twelve-month lease. I wish I had only signed a six-month lease," he said. "Then I could move into a better place right now, and it would cost less."

"Did you pray about it when you rented the place you're in right now?" I asked him.

"Yes," he replied.

"Then don't grieve over your decision. If you prayed about it and made the best decision you could at the time, then you need to trust God. You need to understand that God has a way to eventually turn your decision for your good. Who knows? In six months, you might find an even better place to live, for even less money. Or you could even be living in another city by that time. You don't know what God has planned! We don't know everything the future holds."

Less than a week after our conversation, he went to the apartment office to find out how to get out of his lease. He thought he had signed a twelve-month lease, but he learned he had actually signed a six-month lease and received the benefits of a twelve-month lease, which was one month of free rent. He was able to move into the better place for less money, and he learned the valuable lesson that God is in control, even when we think we've messed up and there's no way out!

When you have prayerfully made a decision and you're not sure whether it was the right one or the best one, don't get upset second-guessing yourself about it. Don't say, "Oh, that was probably a terrible decision. I shouldn't have done that"—as though one mistake will derail you from your destiny. Instead, trust God is in control. Say, "God, I believe You are working out Your purposes in my life. You can take this decision and turn it for my good. I know You are in control, so please show me what You are doing in this situation." Also, remember that if you fail one of these character tests, you can take it again and again until you pass it because God *wants* to take you to your destiny.

God is absolutely and totally in control. You must believe that, because if God is not in control, you need to find out who is and pray to him instead. Some Christians act as though they believe the devil is in control instead of God, but he definitely is not!

I don't know if you know this, but God and the devil are not in a fight with each other. We might be in a fight with the devil, but God is certainly not! He has already won the fight and defeated the devil.

God and the devil are nowhere close to being equal—they are not comparable in any way! Satan has no power compared to God's awesome might. God has all the power in the world (and out of the world). If we are serving God, we do not need to be afraid of Satan.

God is the One who has the power! We serve the God of all power, and He is in control of our lives, so even when we mess up, God can make everything ultimately work for our good. When we truly understand that, we won't grieve over mistakes we have made.

Romans 8:28 tells us, "And we know that all things work together for good to those who love God, to those who are the called according to His purpose." If we love God, He will work it out. This Scripture also says God has called us "according to *His* purpose" (emphasis added). God has a purpose for us! He has a *divine* purpose and eternal plan for all humanity, and each one of us is called to be part of His purpose collectively. God also has a *specific* purpose and plan for each one of us individually that is part of His larger plan and His larger purpose.

Within those eternal plans, God is working everything for our good! He is working in your life to bring about His plans and purposes. He is working in every situation you might face. And because He is in control, He can even turn bad decisions into good things for you when you are walking with Him.

Isaiah explains this mystery of God's providence:

For as the rain comes down, and the snow from heaven,
And do not return there,
But water the earth,
And make it bring forth and bud,
That it may give seed to the sower
And bread to the eater,
So shall My word be that goes forth from My mouth;
It shall not return to Me void,
But it shall accomplish what I please,
And it shall prosper in the thing for which I sent it. (Isaiah 55:10-11)

This Scripture passage is powerful! Why? Because God is saying that every time He speaks, His words will achieve His purpose. Every time! There will never be an occasion when God speaks that His words do not produce results. His words will never come back to Him empty— they will always achieve the purpose for which He sent them. This is amazing! When God speaks, His purposes will come to pass!

Why is this so exciting? Because *God has spoken over you!* God spoke His purpose over your life when He created you! And the words God has spoken over your life will not return to Him void. They will accomplish the thing He sent them to do.

So trust God. Trust that He is working for your good in every situation. Trust that He has spoken over your life and that His words will accomplish what He purposed for your destiny.

Discover Your Gift

An important aspect to understanding your purpose is discovering the gifts God has given you. Why would God call you to do something and not give you the gifts to do it? He has designed you with a purpose in mind, so the gifts He has given you will always be related to your purpose in some significant way. If you look at the gifts God has given you, they will tell you a lot about your purpose. Your gifts can help you understand your God-given destiny.

If you're not sure what your purpose is, ask yourself these questions: What has God gifted me to do? What am I good at doing? What excites me? What brings me joy? What makes me feel alive? When something energizes you and causes you to get excited, it's probably related in some way to your gift and purpose.

All too often we have incorrect ideas about the plans God has for us and the reasons God made us the way we are. Our thoughts might go something like this: *Well, this particular thing is what truly excites me. This is what I would really like to do with my life. But I suppose it isn't God's will. God probably wants me to do something dull or unpleasant.*

I don't know where we get this sort of thinking. Why would a good and loving God call you to do something you don't even like to do?

God is a good God! He wants you to have fun and enjoy life as you serve Him! Does the Bible say, "For God so loved the world that He gave His only begotten Son—*so He can ruin our lives*"? No, that's not what the Bible says! Jesus said, "I have come that they may have life, and they may have it more abundantly" (John 10:10). Jesus came to give us life that is *more abundant*. A more abundant life is one filled with more good things, not fewer!

God wants to give us good things. He wants us to enjoy the life His Son died to give us. That's why He designed us with gifts and desires suited to His purpose for us. When we use the gifts God has given us, our lives are more exciting and fulfilling.

When we use the gifts God has given us, our lives are more exciting and fulfilling.

That's why it's important for you to discover your giftings! Remember, the gifts God has given you will be something you enjoy doing.

While there are probably as many unique giftings as there are people God has created, the Bible describes three specific sets of gifts: manifestation gifts, ministry gifts, and motivational gifts.

There are nine manifestation gifts from the Holy Spirit: words of wisdom, words of knowledge, faith, healing, working of miracles, prophecy, discerning of spirit, tongues, and interpretation of tongues (see 1 Corinthians 12:7-10). The Bible says the "Spirit works all these things, distributing to each one individually as He wills" (1 Corinthians 12:11). We can all operate within one or more of these gifts at any time.

Similarly, there are five ministry gifts: apostles, prophets, evangelists, pastors, and teachers. These gifts are for the equipping of the saints for the work of the ministry (see Ephesians 4:11-13).

Then in Romans, Paul mentions seven giftings that are often described as motivational gifts—in other words, gifts that spring out of the deep motivations in our nature.

Paul encourages us to use our gifts "according to the grace that is given to us" (Romans 12:6). In other words, all these gifts come to us by the grace of God, so it's important for us to understand and use them according to God's design. We should learn as much as we can about the specific manifestation, ministry, and motivational gifts God has given us.

For a moment, I want to focus on the motivational gifts. Let's read about them:

> For as we have many members in one body, but all the members do not have the same function, so we, being many, are one body in Christ, and individually members of one another. Having then gifts differing according to the grace that is given to us, let us use them: if prophecy, let us prophesy in proportion to our faith; or ministry, let us use it in our ministering; he who teaches, in teaching; he who exhorts, in exhortation; he who gives, with liberality; he who leads, with diligence; he who shows mercy, with cheerfulness. (Romans 12:4-8)

Paul explains that just as our physical body has different parts with different functions, each of us has a different function in the body of Christ. None of the parts of the physical body has the same purpose; each part has a specific purpose that is an important part of the whole. In the same way, we as individuals each have a specific purpose that is an essential part of the body of Christ. If we don't find that purpose and do it, the body of Christ will be missing an important part!

What follows here is a brief overview of the seven motivational gifts. I have given titles to these gifts that may help us to better understand and remember them.

1. *Motivator ("Prophecy" [v. 6]).* A person with the gift of prophecy desires to motivate other people to serve God. This gift doesn't have as much to do with the ministry of the prophetic or the manifestation of prophecy as it does motivating others. Someone with this gift desires to reveal the motives of people and see conformity to God's will. Sometimes they tend to focus on "right" and "wrong" and the motives within people's hearts. (Sadly, when a person with this gift is immature, he or she may be too judgmental about the motives of others.) This is my primary gift. I want to motivate every person I meet to serve God, love God, and know God. That's what makes me tick!

2. *Servant ("Ministry" [v. 7]).* The Greek word for "ministry" in this verse actually means "attendance" as a servant or "service."[1] A person with this motivational gift desires to meet the needs of people on a practical basis. When you go out to eat at a restaurant, a person with this gift will start to clean the table off after you have finished eating. Although the waiter might be standing right there, a person with a "servant" gift just can't resist pulling

the dishes together and wiping the crumbs off the table. People with the gift of serving will be motivated to serve others wherever they go.

3. *Teacher (v. 7)*. A teacher is a person who loves to study and present truths to people. These are people who like to read more than one book at once and have great researching skills. They also send me emails with questions such as, "Pastor Robert, I know that you're busy, but will you please answer one question for me? *Could you please explain the book of Revelation?*" People with a teaching gift just can't seem to get enough of studying God's Word! (By the way, I don't want to get any more of those emails, all right? I can't explain the whole book of Revelation to you when I'm still trying to understand it myself!)

4. *Encourager (or "Exhorter" [v. 8])*. Those with the gift of exhortation just love to exhort and encourage people. We all know people with this gift. No matter what you say, they will try to encourage you. If you say, "I just lost my job," an exhorter will say, "I'm so sorry to hear that. Let's pray and believe that God has something even better for you in the days to come." If you say, "I'd really like to lose some weight," an exhorter will say, "I believe in you and know you can do it!" They have a way of always making you feel good.

5. *Giver (v. 8)*. A giver is a person who desires to meet the material needs of others. Those who have this motivational gift absolutely love to give. They are thrilled when they have the opportunity to meet a financial need, but they also want to provide wisdom and counsel to help people steward their finances and belongings well. I have a good friend who is very successful financially,

and his wife has the gift of giving. I joked with him, "That's why God has blessed you financially—so your wife can give all your money away!"

6. *Administrator (or "Leader" [v. 8])*. A leader is a person who desires to help people through the gift of organization and administration. This is a person who has his or her socks organized by color and by style, and if you get a sock out of order, watch out! My good friend Tom Lane has this gift, and I hired him for that reason. For years he oversaw hundreds of our church staff. His gift is very evident when he comes into my office and happens to notice that something is one inch out of place. His organizational gift will immediately manifest, and he can't help but move that item back by one inch to its "proper" location. (Sometimes when he's not looking, I move it back just to mess with him.)

7. *Empathizer (or "Mercy" [v. 8])*. The person who has this gift desires to identify with people and empathize with them. I want to point out the difference between sympathy and empathy. Sympathy says, "I see what you're saying." Empathy says, "I feel what you're feeling." All of us, as followers of Christ, should be able to empathize with others to some extent, but you will definitely want people with this gift around when you're going through a difficulty. My wife has this gift. (Interestingly enough, she has the gift of mercy, and I have the gift of prophecy—two gifts that many consider to be opposite of one another. I love how God balances each of us through the other's gift!)

Each of these gifts is different, and each of these gifts has a part to play in fulfilling the purposes of God. If you've ever served on a team, you've probably had an opportunity to witness these gifts in action.

For example, if you had a committee meeting, the meeting would probably be led by the administrator who would start by passing out a very important agenda with organized notes meticulously detailing the structure of the meeting. But if someone should mention in passing that "So-and-So" has just lost his job, you would suddenly see all the different motivational gifts jumping into action.

The motivator might say, "Perhaps he has sin in his life. Maybe we should go talk to him about that and help him get the sin out of his life." He's really trying to help, even if it might not sound that way.

The teacher would say, "If he would just do what it says in 1 Timothy 3, he would be fine. There are seven principles in 1 Timothy 3 that give the answer to this problem (they all begin with the same letter, by the way)—and he needs to know what those principles are."

The encourager would already be on the phone with the person who lost his job, saying: "I heard you lost your job, but it will be all right. God has a plan, and what's waiting for you next will be even better!"

The person with the serving gift would have already left the meeting to go buy groceries for him.

The giver would be taking out his or her wallet and saying, "Okay, how much do you think he needs? We could take an offering right here in this room today and help this guy out."

And the mercy-motivated empathizer? Why, they would be sitting in the corner, crying tears of compassion for the man and his family and thinking about picking up a sympathy card for him on the way home!

This is just a light-hearted illustration of the different ways these gifts work to meet the needs of people. No one gift is better than another. Jesus had all seven, and if we want to be like Him, we should seek to operate in more than one as well. For instance, although my main gift is motivator, I often function as a teacher.

Remember, God's heart is always about people, so every one of these gifts has to do with helping people! Whatever your purpose in life, it will be related to other people in one way or another.

Together, all these gifts make up the body of Christ.

As a member of the body of Christ, your gift is an important part of God's plan. It's vital to your destiny that you determine what your gift is and begin moving in it. When you start to operate in your gift, it will give you a direction.

Your Purpose Gives Direction, Not Specifics

You may not have a specific picture of your complete destiny, but you do have a gift. And when you determine what your gift is, that will help bring *direction* to your life. Your purpose provides *direction* toward your destiny, but it's important to understand that your purpose does not contain the *specifics* of your destiny.

Joseph had a dream from God, and it gave him vision and direction. But he didn't know what the final manifestation of the dream would look like. Joseph also had a gift from God, and that gift gave him purpose in his everyday life. But he didn't know the *specifics* of how that gift would be used in his destiny.

It's pretty obvious Joseph had a gift of administration, but he didn't wait until he got into a place of authority to lead. While Joseph was a slave in Potiphar's house, he organized the house and became its overseer (see Genesis 39:3-5). And when Joseph was in the prison, he organized the prison and became the overseer of it as well (see Genesis 39:21-23). We don't know much about the pit, but my guess is that it was the most organized pit ever! Throughout his life, Joseph led where he was, no matter his position.

Many people want to wait until they get into a better position to use their gifting. They say, "When I get a better job, then I'll really help people." Please hear me: start now, wherever you are. Even if you're in a pit or a prison, minister to others with your gift and watch the doors of favor and blessing open for you like they did for Joseph.

Joseph seemed to understand he had a gift of administration, and he was faithful to use his gift wherever he went. However, Joseph didn't know the *specifics* of how his gift would play a part in his destiny. While he was serving as a slave in Potiphar's house and while he was organizing things in the prison, Joseph had no idea he would one day be doing that for the entire nation of Egypt. God never showed Joseph the specific details about the destiny He had planned.

It's important to understand this truth if you want to pass the Purpose Test: your gift and purpose will only point you in the *direction* of your destiny, but they will not provide the *specifics*. This is where faith comes in. It takes faith to keep moving in the direction of your purpose, especially when you don't know the specifics of what waits at the end of the journey!

Are there specifics to your destiny? Yes, there are.

Can you know the specifics of your destiny? Yes, you can.

When can you know the specifics of the destiny God has for you?

After you have carried them out!

When you finally step into the destiny God has for you, you will understand the specifics of His plans for your life—but not before then! Why doesn't God reveal all the specifics of your life story right away? I think it's because the details would scare you to death! God gave Joseph a dream about being a leader someday, but He left out all the enslavement and imprisonment parts. It would have been too much for Joseph to handle.

Another reason God waits is so as you move toward your destiny, you will have to keep walking by faith. You will have to remain close to the Lord. So don't become upset or frustrated that you don't know the specifics. All you must really know for certain is you have a gift and a direction from God, and you must *be faithful* to your gift. You must *be faithful* to the direction God has given you.

After you have stepped into your destiny, you will look back, just as Joseph did (see Genesis 45:5–8) and understand the specifics of your purpose. You will say, "Oh, now I understand why I had to go through that! Now I know why God brought me here. This is the reason God worked in my life in that way. This is the reason things happened the way they did. Now I understand the purpose of all those things!"

When you finally step into your destiny, you will see the full picture of God's purpose, but not before. You can't see the picture before it happens, but you will be able to see the *direction*. This is a promise we have from God.

The Bible says, "Your word is a lamp to my feet and a light to my path" (Psalm 119:105). Notice that it doesn't say, "Your Word is a bright spotlight that allows me to see three miles down the road." No, it says God's Word is a lamp to your *feet*. That means it shows you the *next step*. It shows you just enough light to take the next step in front of you. And that light is all you need to keep moving toward your destiny.

You may not know what's at the end of the road in front of you, but if you're faithful and keep walking in the direction God has given you, He will guide you into the destiny He has planned for you. Trust that God is in control and allow Him to direct your steps into His purposes. After all, our destinies are always going to be about helping people in some way. God wants that to happen too, so rest in the knowledge of His goodness.

Let me tell you about a man who had a purpose. He was faithful to develop his gifts. He headed in the direction his gifts brought him, but I am certain he had no idea of the *specific destiny* to which his purpose would lead him!

At 22, he lost his job.

At 23, he was defeated for state legislature.

At 24, he failed in business but was later elected to state legislature.

At 26, the woman he deeply loved died before they could be married.

At 27, he had a nervous breakdown.

At 29, he was defeated for Speaker.

At 34, he was defeated for Congress. He was then elected to Congress three years later.

At 39, he was defeated for renomination to Congress.

At 46, he was defeated for Senate.

At 47, he was defeated for Vice President.

At 49, he was defeated for Senate again.

At 51, he was elected President of the United States.

His name was Abraham Lincoln.[2]

Abraham Lincoln became one of the most pivotal presidents in our nation's history, leading our country through a civil war that seemed certain to tear the nation apart. More importantly, he righted one of the greatest injustices in which our country has ever been involved—the institution of slavery. As He had done with Joseph, God put Abraham Lincoln right where He wanted him, at the exact moment in history he needed to be.

Abraham Lincoln faced many obstacles, failures, and tragedies. He had no idea the *specifics* God had planned for him, but he developed the gifts he had wherever he was, and he allowed those gifts to give direction and purpose to his life. He didn't let difficulties thwart him. He stayed focused on the *direction* God had given him. God did the rest.

His gift and his purpose was to be a leader. But his destiny was to change the world.

Set Your Course and Be Faithful

We can all learn a lesson from Abraham Lincoln's example. Determine what your gift is and allow it to give you direction. Then *set your course* in that direction and simply *be faithful*. Don't get sidetracked trying to figure out the specifics. You get into trouble when you try to dictate the specifics to God.

"But God, I'm supposed to be a pastor. But God, I'm supposed to be in business. But God, I'm supposed to be a teacher. But God, I'm supposed to . . . I'm supposed to . . . I'm supposed to . . ."

What makes you think you can tell God what you're supposed to do? He is God! He created you! Don't you think He already knows what you're supposed to do?

When we imagine the specifics of our lives and they don't happen the way we think they should, we're going to be disappointed. We might choose the city we think we're supposed to live in, the job we think we should have, or the number of children we think we want to have. Then, if things don't unfold the way we planned, we grumble and complain, saying, "God, You're not keeping up Your end of the deal!"

But all the while God is saying to us, "One step at a time. I have it all under control within My plan and purpose. Just keep your eyes on Me and take one step at a time. I will take care of the specifics."

It's when we try to get involved in the specifics of our destiny that we become discouraged. Remember the butler and the baker in the prison? Do you think Joseph would have noticed their sad faces and interpreted their dreams if he were consumed with his own difficulties and the unrealized expectations of his specific destiny? He may have missed the chance. So don't focus on specifics. Instead, set your course in the direction God has shown you. Be faithful to what He has called you to do. Your faithfulness will carry you through to the destiny God has planned.

Be faithful to what He has called you to do. Your faithfulness will carry you through to the destiny God has planned.

The Lord created every one of us with a purpose, but it's up to us to determine what we will do with that purpose.

The Lord sets a direction in front of each one of us, but it's our faithfulness that determines how far we will go.

I was born with a gift to speak and teach, but I believe the number of people I can reach and help is determined by how many tests I pass and how faithful I stay to the Lord.

There are many tests you must go through on the way to your destiny, and all of these tests are important. Humility, character, stewardship, integrity, perseverance—all of these are important to fulfilling your destiny. But they can all be summed up in one word: faithfulness.

Faithfulness is the answer to all the tests God will give you. If you will remain faithful to the direction God has revealed to you, you will ultimately fulfill the destiny He has on your life.

Will you be faithful to what God has called you to do?

What follows is a summary of excerpts from the diary of a man who set his course and was faithful. His name was John Wesley.

Sunday, A.M., May 5

Preached in St. Anne's. Was asked not to come back anymore.

Sunday, P.M., May 5

Preached in St. John's. Deacons said, "Get out and stay out."

Sunday, A.M., May 12

Preached in St. Jude's. Can't go back there, either.

Sunday, A.M., May 19

Preached in St. Somebody Else's. Deacons called special meeting and said I couldn't return.

Sunday, P.M., May 19

Preached on street. Kicked off street.

Sunday, A.M., May 26

Preached in meadow. Chased out of meadow as bull was turned loose during service.

Sunday, A.M., June 2

Preached out at the edge of town. Kicked off the highway.

Sunday, P.M., June 2

Afternoon, preached in a pasture. Ten thousand people came out to hear me.[3]

John Wesley knew his purpose. He didn't see the *specifics* of his purpose, but that didn't stop him from preaching and developing his gift. He allowed his gift to provide direction to his life. Then he set his course and remained faithful. Even amid setbacks, his faithfulness carried him through to his destiny as the theological leader of a spiritual revival in England.

More than anything else, faithfulness kept Joseph true on the path to God's destiny for him—saving millions of people. Faithfulness must also be the foundation for *our* lives. We must be faithful to God through all these tests. As we travel the road to our destiny, faithfulness is the anchor that will hold us steady through every storm. And faithfulness will keep us going until we pass every test and step into the fulfillment of our destinies in God.

Stay the Course

C hances are, as you read this, you're currently in one of two places. Maybe you're in a wilderness land somewhere between your dream and your destiny. Or maybe you're already walking in your destiny. No matter where you are, there are more tests ahead for you to face and pass.

You see, some of the tests we've examined in this book occurred in Joseph's life after his dream but before his destiny. Others occurred after he had already stepped into his destiny. But in order to fulfill his destiny to the fullest, he had to *continue* passing these tests. And the same is true for you.

As you go through each of these tests, remember that God is never going to test you beyond your ability (see 1 Corinthians 10:13). When you were in the third grade, your teacher didn't give you a calculus test. No, you were tested with content that was challenging but suitable for the third grade. And it's the same with the tests you'll take to reach your destiny. In fact, God is the best teacher ever! So don't be afraid. There's no test God will ever put before you that He won't give you a way to pass. By the power of the Holy Spirit, you *can* pass each of these character tests.

You may be in the midst of a real challenge right now. Be encouraged! You're that much closer to your destiny. God gave you the dream, and this is how He is preparing you for your destiny. And the good news is that God *wants* you to pass this test and move to the next level!

Your Destiny Is a Journey

I truly believe I am walking in the destiny God has for my life right now. There is incredible satisfaction in being where I am, and I feel extremely blessed. Yet it's also hard work. That's why we all go through these tests—so we are prepared for the blessings *and* the work that comes with fulfilling our destiny.

And just because we step into our destiny doesn't mean we have "arrived"—our journey doesn't end there! God still had more for Joseph as he moved forward in his destiny, and He has more for me too. Even now, twenty years after I've written this book, God is moving me into new heights of my destiny.

Your destiny is not a one-stop destination. Your destiny is a journey.

Your destiny is not a one-stop destination. Your destiny is a journey.

So, yes, I've written this book about reaching your destiny, but I haven't arrived either. As long as I'm breathing, God has more for me to do! And I'll continue to experience some of these tests as I journey toward new depths of my destiny. That's why it's not hard for me to let go of anything that isn't really part of His plan. I've come to understand that God's dreams for us are much better than any dreams we could dream for ourselves. God's destiny for us is much bigger than anything we can imagine. The more we seek to know Him, the more this realization will sink into our hearts and minds.

I've found the key to moving forward is being faithful with the basics. Let me explain.

Before a pilot can fly his plane, there's a checklist he must go through. He has to check to see if any water has gathered in the fuel tank. He has to check to make sure the radio works. He has to check to ensure the altimeter is functioning, and so on. He must go through this checklist *every time* he flies his plane. Even if he's been a pilot for thirty years, he still needs to go through the list to make sure everything has been checked. He knows that if he misses one thing, it could be disastrous for him and everyone else on the plane.

For believers, the basics are essential: reading and knowing God's Word (Psalm 119:105; Hebrews 4:12), praying (Philippians 4:6; Matthew 6:9–13), gathering with other believers (Hebrews 10:25), faithfully stewarding your body and resources (1 Peter 4:10; Colossians 3:23), confessing and repenting of your sins (1 John 1:9; James 5:16), and loving other people (John 13:34). These are foundational activities of a healthy and faithful Christ-follower.

No matter where you are in your journey, you must always do these things. Just because you're living in your destiny doesn't mean you can quit having your quiet time with the Lord or wisely stewarding your resources or any of the other things you've learned through all the character tests. If you've been a Christian for sixty years and you're walking in your extraordinary destiny, you still need to be in the Word and have an active prayer life.

You must *continue* to do all the things you've done to get to where you are so you can move forward in your destiny. Galatians 6:9 encourages us, "And let us not grow weary while doing good, for in due season we shall reap if we do not lose heart."

God doesn't present you with these ten character tests because He's skeptical you'll pass them or because He's waiting for you to fail. He uses these tests to refine you, to prepare you for your destiny, and to make you more like Him. And I believe we will all look back one day on the tests we've taken and say, "Thank You, God!"

These tests also help you develop the strong character necessary to support your God-given destiny. That's why it's so important to allow God to work in these areas of your life and to allow Him to develop patience, purity, perseverance, and true prosperity. Allow God to remove pride and the wrong motives for wanting power. Allow your heavenly Father to give you the grace to pardon those who have wronged you. Allow Him to reveal to you the glorious purpose for which He created you.

God's Purpose for You Is Extraordinary

Remember, the dreams God gives you are tailor-made just for you. Like Joseph's dreams, they might not make sense right away or feel very significant. But trust that God is leading you toward an incredible and unique destiny. You might have a dream to be a hairstylist, a business owner, a golfer, a schoolteacher, a plumber, a comedian, or even a politician like Joseph! God is the giver of *every* dream, and they are all good. Let me share some encouraging stories with you.

My friends Teresa and Bruce McGaha had a dream of starting a hair salon that was different from any other. As they pursued God and this dream, their salon morphed into something beyond what they ever imagined possible. Yes, it's a quality place with masterful hairstylists, but it's also become an undercover base for God's kingdom. Individuals who would never step into a church have come for a hair appointment and experienced a holy appointment with the King of kings. Bruce and Teresa have led people to Christ right beside hairdryers, curling irons, and perms.

Several years ago, a few women were getting their hair cut and mentioned they were dealing with infertility. The hairstylists paused and prayed for the women, and God answered! He started miraculously opening wombs! When the word got around, women were suddenly showing up to the salon because they heard it was the place to go to get pregnant! Bruce and Teresa had the opportunity to explain that it wasn't their salon that made the difference—it was God who did it. He alone opens wombs. And then they'd pray with the women, sometimes introducing them to Christ for the first time.

Teresa's dream to create a hair salon that was different has certainly come true but in a way that ministers deeply to people in need. It's amazing how something as ordinary as a hair salon can be the platform through which God's destiny is fulfilled.

Similarly, my friend Steve Dulin had a vision to start a construction company dedicated to quality work and honest values. He saw a deficit of integrity in this field and felt like God had given him a dream to do something about it. In the twenty-two years Steve owned his company, God blessed him so tremendously that he gave over 50 percent of his income to the kingdom, and he had regular opportunities to share God's love with clients and other businesspeople.

One time, a woman contacted Steve and asked him to build an abortion clinic. Steve felt like he needed to go talk to her in person and explain why he didn't feel he could be part of this project. He approached her and lovingly shared his beliefs with her. She was so surprised by the Christian love he expressed, and he and his wife, Melody, were able to develop a friendship with her. He was integral in her leaving the abortion business, and it all started with a dream to build a quality, honest construction company.

My friend Michael Jr. is a comedian. When we met, he was doing comedy in Los Angeles and had appeared on the *Tonight Show* and at other big comedy venues. I saw his comedy routine at a charity event and thought he would be a great addition to the entertainment at our Gateway staff Christmas party. I went up to talk to him after his show, and we immediately became friends. I learned he was a Christian and had an incredible testimony. We joked back and forth a lot, and then I said to him, "Have you ever thought about using your gift for the Lord?" Michael seemed puzzled and responded, "I'm a comedian? How would I do that?" I told him he could go around to churches, do comedy, share his testimony, and then invite people to accept Christ.

We had that conversation twelve years ago. Since then, Michael has spoken at thousands of churches, large events, and gatherings. If you've seen his show or heard him speak, you know he's hilarious and a total genius. The way he thinks about things and breaks them down is unlike any other. He speaks truth in a funny and unassuming way, and *thousands* of people have chosen to accept Christ. One year alone, twenty-seven thousand people accepted Christ at his comedy shows! He has written books, starred in movies, and been invited into rooms he wouldn't have been otherwise. He's a completely yielded vessel through which God can move. Michael's dream to be a comedian has turned into a destiny beyond what he could have imagined.

Isn't God amazing? His purpose for each one of us is extraordinary!

The journey may not look the way you expected, and it may be long and filled with trials, but do not lose heart! God gave you the dream, and He is preparing you for your destiny. May you continue to allow God to strengthen and deepen your character. May your God-given dream become your God-fulfilled destiny!

Afterword

My daughter, Elaine, and her husband, Ethan, planted a church in Houston, Texas, a few years ago. It has grown tremendously, and they're impacting thousands of people. But as many pastors and church leaders can attest, the demands of ministry can take a toll. There's a lot of spiritual warfare, and there are a lot of sleepless nights.

Elaine called me one evening after a particularly rough day and asked, "Dad, is it worth it? Is all this worth it?"

Elaine's question sounded very familiar. As a young man, God told me that Gateway was destined to be a large church and that I would write books, speak, and equip people around the world in their walk with the Lord. But along the way, and even now that I'm walking in my destiny, it has felt different than I expected.

I never expected the burden of responsibility that would accompany my great destiny. No one told me that with every new level of influence come new guidelines, new obligations, new restrictions, new blessings, and new relationships. With every step, I've had to learn to manage my time, energy, and money better. The habits and schedules that worked for me, my family, and Gateway twenty years ago do not work today. I can no longer personally interview every potential staff hire or accept every invitation to speak. I can no longer attend every meeting, and I've had to learn to trust others to catch the vision of Gateway and pass it on.

Over the years, I've had to let go of certain things in order to pick up others, such as the privilege of mentoring a younger generation of leaders. And while it's challenging, it's also an incredible and exciting place to be!

Sometimes I think about Joseph when he was named second in command of Egypt. He had finally stepped into his God-given destiny, yet it wasn't entirely light and easy for him. Yes, he was rich and powerful. Yes, he was blessed with children and influence. But he had to make hard decisions. He had to manage an entire country's worth of food in a famine, steward land and resources wisely, and negotiate difficult trades.

He also had to deal with the hurts of his past and forgive his brothers' atrocious acts toward him. He probably had wounds from slavery and prison that took time to heal. He likely had some really difficult days. Just because he stepped into his destiny didn't mean he had "arrived" and life was suddenly going to be without hardship or trouble.

Even though he helped save *millions* of lives during the famine, I imagine Joseph also had moments where he said, "Lord, is all this really worth it?" And I think God replied, "It would have been worth it to save just *one* person."

Through every test on the way to our destiny, we need to remember this about our Father: every single person is precious to Him. *You* are precious to Him.

In Luke 15, Jesus tells the parable about a shepherd who has a hundred sheep but loses one. So the shepherd leaves the ninety-nine to find the one lost sheep. And when the shepherd brings it back, he gathers his friends and neighbors together and rejoices! Jesus is this Good Shepherd. He knows and loves every one of us individually, and He rejoices when we are by His side.

God will not let you get lost in the midst of these character tests. Hebrews 13:5 says, "He Himself has said, 'I will never leave you nor forsake you.'" He is with you every step of this journey. God *wants* you to reach your destiny. But it's not just for your personal fulfillment and relationship with Him. It's for every precious person you're supposed to help.

He is with you every step of this journey.
God *wants* you to reach your destiny.

So when Elaine asked me if all the tough times were worth it, I responded, "For whom?"

"What do you mean?" she asked.

"Are you asking if it's worth it for you or worth it for the people you're helping? Because for the people you're helping, it's worth it. It's worth all the hard conversations, all the tough meetings, all the tests and late nights. It's worth it for *them*. God called you to do this, not so you could pastor a large church. He called you to this so you could help people."

I fully believe what I said to Elaine. Every test, trial, and difficult day has absolutely been worth it. And it has absolutely been worth it for me personally! My relationship with the Lord is stronger. My trust in Him is unshakeable. He's blessed me and my family beyond anything we could have imagined.

I'm so thankful for every single one of these character tests. I never would have been able to stand strong in my destiny without the preparing work God did in my life through these ten tests. And if God can take someone like me through to my destiny, He can surely do the same with you if you don't give up.

Yes, every bit of the journey from my dream to my destiny has been worth it. And I know yours will be too!

Dream to Destiny Icons Explained

The Pride Test: Sun, Moon, and Eleven Stars

The sun, moon, and eleven stars icon represents one of the dreams Joseph had about his brothers bowing to him. Joseph bragged about the dream and therefore failed the Pride Test.

The Pit Test: A Pit

This icon is a view of the night sky from inside the deep pit where Joseph found himself when his brothers betrayed him and left him for dead. It's also a figurative representation of the pits we sometimes find ourselves in throughout our lives.

The Palace Test: A Palace

This illustrated palace is a representation of the palace that Joseph was given stewardship over when he served Potiphar. It's a reminder to be faithful and that God's presence is what pushes us forward and prospers us.

The Purity Test: A Woman's Eye

The woman's eye represents Potiphar's wife who cast longing eyes at Joseph and attempted to seduce him. It's a reminder that impurity begins in the eye.

The Prison Test: Shackles

Joseph was imprisoned and his feet were hurt with fetters. The shackles serve as a reminder that even though we go through difficult trials and tribulations we can have hope because God can deliver us.

The Prophetic Test: Puzzle Pieces

The puzzle pieces represent the prophetic words God spoke to Joseph. Prophetic words are not the whole picture, just part of the bigger picture, which is like a huge puzzle. God alone knows every piece of the puzzle and how each piece fits together in our lives.

The Power Test: Signet Ring

The signet ring represents the power that Joseph was suddenly given upon his release from prison. We are all given power and influence in some form, and it matters how we respond to it.

The Prosperity Test: Gold Coins

When Joseph was placed in leadership, he ordered grain to be saved during the seven years of plenty, so there would be enough for everyone to survive on during the seven years of famine. The gold coins represent how God desires His people to steward their money and resources faithfully.

The Pardon Test: Key

Joseph had every reason not to forgive his brothers for what they did to him when he was a teenager, but he chose to forgive them. Forgiveness means to release, and the key icon represents releasing others from chains of unforgiveness so you can move forward in your destiny.

The Purpose Test: Gift

God gave Joseph many gifts and talents. Likewise, God gives all of us gifts and talents that He wants us to use to help others. This icon reminds us that discovering and honing our gifts is essential to stepping into our destinies.

End Notes

Chapter Two

1   Josephus, *Antiquities of the Jews*, 12.11 §3, quoted in *Jamieson, Fausset & Brown's Commentary* (Seattle, WA: Biblesoft, 2003), CD-ROM.

Chapter Three

1   *Adam Clarke's Commentary on the Bible* (Seattle, WA: Biblesoft, 2003), CD-ROM.

2   *Biblesoft's New Exhaustive Strong's Numbers and Concordance with Expanded Greek- Hebrew Dictionary* (CD-ROM, 2003), Hebrew ref. no. 6743; Greek ref. no. 2137.

Chapter Four

1   *Biblesoft's New Exhaustive Strong's Numbers and Concordance with Expanded Greek- Hebrew Dictionary* (CD-ROM, 2003), Greek ref. no. 5343.

2   *New Exhaustive Strong's Numbers*, Greek ref. no. 264.

3   The Barna Group and Josh McDowell, *The Porn Phenomenon: The Impact of Pornography in the Digital Age* (Ventura, CA: Barna Group, 2016).

4   Barna Group, *Porn Phenomenon*, 32.

5   Ingrid Solano, Nicholas R. Eaton, and K. Daniel O'Leary, "Pornography Consumption, Modality and Function in a Large Internet Sample," *Journal of Sex Research* 57, no. 1 (2020), 92–103 https://doi.org/10.1080/00224499.2018.1532488.

6   Barna Group, *Porn Phenomenon*, 33.

7   Barna Group, *Porn Phenomenon*, 142.

8   Barna Group, *Porn Phenomenon*, 33.

9   Barna Group, *Porn Phenomenon*, 33.

10   Barna Group, *Porn Phenomenon*, 80.

11   Barna Group, *Porn Phenomenon*, 20.

12   Barna Group, *Porn Phenomenon*, 85.

13   Barna Group, *Porn Phenomenon*, 143.

14   Barna Group, *Porn Phenomenon*, 29.

15   Barna Group, *Porn Phenomenon*, 91.

16   "Pornography: A Gateway to Human Trafficking," Freedom Youth Project, July 21, 2011, accessed January 2016, http://www.freedomyouthproject.org/2011/07/pornography-and-child-sex-trafficking.html.

17   "How the Porn Industry Profits from Nonconsensual Content and Abuse," Fight the New Drug, accessed January 9, 2023, https://fightthenewdrug.org/how-the-porn-industry-profits-from-nonconsensual-content-and-abuse/.

18   Barna Group, *Porn Phenomenon*, 97–98.

19   Sebastian Hökby et al., "Are Mental Health Effects of Internet Use Attributable to the Web-Based Content or Perceived Consequences of Usage? A Longitudinal Study of European Adolescents," *JMIR Mental Health* 3, no. 3 (July–Sept. 2016), e31. https://doi.org/10.2196/mental.5925

20   Victor Cline, *Pornography's Effects on Adults and Children* (New York: Morality in Media, 1993), Scribd.

21   "How Porn Can Affect the Brain like a Drug," Fight the New Drug, accessed January 9, 2023, https://fightthenewdrug.org/how-porn-can-affect-the-brain-like-a-drug/.

22   "We Need to Talk About Porn. Is It As Harmless As Society Says It Is?" Fight the New Drug, accessed March 10, 2023, https://fightthenewdrug.org/3-reasons-why-watching-porn-is-harmful/.

Chapter Five

1   *Biblesoft's New Exhaustive Strong's Numbers and Concordance with Expanded Greek- Hebrew Dictionary* (CD-ROM, 2003), Greek ref. no. 2744.

2   *New Exhaustive Strong's Numbers*, Greek ref. no. 2172.

Chapter Six

1   *Biblesoft's New Exhaustive Strong's Numbers and Concordance with Expanded Greek- Hebrew Dictionary* (CD-ROM, 2003), Hebrew ref. no. 1697.

2   *New Exhaustive Strong's Numbers*, Hebrew ref. no. 565.

Chapter Eight

1   Tim Worstall, "Astonishing Numbers: America's Poor Still Live Better than Most of the Rest of Humanity," *Forbes,* June 30, 2021, https://www.forbes.com/sites/timworstall/2013/06/01/astonishing-numbers-americas-poor-still-live-better-than-most-of-the-rest-of-humanity/?sh=68f6933e54ef.

2   "The World by Income and Region," WDI - The World by Income and Region, accessed December 15, 2022, https://datatopics.worldbank.org/world-development-indicators/the-world-by-income-and-region.html.

3   "American Donor Trends," The Barna Group, June 3, 2013, accessed March 28, 2018, https://www.barna.com/research/american-donor-trends/.

Chapter Nine

1   *Biblesoft's New Exhaustive Strong's Numbers and Concordance with Expanded Greek-Hebrew Dictionary* (CD-ROM, 2003), Hebrew ref. no. 5375.

Chapter Ten

1   *Biblesoft's New Exhaustive Strong's Numbers and Concordance with Expanded Greek- Hebrew Dictionary* (CD-ROM, 2003), Greek ref. no. 1248.

2   "Lincoln's 'Failures'?" Abraham Lincoln Online, accessed March 31, 2018, http://www.abrahamlincolnonline.org/lincoln/education/failures.htm.

3   "From the Diary of John Wesley," Bible.org, last modified February 2, 2009, accessed February 21, 2023, https://bible.org/illustration/diary-john-wesley.